UNPAID PROFESSIONALS

UNPAID PROFESSIONALS

COMMERCIALISM AND CONFLICT IN BIG-TIME COLLEGE SPORTS

With a new postscript by the author

Andrew Zimbalist

PRINCETON UNIVERSITY PRESS   PRINCETON AND OXFORD

Third printing, and first paperback printing, with a new postscript, 2001

Paperback ISBN 0-691-08690-7

The Library of Congress has cataloged the cloth edition of this book as follows
Zimbalist, Andrew S.
Unpaid professionals : commercialism and conflict in
big-time college sports / Andrew Zimbalist.
p.   cm.
Includes bibliographical references (p.) and index.
ISBN 0-691-00955-4 (cloth : alk. paper)
1. College sports—Moral and ethical aspects—United States.
2. College sports—Economic aspects—
United States.   3. College sports—United States—Management.
4. College athletes—United States.   I. Title.
GV351.Z56   1999
796.04'3'0973—dc21   99-17410

This book has been composed in Galliard

The paper used in this publication meets the minimum requirements
of ANSI/NISO Z39.48-1992 (R1997) (*Permanence of Paper*)

www.pup.princeton.edu

Printed in the United States of America

3   5   7   9   10   8   6   4

WITH LOVE, TO

———— Shelley, Alex, Ella, Jeffrey, and Michael ————

Contents

I KNEW something was amiss in the fall of 1992 when my 12- and 13-year-old-sons, Michael and Jeffrey, announced that they wanted to attend the University of Michigan. In March of that year, Michigan had appeared in the NCAA basketball finals. Three years earlier they won the national championship. Michigan hats and sweatshirts were hot items in Northampton, Massachusetts. Jeffrey and Michael, of course, knew nothing of Michigan's fine academic reputation and had no idea what they wanted to study, but for the moment anyway they wanted to become Wolverines.

I had never grown very attached to college sports. I grew up in a suburb of New York City in the 1950s where I enjoyed watching the Yankees win every summer. The Yankees provided all the vicarious thrills I needed. No need to follow St. John's, NYU, or other college powerhouses in the area. My high school band did play every year at King's Point (U.S. Merchant Marine Academy) basketball and football games, but I can't remember a single game that they won.

Then I went off to Wisconsin in 1965, a couple of years after they played in the Rose Bowl. But unlike Michigan, the Rose Bowl at Wisconsin happened only once every three decades. I was there during off years—very off. And the basketball team was no better. So I didn't catch college sports fever while in college.

I did graduate work at Harvard and never came within five hundred feet of the football field. I still don't know where the basketball court is.

Shortly after publishing *Baseball and Billions* in 1992, however, I started to be asked to consult in college sports related litigations. The first solicitation I accepted was in Marianne Stanley's gender equity case against the University of Southern California. This was around the time that my sons revealed their college preference. Since then, I have been an interested and often baffled observer of the big-time college sports scene.

I became still more connected when I was asked four years ago to serve on Smith College's Athletics Committee and two years ago to be the faculty representative to the NCAA (National Collegiate Athletic Association). The NCAA is split into three divisions, according to the seriousness of each school's pretensions to athletic success. Division I is the most serious. Smith College is Division III—not very serious. But as the country has become more sports crazy over the last two decades, even the not very serious athletic schools are somewhat serious. Several years ago, for instance, I received a phone call from one of our coaches to check up on how a student-athlete was likely to do in my class. She was having trouble with her classes and her athletic eligibility was in question. The coach made it clear that any leniency would be appreciated. I had heard and read about such things happening at Division I schools all the time, but I never expected it to happen to me at Smith College.

As faculty representative at Smith, I went to the last mass NCAA Convention in January 1997 (now each division has its own annual meeting and votes on its own legislation). I was impressed with the size of the meeting as well as its democratic, albeit disorganized, character. I was even more impressed by the signs of commercialism wherever I looked.

Commercialism had also blossomed seven miles east of Smith College, at the University of Massachusetts. The UMass basketball team had gone from oblivion to national prominence in a few short years in the early and mid-1990s. ESPN camera crews now came to town. Corporate signage began to fill the Mullins Center arena. UMass beer mugs and Marcus Camby and Lou Roe jerseys became ubiquitous in our placid valley. Coach John Calipari personally copyrighted and sold rights to the slogan "Refuse to Lose," which was actually first used by the UMass football team. Conversation at dinner parties turned from literature, movies, and politics to the latest conquests of the "Minutemen." College basketball fever infected central Massachusetts.

Rooting for UMass was fun, but I was always uneasy about what it meant. A friend of mine played golf with coach Calipari at the Hickory Ridge Country Club in Amherst (where Calipari had a complimentary membership courtesy of his contract with the university) and learned that Calipari enjoyed a compensation package of around $1 million. This was ten times more than the highest paid professor at Smith College and six times more than the Smith president made at the time. I read about six key players on the UMass team who had grade point averages below 2.0. I heard about games starting at midnight and noticed that the team practically spent more time on the road than at UMass. Again, something seemed amiss.

I had been teaching a seminar at Smith on the economics of professional sports since 1990 and decided that whether they paid their players or not, college sports had become professional. College sports was added on to my syllabus. After reading and teaching about it for several years and still being baffled, I chose to commit myself to deciphering what was going on and what needed to change. What follows is what I have figured out and what I think needs to be done about it.

I have not attempted to tackle the entirety of college sports; rather, I concentrate on the basketball and football programs of the top one hundred or so schools in Division I. These are the schools that have most commercialized their programs and most compromised the educational standards of academia.

There is the danger in reading what follows as a description of all big-time sports schools or all the student-athletes at these colleges. My depictions and analysis are not about everyone. I try to emphasize what I see as the dominant tendency within big-time college football and basketball. In so doing, I am abstracting from and simplifying many complexities and variations. For instance, there are many basketball and football players at big-time universities who are serious students. Such individuals exist even at the Division IA colleges with the most modest academic pretensions, but they exist in greater proportions at universities like Cal-Berkeley, UCLA, North Carolina, and Maryland, and in still greater proportions at Northwestern, Duke, and Stanford.

Stanford University, in fact, stands out like a knight in shining armor in the world of college sports. Not only has Stanford won the last four Sears Directors' Cups, awarded to the school each year with the highest ranked teams considering all sports, but it graduates 91 percent of all its athletes, including 94 percent of its football players and 100 percent of its basketball players.[1] Relative to other schools, Stanford does not make many compromises in admissions standards for its men's basketball and football programs. Of the 12 players on Stanford's men's basketball team, the high school grade point average (GPA) was an impressive 3.61; of the 69 players on the football team, the figure was 3.57. Little wonder that Stanford has never stood out in these two sports.[2] Presumably in an effort to retain some competitiveness in these sports, however, even Stanford makes significant concessions for SAT scores: the average combined SAT score was 1047 for basketball players and 1108 for football players, while the average score for the entire freshman class was 1417.[3]

Comprehending college sports is at least as challenging as any intellectual nut I have tried to crack. It has required a lot of patience and support from practitioners, journalists, colleagues, and friends. Ursula Walsh, director of research at the NCAA until 1998, was helpful beyond words. She responded to dozens of pleas for information and for documents. She was a patient and humorous interlocutor and a poignant critic. My debt to her is enormous. Other staffers at the NCAA were also quite helpful: Todd Petr, Daniel Nestel, Keith Martin, Rebecca Wempe, and Mary Johnston. From my experience, the problems with the NCAA do not emanate from the lack of talent or poor intentions of its employees.

Many other individuals provided me information or offered useful suggestions: John Mansell, Stephanie Motter, Lynn Oberbillig, Phil Peake, Bob Merritt, Robert Brewstein, Robert Bryce, Fred Stroock, Bob

Bradley, Kristen Van Gaasbeck, Larry Gerlach, Jim Naughton, Tom McMillen, Alex Wolff, Donna Lopiano, Deborah Brake, Robert Bell, Mike McGraw, Kathy Flynn, Sue Pearson, Al Rufe, Jim Leheny, Ruth Yanka, Bill Brandt, Christine Grant, Rich Sheehan, Murray Sperber, Tom Weisskopf, Chris Shelton, Rene Gernand, Armen Keteyian, Wally Hendricks, Dennis Dresang, Dan Fulks, Rick Edwards, Glenn Wong, Medea Benjamin, Keith Dunnavant, James Loughran, Sonny Vaccaro, and Sue Levin. Nikki Carlson and Betsy Hosler were wonderful research assistants.

Several colleagues and friends read parts or all of earlier drafts. I am deeply indebted to each of them: John Siegfried, Steve Goldstein, Mike Cross, Roger Noll, Marty Dobrow, Barry Werth, Gary Roberts, Steve Fraser, and Eleanor Abend.

My greatest debt goes to my wife, Shelley, who was more supportive and loving than I had a right to expect. She is also responsible for many improvements in the manuscript. Love and thanks to Michael and Jeffrey for tweaking my intellect (they ended up, not at Michigan, but at Tisch/NYU and Brown, respectively). Finally, here's hoping that when our twins Alex and Ella are ready for the university in seventeen years, college sports will be alive, well, and more congruent with the educational mission of academia.

UNPAID PROFESSIONALS

CHAPTER ONE

Introduction

*A college racing stable makes as much sense as college football. The
jockey could carry the college colors; the students could cheer; the
alumni could bet; and the horse wouldn't have to pass a history test.*
    —Robert Hutchins, former president of the University of Chicago

*According to legend, Haverford College's baseball team had just been
clobbered by Villanova in the first game of a doubleheader. Prior to
the second game, Haverford's coach gave the team a pep talk which
provoked an animated exhortation from one of the Haverford players: "Let's take the field and do what we do best—study!" Not long
into the second game, Villanova's shortstop hit a three-run homer,
inducing Haverford students in the stands to chant: "That's all
right, that's okay, you'll be working for us some day."*

ON PAGE ONE of the 1997–98 NCAA Manual the basic purpose of the
National Collegiate Athletic Association is written: "to maintain intercollegiate athletics as an integral part of the educational program and
the athlete as an integral part of the student body and, by doing so,
retain a clear line of demarcation between intercollegiate athletics and
professional sports." Some may wonder whom do they think they are
kidding.

In December 1996, Notre Dame was playing its final regular season
football game against the University of Southern California. The Notre
Dame placekicker missed an extra point at the end of the fourth quarter
and the game went into overtime where Notre Dame lost, 27–21. The
loss quashed Notre Dame's bid to go to an Alliance Bowl game, which
would have been worth $8 million to the school. The Fighting Irish
turned down an invitation to the $800,000 Independence Bowl. The
placekicker blew an $8 million extra point![1]

Notre Dame has a 7-year, $45 million contract with NBC to televise
its regular season football games. The major conferences have a $700
million, 7-year contract with ABC to televise the bowl championship

series beginning in 1998–99.² The NCAA has a $1.725 billion 8-year contract with CBS to broadcast its annual men's basketball tournament.

Like the professional leagues, the NCAA promotes its own line of licensed clothing, as do its leading colleges. Like the National Basketball Association (NBA) and the National Football League (NFL), the NCAA has its own traveling tent show—NCAA Hoop City. It has its own marketing division. Its corporate sponsorships have increased roughly sevenfold in the nineties, with guaranteed income of $75 million between 1997 and 2002. It has its own real estate subsidiary and even its own Learjet. In 1997, the NCAA cut a deal with the city of Indianapolis to build it a new headquarters and provide an estimated $50 million in subsidies, leaving three hundred employees and forty-five years of tradition behind in Kansas City.³

The NCAA's total budget, which surpassed $270 million in 1997–98, has grown at an annual rate of 15 percent since 1982. Its Executive Director, Cedric Dempsey, has done even better than this. His salary and benefits package grew 30.2 percent in fiscal 1997 to $647,000, as part of a new five-year deal. Dempsey replaced Dick Schultz in 1993 when the latter ran into ethical problems. As punishment, the Association gave Schultz a golden parachute worth at least $700,000.⁴

Dempsey also gets treated well when he attends the Final Four of the annual basketball tournament. The *Kansas City Star* reports that "the manual for cities holding Final Fours requires a series of gifts to be delivered every night to the hotel rooms of NCAA officials. These momentos cost Indianapolis an estimated $25,000 [in March 1997]. . . . At a minimum, gifts for each official included a Samsonite suit bag, a Final Four ticket embedded in Lucite, a Limoges porcelain basketball and Steuben glass."⁵ And to maximize revenue at the Final Four, the NCAA has spurned normal basketball-sized venues and instead has chosen cavernous arenas such as the New Orleans Superdome, the San Antonio Alamodome, the St. Louis Trans World Dome, the Indianapolis RCA Dome, and the Georgia Dome, all with seating capacities in excess of forty thousand.

With big bucks dangling before their eyes, many NCAA schools find the temptations of success too alluring to worry about the rules. Schools cheat. They cheat by arranging to help their prospective athletes pass standardized tests. They cheat by providing illegal payments to their recruits. They cheat by setting up special rinky-dink curricula so their athletes can stay qualified. And when one school cheats, others feel compelled to do the same. Then the NCAA passes new rules to curtail the cheating. Sometimes these rules are enforced, sometimes not, but rarely is the penalty harsh enough to be a serious deterrent. The solution, it turns out, is more rules. The NCAA Manual has grown in size from 161 pages in 1970–71 to 579 pages in 1996–97 (and the pages increased in size from 6 × 8½ inches prior to 1989 to 8½ × 11 inches after). In 1998–99, the Manual became so long that the NCAA broke it into three volumes, with 1,268 pages (some are repeats).

So what is "the clear line of demarcation between intercollegiate athletics and professional sports"? It certainly is not the presence or absence of commercialism and corporate interests. Rather, two differences stand out. First, unlike their handsomely remunerated coaches and athletic directors (ADs), college athletes don't get paid. Second, the NCAA and its member schools, construed to be amateur organizations promoting an educational mission, do not pay taxes on their millions from TV deals, sponsorships, licensing, or Final Four tickets.

The tension between professional and amateur in college sports creates a myriad of contradictions. And, as the NCAA can well attest, contradictions in 1990s America mean litigation.

Consider the legal toll on the NCAA during 1997–98. It settled a long-standing dispute with basketball coach Jerry Tarkanian over due process for a hefty $2.5 million in the coach's favor. It was told by the 3rd Circuit Court of Appeals in Philadelphia that since NCAA schools receive federal funds, the NCAA itself was subject to Title IX (federal gender equity rules).* Among other things, this ruling called into question the legality of NCAA regulations about scholarships for athletes. And, potentially most significant, the NCAA was hit with a $67 million court judgment over one of its rules that restricts the earnings of certain coaches. This ruling, if it stands, might be used to challenge a panoply of NCAA restrictions on the operation of markets, including prohibitions on paying athletes, restrictions on how much they can earn outside their sport, and limitations on the number of games played or the number of players on a team. In the end, it may challenge the modus operandi of the Association. As I write in the late summer of 1998, the NCAA faces a new $267 million antitrust suit by Easton Sports over proposed specifications to reduce the pop in aluminum bats and another multimillion suit by Adidas over limitations on logo sizes on uniforms.

In the end, college sports leads a schizophrenic existence, encompassing both amateur and professional elements. The courts, the IRS, and sometimes the universities themselves cannot seem to decide whether to treat intercollegiate athletics as part of the educational process or as a business. The NCAA claims that it manages college sports in a way that promotes both the goals of higher education and the financial condition of the university. Critics say it does neither.

---

* This ruling was appealed and was scheduled to be heard by the U.S. Supreme Court on January 20, 1999.

The NCAA wants it both ways. When confronted by the challenges of Title IX and gender equity, the NCAA and its member schools want to be treated as a business. ADs argue that it is justifiable to put more resources into men's than women's sports, because men's sports generate more revenue. But when the IRS knocks on its door, the NCAA and its member schools want their special tax exemptions as part of the non-profit educational establishment and they claim special amateur status in order to avoid paying their athletes.

Big-time intercollegiate athletics is a unique industry. No other industry in the United States manages not to pay its principal producers a wage or salary. Rather than having many competing firms, big-time college sports is organized as a cartel, like OPEC, through the NCAA. To grasp its *modus operandi*, it is necessary to consider each of its component parts: its unpaid athletes (discussed in chapter 2), its athletic directors and coaches (treated in chapter 4), its relations to the media (in chapter 5), to the government, to the athletic shoe companies and other businesses (in chapter 6), and, finally, its relation to the NCAA cartel (in chapter 8). Chapter 3 explores how Title IX and gender equity have changed the economic landscape of college sports. Chapter 7 analyzes the budget of big-time athletic programs and its impact on university finances.

Externalities is the word economists use for a phenomenon that arises when a producer or consumer takes an action but does not bear all the costs (negative externality) or receive all the benefits (positive externality) of the action. College sports generates both positive and negative externalities. Among the positive externalities are that they provide a source of entertainment for tens of millions of Americans and of school spirit for college students.[6] Among the negative externalities are that college sports compromise the intellectual standards and educational process at U.S. universities. The challenge is to reform the system in a way that preserves the positives and minimizes the negatives. If the experience with the contradictions and imperfections of college sports over the last hundred years has taught us anything, it is that there are no quick fixes or ideal outcomes. The system, however, can be improved and ideas for such improvement are offered in chapter 9.

INGLORIOUS BEGINNINGS

Intercollegiate sports in the United States lost its innocence on day one. In 1852, at bucolic Lake Winnipesaukee in New Hampshire, the Harvard and Yale boat clubs gathered for a rowing contest. The setting was harmless enough, but already commercial interests were at work. The

superintendent of the Boston, Concord and Montreal Railroad organized the event, luring the Harvard and Yale rowing crews with "lavish
prizes" and "unlimited alcohol," in order to attract wealthy passengers
up to watch the event.[7] In the 1855 boat race between Harvard and Yale
the first known eligibility abuse occurred. The Harvard coxswain was
not a student, but an alumnus.[8] Four years later, Brown, Harvard, Yale,
and Trinity organized the College Rowing Association. College baseball, track and field, and football followed in the ensuing two decades.

The pervasive and transformative impact of intercollegiate sports was
soon to be apparent. President Harry Barnard of Columbia University in
the 1870s congratulated the crew team after a victory: "[you have] done
more to make Columbia known than all your predecessors . . . because
little was known about Columbia one month ago, but today wherever
the telegraph cable extends, the existence of Columbia College is known
and respected."[9]

But football quickly eclipsed crew in popularity. By the late 1880s the
traditional rivalry between Princeton and Yale was attracting forty thousand spectators and generating in excess of $25,000 (approximately
$420,000 in 1998 dollars) in gate revenues.[10] Woodrow Wilson, Presi-
dent of Princeton University in 1890, told alumni: "Princeton is noted
in this wide world for three things: football, baseball, and collegiate in-
struction."[11] And, President Charles Eliot of Harvard bemoaned: "Colleges are presenting themselves to the public, educated and uneducated
alike, as places of mere physical sport and not as educational training
institutions."[12]

Media coverage of these sporting contests was seductive and college
administrators seemed to be increasingly consumed with their competitive success on the playing field. Already in the 1880s Yale had a
$100,000 slush fund to aid football.[13] Teams regularly used graduate
students and paid ringers to play. In 1896 Lafayette College enrolled
tackle Fielding Yost, a student at West Virginia University, in time to
play in the game against the football powerhouse of the University of
Pennsylvania, which had won thirty-six consecutive games. With Yost's
assistance, Lafayette beat Penn, 6 to 4; then Yost was sent back to West
Virginia. A few years later, Yale lured tackle James Hogan by offering
him free meals and tuition, a suite in Vanderbilt Hall, a trip to Cuba, a
monopoly on the sale of game scorecards, and a job as cigarette agent
for the American Tobacco Company.[14]

Football coaches' salaries began to exceed those of the highest paid
professors.[15] Horrified faculty members formed committees to attempt
to take control over the situation. But powerful interest groups and
competitive pressures effectively thwarted burgeoning reform move-
ments. On three different occasions in the 1880s the Harvard Board of

Overseers voted to ban football at the school, but each effort was undermined by alumni groups. The Big Ten Conference in 1895 acted to curb what was then considered to be a major abuse and prohibited the use of freshmen and graduate students, but when the Ivy League failed to follow suit the Big Ten lost out competitively and was forced to retract its reform.

W. F. King, the 30-year president of Cornell College in Iowa, observed in May 1893: "The hot competition in these games stimulates certain unfortunate practices, such as the admission of professionals into college as nominal students at the expense of the team, tendencies to betting, the limitation of the benefits of the games to a very few persons, and with these the interest is too intense to be compatible with educational advantages."[16]

The disproportionate drive to victory became tragically manifest in 1893 when seven fatalities were reported in college football. Twelve more deaths occurred in 1894. In 1905, eighteen players were killed in college football games (bringing the 1890–1905 total fatalities to 330), and scores more seriously wounded, largely from use of the flying wedge formation and the absence of protective gear.[17] Columbia, Northwestern, Stanford, and California declared that they would no longer sanction football at their schools.[18]

President Teddy Roosevelt summoned representatives of Harvard, Princeton, and Yale to the White House to discuss the growing violence of college football. (Roosevelt's own son had recently broken his nose in a freshman football game at Harvard.) Carrying a big stick, he threatened to proscribe intercollegiate football unless the game was reformed. The National Collegiate Athletic Association (NCAA) was formed later in 1905 to address this problem.[19]

With a few rule modifications, intercollegiate football was poised for a boom. As attendance at games soared, forty new, large stadiums were built between 1920 and 1940. But more popularity and greater investments only made winning more important. Cheating and financial scandals abounded. A 1929 report issued by the Carnegie Commission concluded that "the heart of the problem facing college sports was commercialization: an interlocking network that included expanded press coverage, public interest, alumni involvement and recruiting abuses. The victim was the student-athlete in particular, the diminishing of educational and intellectual values in general. Also, students (including non-athletes) were the losers because they had been denied their rightful involvement in sports."[20] Three-quarters of the 112 colleges studied by the Carnegie Commission were found to be in violation of NCAA codes and the principles of amateurism. A follow-up survey conducted by the *New York Times* in 1931 found that not a single college had changed its practices to adhere to the NCAA codes.[21]

Voices of reform grew more outspoken in the thirties. Hollywood movies from the Marx Brothers' *Horse Feathers* to *Saturday's Heroes* and *Hero for a Day* mocked the duplicity of college sports.[22] Robert Hutchins, President of the University of Chicago, wrote in 1931: "College is *not* a great athletic association and social club, in which provision is made, merely incidentally, for intellectual activity on the part of the physically and socially unfit. College is an association of scholars in which provision is made for the development of traits and powers which must be cultivated, in addition to those which are purely intellectual, if one is to become a well-balanced and useful member of any community."[23] Without meaningful reform in the system, the University of Chicago dropped its football team in 1939. Ironically, what seemed to be a deliberate repudiation of brutality and irrationality was transformed into what many believe to be the quintessence of the same—the stadium locker rooms at the University of Chicago swiftly were converted into secret laboratories for the federally funded Manhattan Project, dedicated to developing the atom bomb.

The Depression affected ticket sales at college football contests in a predictable fashion, but colleges continued to compete against each other in their efforts to recruit top high school players. The scarcity of players led to still more abuses during World War II as well as to the relaxation of player substitution rules and the introduction of two-platoon football.[24] By war's end it seemed to some that transgressions of the amateur code had reached unconscionable proportions. Stanley Woodward, the sports editor for the *New York Herald Tribune*, wrote in November 1946: "When it comes to chicanery, double-dealing, and undercover work behind the scenes, big-time college football is in a class by itself. . . . Should the Carnegie Foundation launch an investigation of college football right now, the mild breaches of etiquette uncovered [in the 1920s] . . . would assume a remote innocence which would only cause snickers among the post-war pirates of 1946."[25] The payrolls of several college teams reached $100,000 and the coach at Oklahoma State estimated that its rival Oklahoma spent over $200,000 a year on players (approximately $1.8 million in 1998 dollars).[26] The conjuncture of falling revenues and rising costs, along with a sharp rise of gambling on college contests, led the NCAA to grow increasingly concerned about the absence of an effective enforcement mechanism to uphold its principles of amateurism.

While the search for an enforcement mechanism was postponed by World War II, it resumed in July 1946 when the NCAA convened a

"Conference of Conferences" in Chicago.[27] This meeting produced a draft of the document "Principles for the Conduct of Intercollegiate Athletics." It became known as the "Sanity Code" because, by threatening to expel violators from the NCAA, it purported to bring order and sanity back to college sports.

Section Four of the document stipulated conditions and limitations on financial aid to athletes. Aid could not be given solely on the basis of athletic prowess, but must also consider a student's need and scholarly accomplishments. Aid was to be limited to tuition and incidental fees. The Sanity Code was officially adopted at the 1948 annual NCAA convention.[28]

Players at the University of Kentucky, among other places, though, had found a way to circumvent this new effort to deprive them of compensation. Five basketball players were convicted of point fixing on their games during 1948–50, a stretch that saw the Kentucky team win two national championships. Ten players on the team also received illegal outside aid, and their famed coach, Adolph Rupp, was condemned for "consorting with bookmaker Ed Kurd."[29]

The New York judge who heard the Kentucky point fixing case did not pull any punches in his opinion. Judge Streit wrote that the University of Kentucky's athletics program was "the acme of commercialism and overemphasis, [including] undeniable evidence of covert subsidization of players, ruthless exploitation of athletes, cribbing on examinations, illegal recruiting, a reckless disregard for the players' physical welfare, matriculation of unqualified students, demoralization [corruption] of the athletes by the coaches, the alumni, and the townspeople."[30]

Economists who have studied the NCAA argue that the Sanity Code marks the beginning of the NCAA behaving as an effective cartel. In this instance, colleges are colluding to set rules that limit the price they have to pay for their inputs (mainly the "student-athletes"), something the colleges could not do if they openly competed with each other for the best athletes. Thus, what appears to some to be a meritorious effort to treat athletes roughly the same as other students with regard to financial aid and to hold back the forces of professionalism and commercialism in college sports, appears to others to be little more than an insidious conspiracy to reduce costs and enlarge profits.

Over time the limitations on financial aid have been somewhat relaxed, allowing aid based on athletic ability alone and expanding the potential aid package to include room and board and books. At the 1997 NCAA Convention, under certain conditions "living expenses" were added to the possible aid package. Even with this relaxation, however, an athlete's financial aid package tops out at around $30,000 in the late-1990s. Given that the leading college basketball teams generate over five million dollars and the leading football teams over twenty million dollars annually in revenues,[31] it seems obvious that the star players on these teams are worth many times more than their financial aid packages. One study, based on data from 1988–89, estimated that the top college football players generated over $500,000 in revenues annually for their schools.[32] The figure today would be at least 50 percent higher.[33] Another study estimates that individual top college basketball players in the early 1990s produced revenues of $870,000 to $1 million each year.[34]

Herein lies a powerful incentive for colleges to cheat. Since schools are not allowed to offer overt cash payments to athletes, schools are obliged to seek more creative or surreptitious forms of remuneration to their student-athletes.[35] Still, payment to the players is constrained, so the schools divert large sums, on the one hand, to compensate more handsomely their top coaches and athletic directors and, on the other, to recruit their student-athletes and to build facilities that appeal to the athletes. While some of the more egregious forms of covert compensation have been curtailed in recent years, the NCAA has never devoted sufficient resources or energy to ameliorate the problem significantly. Rather, it seems that the NCAA has concentrated its meager efforts on levying exemplary punishments on select schools which, some allege, are out of political favor with the Association. Tom McMillen, University of Maryland and NBA star, former U.S. Congressman, and presently co-chair of the President's Council on Physical Fitness, commented during a congressional hearing in July 1991: "The NCAA's response to the crisis has been inadequate: its members have promulgated an ironic system of rules that severely penalize the most minor infraction while ignoring the larger, corrupt practices which are evident in the system."[36]

Even after under-the-table payments from boosters and player agents, the special dormitories and meals, the high-paying summer sinecures, solicitous tutors, tailored gut courses, free clothing, and a myriad of other perquisites, the majority of the top student-athletes are creating considerably more value for their colleges than they are receiving. And this disparity becomes even more glaring when one takes into account that only 50 percent of Division IA football and 41 percent of men's basketball players receive college degrees; among black athletes these proportions fall to 44 percent and 35 percent, respectively.[37]

One reason student-athletes without any academic pretensions accept this state of affairs is that they have little or no alternative. Another is that many student-athletes from high school and college believe that they will make it to the pros. According to a 1990 survey, among blacks this share is alarmingly high and utterly unrealistic: 43 percent of black high school athletes (vs. 16 percent for whites) and 44 percent of black college athletes believe that they will one day become professionals. In fact, only one in several thousand high school athletes makes it to the professional level. Yet when Congress introduced the "Right to Know Act" to require universities to make public the graduation rates of its student-athletes, the NCAA lobbied forcefully against it. While the Act passed Congress over the Association's objection, the incident highlighted for many the troubling fact that intercollegiate sports are self-regulated by the NCAA, whose own structure has been adapted, most recently with "restructuring" in 1997, to promote commercialization. To be sure, the efforts to deceive college athletes often goes well beyond graduation rates. In one remarkable incident, Clemson University, in order to attract black athletes to an overwhelmingly white campus, paid blacks from Columbia, South Carolina, to come to campus on weekends when the black recruits were visiting and pretend that they belonged to a fictitious black fraternity.[38]

Complementing this dubious treatment of the student-athletes, the cultural dominance of intercollegiate sports over campus life raises still more serious questions. University administrators' quest for publicity and media coverage leads them to genuflect at the door of the athletic director's (AD's) office. Resources are lavished on the recruitment of top athletes, not top scholars.[39] Full financial scholarships go to the best athletes, not the best students. During the academic year 1993–94, Duke University awarded $4 million to its 550 student-athletes, and only $400,000 in academic merit grants for its 5,900 other undergraduates. The University of North Carolina at Chapel Hill offered almost $3.2 million to its 690 athletes and only $636,000 in academic merit scholarships to the rest of its 15,000 student body.[40]

Special living conditions, meals, and curricula reinforce a class system within the student body. Underqualified students, some without elementary reading and mathematical skills, are admitted, sometimes by arranging for surrogates to take their SAT exams. The institutional logic evolves to support athletic prominence rather than intellectual inquiry. The President of the University of Oklahoma reflected this poignantly when he went before the state legislature in search of a larger university budget and asserted: "I hope to build a university of which our football team can be proud."[41]

A 1989 Harris poll found that 80 percent of Americans surveyed felt that college sports were out of control.[42] The 1991 Knight Commission report on college athletics concurred, and Creed Black, the President of the Knight Foundation, told the U.S. Congress that university athletic programs were being corrupted by big money and "the rules violations undermined the traditional role of universities as places where the young people learn ethics and integrity."[43] When college basketball players seek to protest the working conditions and wages at a Nike factory in

Asia by taping over the Nike label on their sneakers, but their school's endorsement contract with the company obligates the players to remove the tape, then has not the sacred principle of free speech been violated?

Acknowledging that intercollegiate sports have lost all sense of proportion, however, is not to deny them their rightful place in the university. Participation in sports can promote physical and emotional well-being. Physical activity, whatever its form, is a healthy antidote to the sedentary lifestyle of a student. Participation in competitive sports can enhance one's self-image and teach discipline. Team sports can build character, friendships, and community. Spectator sports can provide release and enrich school spirit. Athletes need not be counterposed to students.

This is clear in the case of women participants in school sports. An emerging body of research has found that female participants in school sports are more likely to graduate high school,[44] 92 percent less likely to use drugs, less likely to be depressed or experience low self-esteem, and 55 percent less likely to have an unwanted pregnancy.[45] At the university level, women student-athletes graduate at a 69 percent rate, compared to 59 percent for all women. Eighty percent of women who were identified as key leaders in Fortune 500 companies had a background in sports.[46] Regular exercise has also been shown to reduce significantly the risk of breast cancer, and to lower the incidence of obesity (currently experienced by 25 percent of children and 30 percent of adults in the United States) and of osteoporosis (loss of bone mass).[47]

It is precisely these positive attributes of sports participation along with an abiding ethos of fairness that drive the struggle for gender equity in athletic programs. In 1972, notwithstanding an aggressive NCAA lobbying effort against it, Congress passed Title IX of the Educational Amendments to the 1964 Civil Rights Act. Title IX declared it to be illegal for institutions receiving federal aid to discriminate in any of its activities on the basis of sex. While the initial implementation of Title IX in intercollegiate athletics was delayed and its progress proceeded in fits and starts, by the mid-1990s enormous gains for female student-athletes had been achieved. For instance, the number of women athletes involved in intercollegiate sports increased from 31,852 in 1971–72 to 129,285 in 1996–97. Still, in 1996–97 women represented only 39 percent of all student-athletes and received a smaller (37.3) percentage of all scholarship aid to athletes. Thus, much ground remains to be traveled before gender equality is attained.

It is no longer fashionable for the NCAA, its member schools, or athletic directors to argue against the principles of gender equity. Virtually all proclaim their commitment to the goals of Title IX; the only impediment, they say, is economic. There is simply not enough money to go around. Men's football can have eighty-five full athletic scholarships and men's basketball can have coaches with salaries above $1 million because, they contend, these teams generate sufficient revenue to pay for these expenses. Women must be patient.

The courts and the U.S. Department of Education's Office of Civil Rights (OCR), however, seem to be sending a different message: women have waited long enough. Title IX is not conditioned on financial returns, but on the principle of educational equity.

Since the vast majority of college athletic programs operate in the red, finding funds to promote equal athletic opportunity for women is no easy matter. Title IX not only presents a budgetary problem for U.S. colleges, it raises the basic question of the role of athletics in the university.

College presidents see two difficult choices: attempt to develop new revenue sources by further commercializing intercollegiate athletics or move decisively away from big-time athletics. While level-headed thinking might seem to dictate the latter option, cultural momentum and key alumni, boosters, and corporate interests favor the former.

The business of college sports took a dramatic turn in 1984 when the Supreme Court struck down the NCAA's centralized control over the national televising of college football. This decision ended the NCAA's monopoly and resulted in more games being televised. So far, so good (suspending critical judgment about its cultural impact). The other outcome of the high court's ruling was that strong football schools and conferences began to earn television revenue for themselves instead of sharing it with all NCAA colleges. The rich programs eventually got richer, and the middle and poor programs got poorer. This growing inequality has been enhanced in the 1990s by increased corporate penetration of the top programs, the formation of the Bowl Championship Series (né Bowl Super Alliance), and the NCAA's "restructuring" which allows for Division I colleges to run their own show as well as for control to be vested in the Division's most powerful conferences.

Thus, many of the sixty-odd top schools in the Big Ten, the Pac-10, the Big East, the Atlantic Coast Conference, the Big 12, and the Southeastern Conference are being bathed in cash, while the 40 Division IA schools in other conferences, the 198 schools in Divisions IAA and IAAA, the 267 schools in Division II, and the 387 schools in Division III are drowning in red ink. Save the handful of colleges with excellent academic reputations, college public relations, admissions, and development departments behave as if successful athletic teams are the *sine qua non* of financial health and more qualified student bodies. The logic is that athletic triumphs bring notoriety which, on the one hand, entice more student applications, thereby allowing for greater selectivity in admissions, and, on the other, stimulate alumnae and local boosters to open their wallets for the school's endowment. The evidence, as we shall see, is otherwise.

The struggle for gender equity has put the traditional conflict of college sports between professionalism and amateurism into sharp relief. At once, the NCAA must deal, *inter alia*, with growing legal challenges to its rules and regulations, the rigidifying class structure among its member schools, the push for sexual parity, the unpaid professional athletes who are jumping early to the pro leagues, and the glut of sports programming on television. Intercollegiate athletics is at a crossroads. This book is about how it got there and about the difficult choices that lie ahead.

CHAPTER TWO

The Student as Athlete

Thus, a youngster gambling his future on a pro contract is like a worker buying a single Irish Sweepstakes ticket and then quitting his job in anticipation of his winnings.
　　—Tom McMillen, former basketball star at the University of Maryland
and the NBA, former member of the U.S. Congress, and cochair of the
President's Council on Physical Fitness

Resolved: That as ministers of the Kansas conference, being more fully convinced than ever that intercollegiate games are dangerous physically, useless intellectually, and detrimental morally and spiritually, we respectfully request, with renewed emphasis, the trustees and faculties of our institutions of learning to do all in their power to abolish such games.
　　—Kansas Annual Conference of the Methodist Episcopal Church,
March 1894

IN 1996 the Wildcats of Northwestern University went to the Rose Bowl for the first time since 1949. The Wildcats had not had a winning record since 1971. In September 1995 their odds of making it to the Championship Game of the Big Ten and Pacific Ten Conferences could not have been much better than Ross Perot's chances of being elected president. There were good reasons for Northwestern's 47-year Rose Bowl drought. Northwestern spent $363,000 on recruiting (just three-fifths what their competitors in the conference spent) and graduated a Big Ten high 93 percent of their student-athletes (compared to an average of 66 percent for the rest of the conference).[1] Overall, the graduation rate of scholarship athletes for the entering classes of 1987, 1988, 1989, and 1990 at Northwestern was an impressive 85 percent, compared to the NCAA Division I average athlete graduation rate of 58 percent.[2]

The star running back on Northwestern's Cinderella team, Darnell Autry, was majoring in drama and attempting seriously to pursue a career in acting. He was offered a part in a movie being filmed in Rome during the summer of 1996. Since the NCAA had a rule that one cannot be an amateur qualified to play in intercollegiate competition and still receive remuneration in any activity connected to one's sport, Autry thought it best to ask for the Association's permission to accept the role.

The Association reasoned that former football stars, such as Jim Brown, O. J. Simpson, and Alex Karras, used their football careers to launch acting careers and that Autry would not have been offered the role had it not been for his football accomplishments; thus, if Autry went to Rome he would have to abandon his status as an amateur football player and forfeit his remaining two years of eligibility. After several months of unsuccessfully trying to persuade the NCAA, Autry took his case to court and obtained a temporary restraining order which permitted him to undertake his unpaid part (only his expenses were covered) and retain his eligibility. Since Brooke Shields was able to earn a million dollars in a movie while enrolled at Princeton and countless other undergraduates were allowed to pursue remuneratively their careers during the summer months, the NCAA, ever flexible, modified the rule at their 1997 Convention. Future Darnell Autrys will be able to go to Rome—on the condition that they are not compensated for their services.

Unhappily, Autry's experience is just the tip of the iceberg for Division I athletes. In March 1985, Kenny Blakeney was a starting senior basketball guard for the Duke Blue Devils.[3] Blakeney had a "full ride" grant-in-aid (the NCAA has used this felicitous phrase since 1956 for financial support to athletes, rather than the more common "scholarship," for reasons which should be, or will shortly become, obvious) for his four years at Duke, nominally covering his tuition and fees, room and board, and books. Blakeney received a $725 monthly scholarship stipend; of which, $337.50 paid the rent at his off-campus apartment, $143 went for utilities and phone, $20 for cable television (apparently *de rigueur* for college students in the 1990s), $181.50 for food (training table did not cover all his meals), $32 for dry cleaning (team dress code required a jacket and tie on the road), and so on. Blakeney did not come from an affluent family. His mother, a clerk at a grocery store in Washington, D.C., sent him $60 a month so he could meet his bills. It was not uncommon for Blakeney to have a Snickers bar and Gatorade for breakfast and to call a $2 rental movie a "date."

Yet Blakeney followed a six-day-a-week practice schedule, including team workouts, film sessions, conditioning, and weightlifting. He suffered injuries and he played hurt. During his years at Duke the team won two national championships and appeared in three Final Fours. Duke's Associate Athletic Director said that the team averaged $750,000 a year in revenue sharing from the Atlantic Coast Conference during Blakeney's years at the school. Duke's basketball coach, Mike Krzyzewski, is reputed to receive compensation in excess of $1 million yearly.[4] Blakeney said he and his teammates talked about these financial contrasts all the time: "End of the month, we all talk about it. We're hanging together—broke. A scholarship just isn't enough."

But Blakeney at least received his full ride for four years. Chad Wright was recruited in 1993 to play football at the University of Washington.[5] At the time, he remembers being promised a full scholarship until he graduated. Wright suffered a spinal cord injury while participating in the team's weight-training program, ending his football career. Unfortunately, it also ended his grant-in-aid. Since 1973 the NCAA has only allowed athletic scholarships on a year-to-year basis. Thus, when a student's services as an athlete are no longer required, his hopes for a degree are frequently shattered.[6]

Autry, Blakeney, and Wright are just three of thousands who are yearly caught in the web of contradictions that is intercollegiate athletics. The NCAA maintains a myriad of restrictions, all in the virtuous name of preserving athletics' subservience to the educational mission and amateurism in intercollegiate sports:

- pay for play is prohibited;
- athletes are not allowed to hold a job during the school year (modified beginning 1998–99 academic year);
- the number of grants-in-aid per sport is restricted;
- the size of the maximum grant is limited;
- athletes cannot sign with an agent and still retain their eligibility;
- first-year students must have attained a certain SAT score and high school grade point average (GPA) to be eligible to compete;
- athletes who sign a letter of intent to attend a college must go to that school or they are forced to sit out a year before competing for another school (even if the coach who signed them departs for another school or the NBA);
- athletes who transfer from one college to another must sit out a year;

and so on. There are hundreds more such rules. Trying to keep together an association of 900-odd colleges, to get them all to follow a similar code of behavior, and to reconcile a multibillion-dollar industry with the alleged principles of amateurism is complicated.

Most economists look at the NCAA's rules and see a cartel, endeavoring to maintain a player reserve system and contain its costs. The NCAA, in contrast, maintains that it is upholding the ethical standards of amateurism, as is proclaimed, for instance, in Rule 2.15 of the Manual: "The conditions under which postseason competition occurs shall be controlled to . . . protect student-athletes from exploitation by professional and commercial enterprises." *Sports Illustrated*'s Steve Rushin adds: "With the exception, one presumes, of the Thrifty Car Rental Federal Express Poulan Weedeater Tough-Actin Tinactin Ty-D-bol bowls at the end of the season."[7]

Walter Byers was Executive Director of the NCAA from 1951 to 1987. Indiana University basketball coach, Bob Knight, says of Byers: "[He] has done more to shape intercollegiate athletics than any single person in history. He brought a combination of leadership, insight and integrity to intercollegiate athletics that we will never again see equaled." Byers oversaw the introduction of academic rules, the Association's enforcement system, the development of grants-in-aid and he signed more than fifty television contracts with ABC, CBS, NBC, ESPN, and Turner Broadcasting. Byers has an unequivocal view on exactly what values the NCAA is upholding: "Collegiate amateurism is not a moral issue. It is an economic camouflage for monopoly practice."[8]

Whatever the motives, it is clear that disallowing over-the-table compensation for college athletes has fostered a perverse system of incentives as well as some bizarre behavior. Like the airlines which, unable to compete over prices prior to deregulation, lavished resources on travel amenities and advertising, college coaches, unable to compete over top high school prospects with salary offers, lavish millions of dollars on recruitment and special services for athletes once in college. Then they arrange for "boosters" (usually sports-crazed local businessmen) to make payments on the side to the athletes, while salivating sports agents and their lackeys dangle dollars before the immature, impecunious athletes attempting to induce them to sign over 5 percent of their future earnings should they become pros.

When star athletes who generate $1 million or more in revenue for a school receive compensation worth only $10–40,000, there is a lot of surplus left over. The beneficiaries of this surplus are the football and basketball coaches, the athletic directors, the conference commissioners, the "non-revenue sports" (in the NCAA lingo, all sports other than men's basketball and football), and Divisions II and III. In effect, college sports is an elaborate system of cross-subsidies.

Testifying before Congress in 1992, Charles Farrell expressed the transfer pattern in stark terms: "The majority of football and basketball players in Division I, the NCAA's top competitive division, are black, yet blacks receive only 10 percent of the athletic scholarships awarded in the division. In essence, it is the black athlete who provides the blood, sweat and tears that support college sports."[9] LSU basketball coach Dale Brown is equally strident: "This one-billion dollar TV contract is the paramount example of the injustices in the game. Look at the money we make off predominantly poor black kids. We're the whoremasters."[10]

Byers writes that colleges have appropriated the right to "financially exploit their young players and designate others (such as athletics conferences and the NCAA) to exploit them."[11] When college sports entered the second half of the twentieth century, the NCAA coexisted with other prominent sports organizations in the United States, such as the U.S. Lawn Tennis Association, the U.S. Golf Association, and the U.S. Olympic Committee. The latter three associations have since overseen the professionalization of their industries. Today, golf and tennis stars make millions, and the U.S. Olympic Committee provides grants of up to $15,000 a year to athletes in training, in addition to covering various expenses, allowing the athlete to pursue commercial opportunities, and offering bonus payments for winning Olympic medals. Mike Moran, the U.S. Olympic Committee's Director of Public Information, explains why his organization no longer claims to embody the principles of amateurism: "We wanted to rid ourselves of the hypocrisy."[12] Gulp.

But the NCAA continues to defend the principles of amateurism and nominally maintain the subservience of athletics to the educational mission of academia. Many in the university wonder whether the hypocrisy hasn't gone far enough. Gary Becker, Nobel Prize–winning economist from the University of Chicago, for instance, writes: "An association of companies that limits payments to employees and punishes violators would usually be considered a labor cartel. Why should the restrictions on competition for athletes among . . . the members of the NCAA be any different? And especially since these restrictions primarily affect the low-income athletes—most of whom are black or from other minorities—who dominate big-time college football and basketball."[13] To see what can be done about the present state of affairs, it is important to inquire into the details of collegiate amateurism and how it has come to be what it is today. In this chapter, we consider, first, the evolution of uneven and ambivalent efforts to enforce academic standards on athletes and, then, the pluses and minuses of the college experience for unpaid basketball and football players.

THE STRUGGLE FOR ACADEMIC STANDARDS

Since the first intercollegiate football game in 1869 when Rutgers beat Princeton with the help of ten freshmen, three of whom were failing algebra, college presidents have been preoccupied with maintaining academic standards. In 1889, Harvard president Charles Eliot undertook a study on the relationship between academic success and football participation among Harvard freshmen. Over a two-year period he found that freshmen football players had nearly four times as many D's and F's as A's and B's. He reasoned that first-year students should be ineligible for athletics while they sought their social bearings and established themselves intellectually. Further, allowing first-year "students" to play facilitated the use of ringers or "tramp athletes" who could matriculate one day and play football the next. Eliot's appeal was too enlightened for the Harvard alumni and student body at that time. Six years later, however, the Big Ten Conference declared that transfer students must be enrolled for six months prior to playing in a game and that athletes delinquent in their coursework would be ineligible. Then, in 1903, Harvard became the first big-time school to establish freshmen ineligibility, but many other institutions soon followed Harvard's lead. In 1906, Amherst, Wesleyan, Williams, and the Big Ten Conference prohibited freshmen participation for students who fell below certain threshold qualifications. Most big-name schools adopted restrictions on freshmen participation prior to World War I. With the exception of the two World Wars and the Korean War when the ranks of young men in college were sharply depleted, these restrictions stayed in place until the 1960s.

Other than a 1939 NCAA rule that excluded freshmen from participation in national championships, there was no NCAA-wide policy on the issue. Conferences and schools were free to adopt any policy they wanted. Indeed, several conferences were formed around agreement to restrict freshmen eligibility. Some up-and-coming conferences, though, sought advantage in attracting the best high school talent by allowing their first-year students to play varsity football. Other conferences, responding to this competitive threat, initiated freshmen-only (junior varsity) football programs that were somewhat less demanding on the students' time. These programs, however, became increasingly expensive, especially after the NCAA introduced its grants-in-aid policy in the early 1950s, and financial considerations provoked a discussion of the need for a national policy.

The first Association-wide policy dealing with freshman eligibility (Rule 1.6) was passed at the 1964 Convention to take effect the following year. Rule 1.6 stipulated that for a freshman to receive an athletic grant-in-aid, he or she would have to have a high school GPA, class rank, and standardized test score that would predict (based on statistical correlation for a sample of 40,900 students at 80 colleges) a college GPA of 1.6 (on a scale of 1–4) or better. The 1.6 standard translates roughly into half D grades and half C grades.[14] Not too stringent a standard, but stricter than no standard at all. And it promised to curtail the wanton use of "tramp athletes," modestly reduce athletic aid costs, and provide a public relations boost on behalf of academic integrity.

The NCAA soon found a more effective way to save money for its schools. In 1968 the NCAA declared freshmen eligible for all sports but football and basketball, and in 1972 football and basketball eligibility were added. Since the colleges were offering athletics scholarships to first-year students, it was economically inefficient not to take advantage of their athletic talents. What was a gain for athletic department budgets was a loss for the academic integrity battle begun by Harvard's Charles Eliot eighty-three years earlier.

Having made freshmen eligible, the NCAA struck another blow against academic integrity in 1972 by repealing Rule 1.6. Apparently, half C's and half D's were too much to expect of student-athletes. The new standard to qualify for an athletic scholarship was a 2.0 high school GPA, without regard to what courses were taken, class rank, and performance on the SAT or ACT exam.

One college president rebelled. In the spring of 1989, University of Iowa president Hunter Rawlings, humiliated after several Iowa football players admitted that they majored in Water Coloring and Archery, declared that if the NCAA did not abolish freshmen eligibility he would do so unilaterally. Iowa's football coach Hayden Fry called a press conference and threatened to quit and Iowa's governor Terry Branstad called Rawlings "insufferably naive." Freshmen still play at Iowa.[15]

Pay for Play

As the NCAA struggled to find an acceptable compromise policy to bolster academic standards, there were equally troublesome issues to confront regarding amateurism. A 1929 Carnegie Commission Report on college athletics found that three-fourths of all colleges violated the NCAA's codes and principles of amateurism and that the practice of compensating athletes was widespread. The Big Ten established a committee in 1923 to investigate the payment of football players. Six years later the University of Iowa was expelled from the conference for giving athletes "a share of the commission on the sale of yearbooks" and utilizing "a businessman's slush fund to subsidize teams, refund tuition and fees and failure to certify athletes as bona fide students."[16] But Iowa alumni fought back, creating their own investigation of other Big Ten schools. When they threatened to go public with their findings, Iowa was readmitted into the conference.

In the 1940s Hugh McElhenny, a star halfback at the University of Washington, had been recruited out of high school by dozens of colleges. He reputedly followed a trail of fifty-dollar bills all the way to Seattle, and when he left college to join the National Football League McElhenny became known as the first college player "ever to take a cut in salary to play pro football."[17]

Also in the 1940s, five basketball players, unsatisfied with the compensation packages arranged for them by the University of Kentucky, turned to a gambling ring and engaged in point shaving. Apparently these activities were facilitated by Kentucky's legendary coach Adolph Rupp, who was later found by the Southeastern Conference to have arranged for illegal cash payments to his players on more than one occasion.[18] There is ample evidence that there were players at many other schools engaged in point fixing, including NYU, Bradley, Long Island University, DePaul, Manhattan, and the University of Toledo.[19]

When it was formed in 1905, the NCAA's principal task was to develop new uniform rules for football that would make the sport less violent and more palatable. It was in the interests of all the Association's members to cooperate in reforming the rules of the game and then in adhering to those rules. The NCAA also developed principles of amateurism which proscribed compensation for athletes, but until 1948 the NCAA had no effective enforcement mechansim.

Cartels are established, of course, to benefit their members. Cartels generally attempt to restrict output, thereby raising its price, or place restrictions on inputs, thereby lowering their prices. While cartels thus succeed in raising the profitability of their members at the expense of consumers, each member of a cartel can become even more profitable by cheating on the cartel's rules (provided, of course, the majority of other schools don't also cheat, which would negate the profit-promoting intent of the cartel). All cartels have problems policing their members. The NCAA is no exception.

In 1948 the NCAA undertook a serious cartel effort to reduce costs by banning a full athletic scholarship with the passage of its so-called Sanity Code. Under the Code, a student-athlete could receive a tuition and fees scholarship (not room and board) if the student had a demonstrated financial need *and* met the school's *normal* admissions requirements. This amounted to a scholarship based on athletic merit. Prior to the 1950 NCAA Convention seven schools turned themselves in as violators.[20] Several southern institutions led a critique of the Code, arguing that it favored the elite colleges which already got the better students and had wealthier alumni who could give secretly to the athletic programs. The membership refused to discipline the seven violating schools, and the Code in essence was dead.[21]

Growing booster payments to athletes, however, forced the NCAA's hand and in 1956 the Association voted to allow full grants-in-aid (tuition, fees, room and board, books, and $15 a month "laundry money"). But schools and their booster groups still sought competitive advantage and devised new ways to pay their athletes on the side.

As early as the 1960s, an intense Southwest Conference football rivalry led to serious violations at Southern Methodist University (SMU), Texas Christian University (TCU), and the University of Texas. According to Walter Byers, boosters at SMU were providing over $400,000 to support the school's football program.[22] Players were provided with cars, cash, and sex parties, among other benefits.[23] To stay competitive in the conference, the transgressions of one school became the perceived imperatives of the rival schools. SMU was finally caught and disciplined by the NCAA in 1985, which penalized the football team with no television appearances and no scholarships to freshmen for one year. Yet, apparently, Bill Clements, chair of the SMU Board of Governors and soon-to-be-elected Governor of Texas in November 1986, was not deterred by the penalty and insisted that the players continue to be paid, fearing that otherwise they would go to other schools in the conference. One player admitted to the NCAA enforcement staff that he was paid $25,000 to sign his letter of intent plus monthly cash payments of $25,000. Eventually, as the full scandal broke, the NCAA suspended the SMU football team for one year (the school was prepared to accept a two-year suspension) and forced the resignation of SMU's athletics director (AD), head football coach, and assistant coach, all deeply complicitous in the payment scandal. The AD had to surrender his Cadillac, but was given $246,442 in termination payments. The head coach received a severance payment of $556,272 and the assistant got $60,299.[24] With deterrents like this, it is small wonder that violations proliferate. Meanwhile, TCU was paying its players as much as SMU.

Indiana basketball coach Bob Knight told the *Chicago Tribune* in 1985: "Be sure to say that I say that some basketball players are being paid more money to attend college than the professors who teach at the schools they attend."[25] In 1982 Notre Dame coach Digger Phelps charged that the going price for top high school prospects was in the five figures. Charles Shackleford, who left North Carolina State after his junior year to go to the NBA in 1988, admitted taking some $65,000 from agents.[26] Alex Wolff, college basketball reporter for *Sports Illustrated*, and Armen Keteyian, director of sports programming for CBS News, write in their 1990 book *Raw Recruits* that the market price for top prospects "has spiraled well above that, of course," with the dollars coming from booster slush funds being winked at by coaches and ADs. In September 1987, the University of Illinois assistant basketball coach offered LaPhonso Ellis, a high school star from East St. Louis, $5,000 to sign with the school and $5,000 for each year that he played.[27]

Player agent Jim Abernathy told *USA Today* in 1987: "Everyone is being paid and signed. If anyone says otherwise, they're really stupid, blind or they're lying."[28] In a 1989 survey of professional football players 31 percent of the respondents admitted to accepting illicit payments while playing in college and 48 percent said they knew of others who took payments.[29] Two years later the vaunted basketball program at the University of Kentucky was caught delivering an undercover payment to one recruit as $1,000 in $50 bills fell out of an Emery Express air package.

During 1995–96, former University of California, Berkeley, basketball coach Todd Bozeman paid the parents of one of his players, Jelani Gardner, $15,000 per year for his services.[30] Two football players at the University of Arizona were charged with fraud in June 1997 for having sixty illegally obtained textbooks in their possession. Apparently, the students bought the books with scholarship money (there is no NCAA-imposed limit on the size of course book purchase reimbursements) and then planned to resell them for cash to other students.[31] In late May 1997, former University of Michigan basketball stars Chris Webber and Maurice Taylor were charged with accepting more than $100,000 each from a booster while in school.[32] During an NCAA investigation the players simply stonewalled and only minimal penalties were levied. Of the twenty-three institutions on NCAA probation during 1996–97, eighteen were involved in some violation regarding excess compensation to athletes.[33]

The NCAA has responded to these and other violations with ever more detailed regulations which attempt to curtail such payments. While overt cash payments appear to be on the wane, the Association's small enforcement staff, inadequate sanctions, more ingenious and subtle forms of remuneration, and payoffs from athletic shoe street agents and player agents have put only a small dent in the larger problem. In 1991–92, for example, the NCAA spent $1.9 million on enforcement, while it spent $2.5 million on legal and government affairs, another $2.5 million on public relations, and $1.9 million on committee entertainment.[34] Tom McMillen says: ". . . the incentives for winning and cheating are even greater now than they were two decades ago and have been largely untouched by the NCAA."[35]

Player agents are not legally bound by internal NCAA rules. The NCAA cannot fine or suspend an agent, the way it can penalize a member school or athlete. Former sports agent Mike Trope stated the agent's point of view quite poignantly: "The NCAA rules are not the laws of the

United States. They're simply a bunch of hypocritical and unworkable rules set up by the NCAA. I would no sooner abide by the rules and regulations of the NCAA than I would the Ku Klux Klan."[36] Agent Jim Abernathy says he spent over $500,000 in one year on recruiting players, and some star athletes have reported being approached by over a hundred agents anxious to represent them.[37] Agent Wesley Spears claims he provided Marcus Camby and his friends with cash and goods worth over $75,000 while Camby played at the University of Massachusetts from 1994 through 1996.[38] Another agent, John Lounsbury, says he gave Camby $28,000.[39]

Still, the yearly remuneration package received by top college athletes, including a full-ride scholarship and side payments, rarely surpasses $30–40,000. Those few who are sufficiently talented to play professional ball will soon earn several hundred thousand to several million dollars annually. There is little economic incentive for them to stay in college, even if they would be among the minority who earn bachelor's degrees.

It should surprise no one that star athletes are leaving college after a year or two, or skipping college altogether to play pro ball. The number of basketball players who left college before their NCAA eligibility elapsed increased from sixteen in 1995 to thirty-five in 1996.[40] The 1997 concession (implemented in 1998–99) by the NCAA to allow student-athletes to earn up to $2,000 in a job during the school year is too little, too late for the top players. The early departure of the Allen Iversons, Marcus Cambys, and Stephon Marburys creates a new problem for college basketball as it loses its marquee players, but the sport still is expected to deliver strong television ratings to justify its $1.7 billion contract. Of course, while it is a problem for colleges if their star athletes leave early, it hardly constitutes a social problem of significant proportions. Indeed, it appears little different for Allen Iverson to leave Georgetown after his sophomore year from Bill Gates dropping out of Harvard to found Microsoft, Steve Jobs dropping out of San Jose State to form Apple, or Jan and Dean dropping out of the University of Southern California to sing surfer songs.

Resurrecting Academic Standards

After the vitiation of standards in 1972 with the elimination of Rule 1.6, embarrassments abounded. The expansion of television coverage of college sports in the 1970s brought with it more and more interviews of inarticulate student-athletes using less than grammar school syntax before national audiences. Functional illiteracy among college football and basketball players came to the public's attention. In 1982 Professor Jan Kemp filed suit against the University of Georgia because she was fired after openly protesting the preferential treatment given to academically unqualified athletes. Kemp eventually won her suit with a jury award of $2.58 million and she was honored by the American Association of University Professors for her "unwavering commitment to academic integrity."[41] The case "vaulted [the academic integrity issue] into national prominence."[42] The American Council of Education, a policy forum and lobbying organization for college presidents based in Washington, D.C., pushed for tougher standards from the NCAA. At its 1983 Convention the NCAA passed Proposition 48, to take effect for the 1986–87 academic year.

Prop 48 (it is common parlance in the NCAA to use the diminutive in reference to legislative initiatives) toughened freshmen eligibility standards in two ways. First, it stipulated that the 2.0 high school GPA had to be achieved in 11 core courses, rather than all courses without regard to their seriousness. Second, it reintroduced from Rule 1.6 the standard of SAT or ACT scores, albeit the threshold was only ankle high: 700 combined score on the math and English SATs.[43] To achieve this a student need only answer one out of four questions correctly (of the 1.5 million who took the SATs in 1982, 85 percent of the men and 80 percent of the women met this standard).

There were vehement protests from certain black coaches and other educators who argued that the SATs were known to be culturally biased and favored white middle-class students. Partially in response to this concern the NCAA weakened Prop 48 at the last minute by adding a "partial qualifier" category. A partial qualifier is one who meets either the 2.0 GPA (in all high school courses) standard or the 700 SAT standard. The partial qualifier at this point was eligible for a full grant-in-aid, but could not practice with or play on the team during his or her first year. The non-qualifier, also barred from practicing or playing with the team, could receive federal Pell grant funds or other need-based aid from the institution, but was not eligible for an athletic grant-in-aid.

There is, however, a gaping loophole. If the partial- or non-qualifying student made satisfactory progress then he or she would be eligible to play on the team the next three years. Satisfactory progress, apart from some basically inconsequential guidelines from the NCAA,[44] was left up to the individual school to decide. With classes in subjects like golf and archery, attentive tutoring, and occasional cheating, virtually all partial qualifiers become eligible to play in their second year.[45]

Chris Washburn, for example, was accepted into North Carolina State to play basketball under coach Jim Valvano. Washburn was a "special admit" (the language has been sanitized since the days of ringers and tramp athletes) with a joint SAT score of 470 (270 on math and the minimum 200 on English).[46] His admission was approved by NC State Chancellor Bruce Poulton who defended his decision as follows: "The SAT . . . is racially skewed. . . . Chris took a full load and passed all the courses." One wonders whether NC State, therefore, applies lower SAT standards for blacks who are not athletes. Washburn's full load included classes in "American Sport" and "Public Speaking."[47]

Kevin Ross, a 6'9" basketball star at Creighton University, was admitted into the school after scoring a 9 out of a possible 36 on his ACT test. The average score at Creighton was 23.2. Initially his application was rejected by the admissions office, but the athletics department asked admissions to take a second look with the aid of the school's vice president. Ross's first year included a rigorous schedule of course work in "Squad Participation," "Theory of Basketball," "Theory of Track and Field," and "Introduction to Ceramics." His GPA was sufficient to qualify him to play his sophomore year.

Stephen Gaines, a 6'3", 300-pound defensive lineman, arrived at Texas Tech as a 17-year-old freshman in 1990. He played in five games his freshman year without earning any course credit at all. He dropped out of school for almost two years and returned to play football in the fall of 1992. He earned enough credits to return by taking a course at a junior college on "coaching basketball" and two summer school courses at Texas Tech, one in "beginning raquetball." During the fall 1992 semester he earned 12 course credits, in four 3-hour recreation courses all taught by the same professor. These 12 credits qualified Gaines to play again in 1993. Gaines injured his knee and never made it to his fourth year.[48]

Dontae Jones played Division I basketball for one season. After two years at a junior college where he developed a deep deficiency in academic credits, he qualified for the 1995–96 season by earning 36 hours of course credit the previous summer. This is the equivalent of nine courses! Two weeks after the Final Four Jones dropped out of college. He now plays for the Boston Celtics.

Miles Simon led the University of Arizona to the national basketball championship in 1997 and was selected as the most outstanding player during the Final Four. Up to that point, Simon played his first three years at Arizona on academic probation. With a cumulative grade point average of 1.6 during the spring semester of 1996, Simon withdrew from seven hours with F's and became disqualified. After sitting out during the fall 1996, Simon took a two-week course in Family Studies 401 which began on December 1. Simon and all the other nineteen students in the class, including five other athletes, got A's. Simon was now allowed to play in the December 21 game against Michigan. The next summer Simon went on a basketball tour of Australia and while on the tour took Family Studies 337 and received a B.[49]

Prop 48, then, did little to impose effective academic standards for many student-athletes. Nor did it provide a very meaningful incentive to these young athletes to take their studies more seriously. Many high school guidance counselors reportedly told athletes to take gut courses to meet the 2.0 GPA cutoff and to skip the standardized tests. The student could then get a free ride to college and the only penalty would be sitting out the first year, when the student could do weight training, conditioning, and practice informally. Another strategy is to have the student enter a junior or community college. If they maintain a C average for two years, taking courses like "Walking for Fitness," then they can enter Division I without taking a standardized test.[50]

The NCAA tried to make amends at the 1989 Convention with Prop 42. As passed in 1989, the main innovation of Prop 42 was that it banned the full ride scholarship for partial qualifiers. Prop 42 was immediately denounced by several leading black coaches. John Thompson, Georgetown University's basketball coach, consultant to and director of Nike, and would-be owner of a lucrative slot machine concession in Las Vegas,[51] staged a two-game walkout. Negotiations went on behind the scenes and at the January 1990 Convention (Prop 42 was not scheduled to take effect until August 1990) Prop 42 was modified. In addition to reasserting the 2.0 GPA in all courses standard, the modification now allowed partial qualifiers to receive full financial aid as long as the funds did not come from the athletics department. In other words, Prop 42 was Prop 48 all over again, but this time with the incentive for the institution to engage in accounting gimmickry, and to allow athletes to use funds previously designated for needy and promising students.

In fact, Prop 42 was favored by football and basketball coaches who were limited by NCAA rules to 95 and 15 full grants-in-aid, respectively, at the time.[52] Prop 42 allowed the coaches to stockpile partial qualifiers and not count them against the scholarship limits in their sports. Gary Roberts, Tulane University law professor and faculty athletics representative, led the opposition to this emasculation of Prop 42, arguing: "Proposition 42 uses SAT scores as a cutoff for distribution of scholarships. Proposition 42 opponents are using points per game as a cutoff."[53]

Michael Orenduff, president of New Mexico State University, put a slightly different cast on the process: "That became the game. The government, the NCAA, passes new rules like Prop 48; the people, the college coaches, make a game of figuring out how to get around them. The NCAA can plug one hole, but someone'll go drill another."[54]

Prop 48/42 and Racial Discrimination

Several prominent black coaches did not mince words when speaking about Prop 48/42. Temple basketball coach John Chaney stated:

> The NCAA says it's concerned about the integrity of education. Hell, image is what it's concerned about. If you're a school like Temple, which is not afraid to take a chance on a kid, give him an opportunity to get an education—and that's what I'm all about, opportunity—[the NCAA] begins to look at you with its nose turned up, saying, "Well, Temple is not as academic as others. They're taking in the sick and the poor." It's like the Statue of Liberty turning her ass and saying to the sick, the poor, the tired, "Get the hell out."[55]

Part of the perceived problem around Prop 48/42 is that these initiatives were passed during a period of federal cuts in aid to education. Further, the early evidence showed that blacks were affected disproportionately. In 1985, the year before Prop 48 took effect, blacks represented 27.3 percent of all athletes in the entering class. In 1986, this proportion fell to 23.6 percent. While the share of black athletes in 1989 rose to 25.0 percent, it was still well below the pre-Prop 48 level.

Blacks also made up a disproportionate share of the partial qualifiers: of 457 partial qualifiers admitted to Division I NCAA schools for the academic year 1987–88, 65.0 percent were black; for 1988–89, the figure was 65.5 percent; and for 1989–90 it was 65.9 percent. During these years between 80 and 90 percent of the partial qualifiers failed to meet the standardized test score requirement. This imbalance should have surprised no one since in the late 1980s the average joint SAT score was 737 for blacks and 937 for whites.[56]

The NCAA responded that such an outcome in the short run was to be expected, but that over time the higher standards would send a message to aspiring athletes that they had to do well in primary and secondary school. Further, the NCAA pointed to the fact that the graduation rate of black athletes increased from 34 percent for the entering class of 1985, to 41 percent for the entering class of 1986, to 43 percent for 1989, and 46 percent for 1990 (compared to 38 percent in 1990 for all black students). At least part of the improved graduation rate was due to the higher standards themselves, rather than any incentive effect on high school students. That is, if less qualified students are excluded, other things being equal, one would expect better academic performance. Another part was attributable to the increasing athletic participation of black females who have a higher graduation rate than black males. Nonetheless, the NCAA could point to the facts that the percentage of blacks among all Division I athletes recovered to its pre-Prop 48 level by

TABLE 2.1
Making the Pros

	Football	Basketball
High School Participants	265,000	150,000
Making NCAA Teams	16,450	3,800
Playing as Seniors	8,930	2,400
Playing in the Pros	215	64
Odds	1 in 1,233	1 in 2,344*

*From *NCAA News*, October 9, 1989. Cited in Clark Kerr and Marian Gade, *The Guardians*, p. 84.

the mid-90s and that the share of blacks among partial qualifiers fell steadily to 51 percent in 1994–95.[57] This share rose again to 58.8 percent in 1995–96, but this was still 7 percentage points below the level in 1989–90 (and was itself probably due to the increase in eligibility standards introduced in 1995–96). It is also significant that although the absolute number of black athletes in Division I fell from 3,589 in the 1983 entering class to 3,491 in 1989, the absolute number of all black students entering Division I schools rose from 49,134 to 53,133 between 1983 and 1989, and the share of black students increased from 9.6 percent to 9.9 percent.

There is, to be sure, something compelling about John Chaney's outrage, but ultimately his argument boils down to a call to do away with all admissions standards. Surely, Chaney must recognize that when funds are allocated for athletic scholarships then there are fewer funds available for need-based academic scholarships. Norman Spencer, principal of Franklin High School in inner-city Philadelphia, states: "Our kids, if they don't get the scholarships, they don't go to college."[58] Does Chaney favor admitting inner-city athletes instead of inner-city academically gifted students?

The scales are already tipped in favor of the athlete. Indeed, the scales may be broken. It is almost a universal perception among inner-city youth that the only ticket out is sports. As was portrayed vividly in the movies *Hoop Dreams* and *He Got Game*, the dream of being a basketball star in college and the pros is all-consuming. Unfortunately, it is also dangerously prevalent. A 1990 Harris Poll of 1,865 high school basketball and football players revealed that 32 percent thought they would make it to the pros; among black students 43 percent believed they would be pros. The real numbers and odds from 1989 are in Table 2.1.

Neither the NCAA nor universities in general should be expected to solve the problems of U.S. society. Educational deficiencies based in broken families, cultural violence, and poorly funded public schools cannot be redressed by the university alone. Nor will incentives from the

NCAA suffice to inspire young athletes to do their homework. These problems must be attacked at their roots and not wished away by ratcheting down academic standards. If the burden for teaching basic literacy and numeracy falls upon the university, then the university will be transformed into a grade school and the most important contribution it can make in fighting prejudice and parochialism—the promotion of free and critical thinking—will be undermined.

The remaining question is whether or not it is necessary to use a culturally biased standardized test as one of the eligibility standards. The reason the NCAA uses the SAT and ACT scores is that for athletes performance on these tests is an important predictor of performance in college. Indeed, standardized test performance explains a somewhat greater degree of the variation in college graduation rates than does high school GPA or rank.[59] The reason for this apparently is that difficulty of classes and grading across U.S. secondary schools is highly variable and that athletes seem to benefit from more lenient grading norms and/or easier classes. Thus, the standardized and more systematic information provided by the SAT and ACT exams is, simply put, very useful in deciding which applicants among the prospective athletes will be successful in college. In fact, the share of black athletes who lost their eligibility as a result of the standardized tests fell to 39.6 percent in 1995–96; that is, the tests are no longer the most important obstacle.[60]

Nonetheless, it would be desirable to perfect the tests to eliminate cultural biases. It clearly is in everyone's interest, not just the athletes, for this to happen. The NCAA should work with the Educational Testing Service and the College Board to this end.

In the meantime, the NCAA and its member colleges should worry about their woeful performance in employing black coaches and administrators. According to a 1988 study by the Center for the Study of Sport in Society, college sports has a worse record for hiring people of color than the NBA, the NFL or Major League Baseball.[61] In Division I, although 61 percent of basketball players and 52 percent of football players are black, only 17.3 percent of men's basketball head coaches, 5.3 percent of women's head basketball coaches, 7.2 percent of football head coaches, and 10.1 percent of athletic directors are black. At the NCAA offices, only 21 percent of its professional staff, 6.7 percent of its support staff, and zero percent of its sales staff are black.

Strengthening Prop 48/42 and the Eligibility Clearinghouse

At the January 1992 Convention the NCAA voted in Prop 16. Prop 16 raised eligibility requirements in two stages. First, to be eligible for fall 1995 freshmen would have to meet the 2.0 GPA threshold in 13, instead of the previous 11, core courses. Second, for the fall 1996 the 2.0 standard would be raised and converted into a sliding scale wherein higher GPAs could substitute for lower test scores, and vice versa. The fall 1996 GPA threshold would be raised to 2.5 in 13 core courses and a 700 combined SAT or a 2.0 GPA and a 900 combined SAT, or various combinations in between.[62] Finally, under the urging of the Presidents' Commission, Prop 16 was softened at the 1995 Convention to allow partial qualifiers to practice with the team and to receive athletic scholarships.

The greatest change in eligibility requirements in the 1990s, however, was the decision to establish the NCAA Eligibility Clearinghouse in 1993 to determine whether high school courses qualified as core. Prior to this the determination of core courses was done by the individual colleges which had little, if any, incentive to cast a discerning eye on course background of their prospective athletic stars. Once again this created the problem of cheating on the cartel and once again the NCAA attempted to rectify the problem with new regulations.

Judging by its first three years the Clearinghouse has been something of a nightmare, making arbitrary and wrongheaded decisions, causing lengthy delays which de facto make the athlete ineligible his or her first year and engendering expensive litigations. On top of this, the Clearinghouse cost the NCAA $1.5 million to operate in 1996–97; and this figure does not include the national office costs of dealing with the Clearinghouse.[63]

The basic standards for a core course are sensible enough. The courses must be in the fields of English, math, and physical and social science, with a few optional courses in areas such as philosophy and foreign language. Further, the courses must be college preparatory; they cannot be remedial, vocational, or personal service (e.g., speed reading) in nature.

The Clearinghouse, with a full-time staff of only 13, has to evaluate the curricula of 24,000 high schools around the country. The obvious happens. The Clearinghouse staff makes its initial determinations, not reviewing the syllabi of the multitude of courses, but by reviewing course titles. Appeals of Clearinghouse decisions must be made by the college, not the affected individual; this can delay the process by several months. In 1995, nearly 16,000 of the 114,747 individuals who applied for eligibility hadn't heard from the Clearinghouse as of November 15, more than two months into their first college semester.

For the academic year 1995–96 the cases of approximately 900 students were appealed. In one case, from Roseville High School in Minnesota, the Clearinghouse rejected an honors English course entitled "Critical Reading." Former Minnesota Governor Arne Carlson says that it is absurd for the Clearinghouse to second-guess a state-approved curriculum. Of the nine hundred appeals, an NCAA subcommittee reversed nearly half, and many of the remaining were appealed again to the NCAA Council. The NCAA is studying ways to simplify its system. For 1998–99 the NCAA had pledged to allow high schools to decide which courses are core, subject to review by the Clearinghouse.

The higher standards of Prop 16 have caused overall eligibility to plummet. Within Division I, the proportion of applicants not meeting the eligibility standards increased from 3.2 percent for the entering class of 1994, to 6.0 percent for 1995, to over 10.6 percent in 1996. More disturbing still, the standards have hit lower-income groups and blacks the hardest. Ineligibility among blacks rose from 8.5 percent in 1994, to 16.3 percent in 1995 (compared to 6.5 percent for whites). And ineligibility was inversely correlated with income. In 1995, students from families with incomes of less than $30,000 had an ineligibility rate of 13.9 percent, while students from families with incomes between $30,000 and $40,000 experienced a rate of 8.7 percent, from families with incomes between $40,000 and $50,000 a rate of 6.2 percent, and from families with incomes above $50,000 a rate of 3.1 percent.[64]

The pattern of inequality continued in 1996. The percentage of black prospective student-athletes who were ineligible rose from 16.3 percent in 1995 to 26.9 percent in 1996. The percentage ineligible from families with incomes above $80,000 rose from 6.9 percent in 1995 to 13.3 percent in 1996, and the percentage ineligible from families with incomes below $30,000 rose from 13.9 percent to 34.7 percent.[65]

These results, of course, reflect an underlying societal pattern of unequal opportunity. Arguably, the amelioration of this inequality should also be focused on the society. At best, the university can only make modest improvements in the short run on this deep-seated structural problem.

Despite the higher standards and tougher enforcement of Prop 16 and the Clearinghouse, the basic pattern of admitting underprepared or unqualified athletes persists. A July 1997 study of the top twenty-five schools in football and basketball revealed a substantial disparity in the GPAs and SATs of athletes and nonathletes. At Berkeley and UCLA the average high school GPA of the freshmen in men's basketball was at least one point below that of other students. At Wake Forest, the average combined SAT score for a freshman basketball player was 829 during 1993–96, fully 400 points below the cutoff for the bottom quarter of the class.[66] At the University of Virginia, the men's basketball team had a combined SAT average 510 points below that of the freshman class. In 1996, at Notre Dame the combined median SAT for all first-year students was 1310, but only 894 for entering football players. At Northwestern this disparity was 1310 for all freshmen and 1028 for football players, while at Michigan it was 1240 and 866.[67] John DiBiaggio, former president of Michigan State, commented on the "special admits" at big-time schools: "You can't tell me that a student with that kind of preparation can play a sport, take a full load of classes, and perform at acceptable levels."[68]

The NCAA must address the contradiction of its efforts. It has created an administrative monster in the Clearinghouse in order to evaluate the legitimacy of high school classes. But the NCAA is an association of colleges, not of high schools, and it has done nothing to assess the substance of college courses. Coach Jerry Tarkanian can take his basketball team on a 16-day summer cruise and reward them with six hours of course credit for studying "Contemporary Issues in Social Welfare." Scores of students can sign up for correspondence classes with the Southeastern College of the Assemblies of God in Lakeland, Florida, and have hired hands do the work.[69] Athletes can do college coursework in "The Theory of Basketball," "College Football USA," and "The Theory of Track and Field."[70] And the NCAA is worried about whether "Critical Reading" at Roseville High is a core course!

Eligibility, as defined by the NCAA, is almost entirely a matter of joining the club. Once you're in, the system protects you. With all the emphasis on clearing the initial hurdle there is a strong incentive to scheme and to cheat. Stories of deviousness abound.[71] Consider the case of Andy Katzenmoyer. Ohio State's Katzenmoyer won the 1997 Butkus Award, given to the best linebacker in college football. By the end of the 1997–98 academic year, however, Katzenmoyer's GPA slipped below 2.0 and his eligibility for the 1998–99 season was threatened. The school arranged for him to take three summer school classes to bring up his GPA. Katzenmoyer's three classes were Golf, Music, and AIDS Awareness. His AIDS Awareness teacher, Randi Love, commented: "I didn't know who he was, but my husband did. If I don't pass him, it threatens our marriage." OSU football coach, John Cooper, had a different perspective: "My only concern is that if they're [football players] in [summer school] classes, they're not on the practice fields, and that affects us, because they're behind."[72] Apparently, Katzenmoyer hits a solid 8-iron; his grade point went above the threshold and he was back on the gridiron playing for the top-ranked Buckeyes in 1998–99.

One recent scandal was uncovered by *Sports Illustrated* in July 1997. Top high school athletes are sent to particular high schools (sometimes traveling across the country) where it has been arranged through payoffs to have their standardized tests adjusted. A variation on this theme was reported in the *Kansas City Star* special 1997 report on college sports: some schools pay to have the answers encoded on pencils for prospective athletes.

The foregoing is not intended to impugn the integrity of NCAA officials. For the most part, they appear to be making sincere efforts, and, in some cases, they are making incremental improvements. The problem is that they are trying to reconcile an ideal of amateurism with the commercial juggernaut that big-time college sports has become.

EVALUATING AN ATHLETE'S COMPENSATION

In the fall of 1996, the athletes at Oregon State University gathered for their annual orientation meeting with the staff and coaches of the school's athletic department. The staff and coaches were wearing T-shirts that on the front read "National Champions. Beavers. 1996." Those who follow college sports might well wonder to what this designation applied. The Oregon State Beavers from the Pacific 10 Conference had gone neither to the Rose Bowl nor the Final Four in 1996. Indeed, the football team had not had a winning season since the price of gold was fixed at $38.50 per ounce. The men's basketball team won only four games in 1996. Nor did it refer to women's basketball or a less prominent sport. The back of the T-shirts provided an answer: "Graduation Rate 95%."

A remarkable record, nearly 40 points above the NCAA Division I average of 58 percent! It is even a more stunning achievement when compared to, say, the men's basketball graduation rates for the teams in the 1996 Final Four of 25 percent,[73] or to any of the nine teams ranked in the final top 25 in 1995–96 which had graduation rates of 0 percent.[74]

President Clinton sat in the stands cheering his home state University of Arkansas Razorbacks when they won the 1994 NCAA national championship. As of fall 1997, none of the five starters on that team had a degree from the university.[75] In 1998, only 35 percent of the 350 players in the NBA had college degrees.[76]

Oregon State employs no special secrets or trickery. Many of the other schools in the Pac-10, such as Stanford or Berkeley, can attract superior students, but Oregon State prioritizes education. Coaches aren't hired unless they want to be evaluated on the academic success of their athletes. The AD keeps a record of the athletes' GPAs and compiles an aggregate GPA for each team. These scores are posted each quarter and the winning team receives an award. When on the road, athletes are provided with laptops and modems. Learning labs with computers are open 24 hours a day. Moreover, the athletics department has devoted these resources to learning and still managed to balance its budget for six consecutive years.[77] The Oregon State recipe for success is straight-forward: they create an atmosphere that is supportive of the educational process.

Pressures to conform, however, became too strong for Oregon State's AD, Dutch Baughman. Boosters, local radio stations, and the university administration were becoming increasingly critical of the school's dearth of football and basketball victories (on the playing field). The Pac-10 probably also applied pressure. Why should the conference want to share its lofty revenues with a school that does not make a commensurate effort to field athletically competitive teams? In August 1997, Baughman resigned, saying: "The criteria [*sic*] isn't education but how many wins you have in football."[78] Trotsky used to say that you can't have socialism in one country.

Of course, athletes are not paid at Oregon State, yet few of them, one would surmise, feel exploited—at least through August 1997. Ninety-five percent of student-athletes at Oregon State leave with a college degree, an achievement that no other Division I school can claim and that few even approach. Although the Division I graduation rate of student-athletes overall, including all sports and both sexes, is 58 percent, compared to 56 percent for all students, the graduation rate in the two big-time sports is appreciably lower, 50 percent in football and 41 percent in men's basketball.

When the issue of exploiting student-athletes is raised, it is generally the football and men's basketball teams that are being discussed. It is predominantly on these teams that the athletes can devote anywhere from thirty to sixty hours a week to their sport, where many of the athletes generate hundreds of thousands of dollars for their schools, and where many do not benefit in any meaningful way from their college education. For these athletes, the question is: should they be paid?

From their admission into college, to their free tuition, room and board, to their special curricula, tutoring, and living conditions on campus, there is no question that student-athletes are treated differently. The term student-athlete itself tells you they are not normal students. This anomalous term was coined by Walter Byers in 1953 to assist NCAA member schools in their fight against workmen's compensation insurance claims for injured football players. If student-athletes were normal university students, then either the term would not be necessary or it would be joined by other terms like student-musician, student-artist, or student-engineer.

The experience of student-athletes varies from school to school and individual to individual. Generally, this experience has both positive and negative features. Potentially, the positive features include: a possible college degree; free tuition, room and board; free, special tutoring; privileged living conditions while in college; various psychological and social benefits, and, for some, payments on the side. These benefits, however, are often diminished by many costs. We evaluate these benefits and costs below.

The Positives

GRADUATION RATES

Other than the athletic training and visibility that the fortunate few who go on to the pros receive, the greatest tangible compensation an athlete can hope for is the credential of a bachelor's degree. But, as we have seen, only around half of Division I football and basketball players ever manage to get this degree, and many who have the degree have learned little or nothing.

Although the average time it takes for a student to graduate is 4.8 years (the average is the same for student-athletes), graduation rates as reported by the NCAA consider a six-year period from the time a student enters college. The most recent data available are for the entering class of 1991–92.

On the whole, Division I student-athletes' graduation rates (57 percent) compare favorably to those of all students (56 percent).[79] One explanation for this relative success of student-athletes is that many of them have all or part of their tuition, room and board, and books covered by their grants. Nonathlete students, in contrast, often drop out early for financial reasons.

When the NCAA began to collect these data for the entering class of 1983, both student-athletes and all students had graduation rates of 51 percent. Thus, the graduation rate for athletes has been rising faster than the overall rate. While some would attribute part of this increase to the impact of Prop 48, it is clear that rising graduation rates for women (who constitute an increasing proportion of all students) account for a substantial part of the improvement. Graduation rates for all female students rose from 53 to 58 percent and for all male students from 50 to 53 percent between 1983 and 1991. The rates for female athletes rose from 59 to 67 percent and for male athletes from 47 to 51 percent. The graduation rate for black female athletes jumped from 41 percent to 56 percent, not only the largest increase in any category but also 11 points above the rate for all black female undergraduates.

While the trend has been upward, there have also been some disturbing setbacks. Most notably, the graduation rate for Division I football players dropped from 58 percent for the class entering in 1989, to

52 percent for those entering in 1990, and to 50 percent for those entering in 1991. Graduation rates for men's basketball continues to lag behind all other sports; 41 percent overall and 37 percent for blacks. Alarmingly, the overall graduation rate for men's basketball players dropped from 45 percent to 41 percent between the entering classes of 1990 and 1991. The basketball schedule encroaches on both academic semesters and tends to cause greater disruption in one's studies. Modern commercial innovations, such as Midnite Madness and the scheduling shift to more mid-week games to accommodate TV programming needs, serve to make a difficult situation worse.

There is little mystery behind this pattern in graduation rates. Student-athletes do better on average than other students, but athletes in the two big-time sports do considerably worse. Men's basketball and football players have lower GPAs and lower SATs than other athletes on average[80] and they devote considerably more time and energy to sports and conditioning than do most other athletes. Further, a high proportion of big-time athletes don't attend college for either an education or a degree, but to take advantage of the only viable route to professional basketball and football. Stephon Marbury, the talented point guard at Georgia Tech in 1996, announced after his freshman year that he was entering the NBA draft and with refreshing candor explained that attending college was "just a way to position myself for the [NBA] draft."[81] Former Iowa State football coach Jim Walden told *Sports Illustrated*: "Not more than 20 percent of the football players go to college for an education. And that may be a high figure."[82] These outcomes convey a very simple and clear message about the conflict between big-time athletics and academic values.

But graduation rates at best give only a quantitative, not qualitative, picture of a program's educational success. David Bennett, a former faculty representative to the athletics department at Syracuse University, puts his finger on a core issue: "There are innumerable 'guts' on every campus, some of them designed specifically for student athletes. There are empty degrees, totally hollow degrees." Even when students enroll in standard courses, the meaning of their grade is often suspect. The athletics department can recommend professors who are lenient to athletes, and in other cases where a student is in trouble there are many big-time coaches who have called professors to ask for favors. For instance, Bailey and Littleton cite the case of one professor at a prominent Division IA school who was asked by the football coach to give his starting quarterback a "B" so that he would qualify to play. In this case, the coach asked the wrong teacher. The professor asked the coach for a favor in return: to start a student of his and Rhodes Scholarship candidate at quarterback.[83]

Anton Gunn was an offensive lineman in the early 1990s at the University of South Carolina. He majored in history despite admonitions from the academic advisor in the athletics department that the subject was too difficult. Instead, he was encouraged to major in criminal justice and was given lists of professors who favored athletes. The assignments for one course he was shuttled into as a freshman were due on computer disk, but a special "tutor" did the homework for all twelve athletes in the class. For exams, test copies were passed among the athletes ahead of time. When Gunn was a senior he took a thesis class that conflicted with practice. Gunn missed practice and incurred the wrath of the coaching staff. Gunn was also told not to join a fraternity because it would interfere with football and was threatened with losing his scholarship. The threats proved hollow; Gunn graduated with his history degree after four years in 1994.[84]

In one recent instance, brought to light by a lawsuit of a former football player at Texas Tech University, athletic administrators procured the answers to a final exam and gave them to the student. Not surprisingly, the student received an A in the course.[85] Texas Tech also gained notoriety in 1997 when it was discovered that two of its football stars played in the Alamo Bowl despite having a fall semester GPA of *0.00*.[86]

In still other instances, students arrange to earn credit through correspondence courses or arrange for hired hands to write papers and even take exams for them. The result is that many athletes spend several years at a college and may even obtain a degree without ever having learned basic reading, writing, and arithmetic. Thus, Alan Page, former lineman for the Minnesota Vikings, described a meeting to go over the team's playbook where only two of eight could read the playbook with ease, two could read it with difficulty, and four couldn't read it at all.[87] Dexter Manley, former star of the Washington Redskins, confessed at a congressional hearing that he is illiterate. The University of Southern California in 1991 ordered a former testing coordinator to "discontinue a study of academically at-risk USC student-athletes [because] administrators didn't want outsiders to learn that athletes were being admitted to USC with serious reading deficiencies."[88]

The issues here go well beyond trumped-up courses in college. Parents and primary and secondary schools need to do a better job. There is no excuse for the situation described in the *Orlando Sentinel* in June 1997 where a high school football coach in Dade County, Florida, asked one of his top prospects to look up in the newspaper where he ranked among the county's receivers and discovered that the player could not even recognize his own name in print.[89]

Again, not all big-time sports schools are alike. A few schools, like Stanford, enforce consistently high academic standards for all or nearly all of their athletes. Other schools maintain an "academic track" for student-athletes who are serious about their studies as well as an "athletic track" for those who are unprepared for the rigor and discipline of true college work. Still other schools find virtually all of their basketball and football players with grants-in-aid on the "athletic track."

For those who go on to get a college degree there is a handsome return. The present value of a bachelor's degree (discounted value of additional lifetime earnings) is over $200,000.[90] This is part of the return for many student-athletes.

It is also time to recognize that college is not for everyone. Athletes should be able to pursue a professional career in football or basketball without having to pretend they are also students. The solution is within grasp and is discussed in chapter 9.

GRANTS-IN-AID

After pronouncing itself against full-ride athletic scholarships to college for several decades, the NCAA capitulated in 1952 when student aid based on athletic skill, rather than financial need or academic merit, was approved. In 1956, the full-ride athletic scholarship was sanctioned and grants-in-aid have been part of the NCAA lexicon ever since.[91] Aside from a momentary pang of conscience in 1976 when the Association narrowly defeated a motion (120 to 112) to make scholarships need-based in Division I, the only changes have come in the name of cost-cutting. The number of full-ride scholarships that could be handed out in Division I football, for instance, was set at 105 in 1973, then reduced to 95 in 1988, and to 85 in 1994.

The full grant-in-aid consists of covering tuition, fees, room and board, and books. The average annual nominal value of such a grant at public universities in 1996–97 was $14,771 per year for out-of-state students.[92] Naturally, at the top private schools this value can rise above $25,000 a year in the late 1990s. Since an athletic grant is tax free, the monetary value of a grant consisting of $25,000 in benefits is equal to the grant divided by one minus the marginal tax rate on the athlete's family income. For instance, if a student's family is in the top federal marginal bracket of 39.6 percent and the state has a 5 percent income tax rate, the monetary value of a $25,000 grant-in-aid package is $46,339.[93] Thus, an athletic grant-in-aid to a student from a wealthy family has a higher monetary value than one to a student from a middle income or poor family. Of course, the actual present value of a college degree in terms of added earning power over one's lifetime can be considerably higher still.

The out-of-pocket costs of attending college exceed the full grant. Students have travel expenses to and from home, clothing and leisure expenses, among others. After the NCAA signed its seven-year, $1 billion television contract with CBS for its basketball tournament in 1989, the Association acted quickly to divert any new criticism that it was enriching itself off undercompensated athletes. Although its action was swift, it was hardly magnanimous. In 1990, the NCAA started a Special Assistance Fund of $3 million annually that student-athletes could use for special needs, such as babysitters, clothing, or trips home to visit sick parents (up to $200 per athlete). The $3 million was shared among the NCAA's 33 Division I conferences, with the average conference receiving just under $91,000 (approximately $10,000 per school). After the upward renegotiation of the TV contract in 1994 to $1.7 billion, at the 1996 Convention the NCAA expanded this fund to $10 million a year. The per-student limit was raised to $500; in 1996–97 there were 18,629 students who received an average grant of $415. The Association also has a catastrophic insurance fund, a grants-in-aid fund, and a modest degree completion fund to assist present and former college athletes.[94]

PELL GRANTS

Pell Grants are federal college scholarships made to relatively low-income students. Until 1982 when an athlete received a Pell Grant (the maximum yearly value of which was $1,800 per student at the time), the money from the grant would be subtracted from the student's athletic grant-in-aid from the school. That is, the federal grant would not work to the student's benefit at all, but it would reduce the school's outlay on athletics scholarships or allow the school to provide athletic aid to other (sometimes wealthy) students. Put differently, the federal government (among its other subsidies to college athletics to be treated in chapter 6) was subsidizing the athletic budgets of Division I colleges. Walter Byers calls it "tapping into federal poverty money for Division I athletic programs."[95]

Pell Grant money was sufficiently attractive to colleges (in fiscal 1998 it totaled around $5 billion) that many schools began the practice of writing out the applications for their athletes. Some schools even submitted false documents to procure these funds. The University of Miami, for instance, was given three years' probation in 1995 by the NCAA for falsifying documents to obtain $213,000 in Pell Grants during 1989–91.[96] A 1997 study by the Government Accounting Office estimates that Pell Grant fraud on behalf of college athletes may have cheated U.S. taxpayers out of as much as $300 million.[97]

At the 1982 Convention it was decided to allow the student to keep half of the Pell Grant, with the other half going to reduce the institution's expenditures on athletic aid. By 1990 the maximum Pell Grant had grown to $2,300 and the student was allowed to keep $1,700; and in 1996–97 the maximum grant was $2,470 and the student was allowed to retain it all, thus ending the NCAA's unhappy reverse Robin Hood era.

Students can now receive a full grant-in-aid from their institution and a $3,000 (the fiscal 1998 maximum) Pell Grant above that. Further, at its 1997 Convention the Association decided to allow athletes to work during the academic year and earn up to $2,000 above a full grant-in-aid. Since boosters are sure to offer phantom jobs, the implementation and monitoring of this provision promises to be another administrative headache. AD trepidation over its complications postponed its introduction until 1998–99. In part for this reason and in part because coaches don't want their student-athletes spreading themselves too thin, athletic departments have strongly discouraged their athletes from seeking these jobs. According to one fall 1998 survey, in fewer than one-third of the schools were there more than ten athletes taking advantage of this new job opportunity.[98]

ACADEMIC TUTORING

In 1982, only twenty-four schools had formal academic support programs for athletes.[99] Then came the embarrassment of the Jan Kemp suit against the University of Georgia and the era of perceived higher academic standards ushered in by Prop 48. Today, the NCAA requires every Division I school to maintain such a program. Several Division II schools also run a program, and together there are five hundred academic support programs in the NCAA. There is also a National Association of Athletic Academic Advisors with nearly six hundred members.

These programs can be very involved and constitute major financial commitments, often consisting of special laboratories, remedial sessions, and assistants who are assigned to wake the athletes up and go to class with them. At the University of Southern California, for instance, the academic support program for athletes is housed in a 10,000-square-foot facility with special computer labs and has a full-time staff of 9, including 3 academic counselors, a tutorial coordinator, a learning specialist, and 2 needs coordinators. The budget in 1996–97 was around $800,000 to accommodate the needs of some 600 student-athletes. In contrast, in the early 1980s, academic support at USC was a one-person shop with a budget below $30,000.[100] At the University of Kentucky, the academic tutoring program for athletes had a budget of only $20,000 in 1977; by 1997–98 the budget was close to $1 million, employing 120 to 140 tutors.[101]

LIVING CONDITIONS

The University of Oklahoma opened the first football-only dormitory in the 1940s, but Bear Bryant at Alabama perfected the practice by building a "palace" in 1965 known as "The Bear."[102] Students likened "The Bear" to a Hilton Hotel and soon Bryant's recruiting success led practically every other school in the southeast to open "its own posh football-only hostelry."[103] Big-time athletes also had their own kitchens and dining rooms, known as "training tables." Coaches found that these luxury lodgings were useful for other reasons: controlling the athletes' lives, imposing curfews, curtailing alcohol consumption, and limiting social activities.

Eventually, the football- and basketball-only abodes became expensive symbols of the athletes' isolation from campus life and the educational process. At the 1991 Convention the NCAA voted to phase out the special athletic dorms by 1996 and to reduce the number of training table meals to one per day.

Ever like a leaking hose, with the hostelry hole patched, the cartel members found new ways to compete and new leaks were opened. Special athletic housing was supposedly abolished, but athletes can still reside in special dormitories as long as 50 percent plus one of the residents are not athletes. The other dwellers can be married graduate students, administrators, faculty, or others.

The new recruiting showpieces have become mammoth training complexes, led by the University of Georgia's $12 million Heritage Hall opened in 1987. The University of Tennessee followed with its own $10 million state-of-the-art sports complex, featuring an ultra-modern weight room, indoor practice field, medical facilities, carpeted suites with private bathrooms and cable television, and electronic surveillance. Football and basketball players can no longer live by themselves full-time in these complexes, but they can share them, or spend a night there before a game (or go to a local hotel) and eat an occasional meal there.

PSYCHOSOCIAL BENEFITS

There is a familiar litany of personal benefits that is recited in connection to participation in high school and college sports. It includes: learning teamwork, dedication, discipline, self-esteem; relieving stress and tension; and, improving health, conditioning, and energy levels.

Henry Wade Rogers, president of Northwestern University in the early 1890s, formulated the following rationale for intercollegiate sports in the face of widespread criticism for corruption, violence, and incompatibility with educational values: "[athletics] teach self-mastery, the ability to control one's temper, and to work with others. They demand steadiness of nerve, coolness, self-reliance, the subordination of animal impulses."[104]

These potential gains were given a different spin by Pat O'Brien in his lead role in the famous 1940 Hollywood biopic *Knute Rockne, All-American*: "We [coaches] believe the finest work of man is building the character of man. We have tried to build courage and initiative, tolerance and persistence—without which the most educated brain in the head of man is not worth very much."[105]

Yes, performed properly and in moderation, competitive team sports can possess these virtues; so can other activities, such as joint science projects, jogging or listening to Bach.[106]

PAYMENTS ON THE SIDE

Eric Ramsey was a star cornerback for Auburn University in the early 1990s. He was drafted in the 10th round by the Kansas City Chiefs, and then cut. In these respects, Ramsey was like many other Division IA football players. Ramsey, however, did something that no other player had done. He secretly tape-recorded (22 microcassettes in all) his conversations with coaches and boosters, offering him cash payments for his athletic services.[107]

Because documented tape evidence is generally not available and because most players don't reveal their transgressions unless obligated to do so, it is not possible to discern how widespread the practice of making cash payments is in the late 1990s. There are plenty of anecdotes and an occasional reported infraction, but these days the methods of cash transfer are surreptitious and subtle.

Some athletes apparently are given ATM codes by boosters. Others accompany boosters on large-item purchases and the cashier is instructed by the booster to pass the change on to his friend. Still others receive "loans" or handsomely remunerated summer jobs from boosters. Many more, like the University of Massachusetts' Marcus Camby, are given cash by prospecting player agents. Scores of athletes receive compensation in kind: here, a gold necklace or leather jacket to Marcus Camby or airline tickets to Kirk King; there, a $40,000 gift to former University of Miami player Benny Blades, or a $300,000 Mercedes for Allen Iverson to cruise around in.[108]

Even Notre Dame, famed for running a pristine program, recently has been entangled in a booster pay scandal. Five former and five current football players were found to have received jewelry, clothing, and trips between 1993 and 1998 from a booster who had embezzled over $1 million from her employer.[109]

There are too many boosters, too many athletes, and too many venues for the NCAA to police. Even when an incident does come to light, such as the Florida State football players' 1993 shopping spree at Foot Locker, the institution or its staff often receives little more than a slap on the wrist. The cost of the penalty does not fit the potential benefit of the crime. In the Florida State case, the school hired the NCAA's second-in-charge of infractions, Bob Minnix, as its Associate AD. Then, the NCAA, following a self-investigation by Florida State, found that the school had not committed any major violation and did not lack institutional control.

The general pattern seems to be that unless a school flaunts and continually repeats its transgressions, the NCAA puts the school on probation and proclaims a *de minimis* restriction on the school's recruiting or scholarship aid for a year or two. The number of so-called NCAA major infractions has stayed steady over time: the average number per year was 14.7 during 1985–87, 11.7 during 1988–90, 13.3 during 1991–93, and 14.0 during 1994–96. Something isn't working.

Evaluating an Athlete's Compensation: The Negatives

DILUTED EDUCATION

In proper proportions, being an athlete and being a student can be synergistic. While this is more likely to be the case in women's sports and the non-revenue men's sports, even in these instances there is evidence of possible parasitism.

The odds for synergy in big-time men's basketball and football appear to be slim. Young athletes set their sights on the sports ticket to college and the pros at an early age, and street agents from the athletic shoe companies and coaches push them along with free sneakers, jackets, summer camps, and more.[110] As Clark Kerr and Marian Gade note in their book, *The Guardians*: "When blue-chip prospects (especially in football and basketball) are repeatedly called out of classes in high school to come to the coach's office to talk with college coaches who are recruiting these prospects, there can be no doubt about the greater priority being placed [on athletics] by both college and high school. . . ." Top high school athletes are likely to be contacted by scores, if not hundreds, of recruiters as early as their freshman or sophomore years. Even if they were inclined to pursue their studies seriously, the frenetic atmosphere of the college recruitment process makes this extremely difficult.[111]

This sense of priorities is reinforced by the utter disregard for classes that is displayed in the scheduling of athletic contests. In 1990, when the NCAA voted to reduce the length of the basketball season by two weeks, some of America's most beloved coaches threw a fit. Bobby Knight of Indiana doubted whether the college presidents who sponsored the reduction were "qualified to tell the athletic departments what the fuck to do," and Rick Pitino threatened "pulling out of the NCAA if the restrictions aren't rescinded."[112] Herein lies an important constraint on the NCAA's ability to violate the commercial interests of the big-time athletics programs. They can always threaten to leave the cartel. Since over 80 percent of the Association's revenues directly come from televising the end of the year basketball tournament, the NCAA has to be careful not to push reform too far. The NCAA learned this lesson firsthand with the College Football Association in the 1980s. The length of the basketball season was restored. Today, Division I schools can play twenty-seven games plus any games played in exempted tournaments and the postseason.

In March 1996, Coach John Calipari brought his University of Massachusetts Minutemen to New York for the Final Four on a Wednesday when the first game was on a Saturday night. School was in session. The team had not been expected to travel until Friday. Calipari explained his motives on ESPN: "We came to New York to avoid the media." That's right, the team left sleepy Amherst, Massachusetts, and went to New York, the world's media capital, to avoid the media. Perhaps Calipari had seen *Casablanca* the night before and listened as Humphrey Bogart's character, Rick, explained that he moved to Casablanca for the waters. Small wonder Division I basketball players have trouble graduating.

But the problems go beyond the gross insensitivity to education that frequently occurs in big-time sports. A 1993 study found in a national sample of athletes that, controlling for pre-college differences among the students, athletic participation in college was negatively linked with scores on standardized admissions tests for graduate school. A 1995 study, based on a 1992 survey of 2,416 students, compared test scores in math, reading comprehension, and critical thinking at the beginning and end of the freshmen year. After controlling for initial differences among the students, the authors found that there were significant differences between male athletes and nonathletes with respect to math and reading comprehension, and significant difference between female athletes and nonathletes with respect to reading comprehension. While the biggest difference was for male basketball and football players (who actually experienced a decrease in the math and reading scores during their first year), the difference was significant for other athletes as well. Further, the authors found that the extent of skill diminution was positively correlated with one's skill deficit when entering college.[113] The observed differences could be a result of a lack of time available for study, selection of classes with less emphasis on these skills, or personal factors.

Finally, many believe that the educational problems engendered by overemphasis on sports and winning transcend inadequate cognitive outcomes. For instance, Ernest Boyer in his 1987 book *The Undergraduate Experience in America*, based on extensive Carnegie Foundation research, concluded that on college campuses "the cynicism that stems from the abuses in [college] athletics infects the rest of student life, from promoting academic dishonesty to the loss of individual ideals. We find it disturbing that students who admit to cheating often excuse their conduct as being set by the college example . . . [of] athletic dishonesty."[114]

DRUG ABUSE, GAMBLING, AND VIOLENCE

In July 1996, a female student at New Mexico State was awakened in her bed by a man who was raping her. She called the police. Two months earlier the police had been notified of a similar incident. In August, James McIntyre, a starter on the school's football team, was charged with both rapes. He had earlier run-ins with the law, but the school did not remove him from the football team, pending the outcome of the rape trials.

The football team at the University of Nebraska won back-to-back national championships in 1995 and 1996. Some of the team's starters had been charged with domestic violence, assault, theft, and shooting a gun into an occupied car. Another team member was indicted for attempted murder. In each case, head coach Tom Osborne decided it was in the player's best interest to stay on the team. After the 1996 season, three players left the school before graduating and were drafted by NFL teams; all three have since been convicted of crimes they committed while on Osborne's team.

Virginia Tech lost to Nebraska in the 1996 Orange Bowl. Eighteen members of their football team were arrested between May 1996 and May 1997; two of them for rape.[115] In January 1997, a student journalist wrote a critical comment about Manny Dies, a 6'9" basketball player. Dies showed up at the student's room, encountered a locked door, and broke the door down. The student escaped by jumping from the second-floor roof.[116]

In October 1996, between thirty and fifty players on the University of Rhode Island football team assaulted a fraternity house. They were retaliating because at a party at the same house the previous weekend two players were asked to leave. The fraternity president described the attack: "They broke windows, smashed down four doors and beat and kicked a number of our members. They even threw one of the brothers down a fire escape." Three students, one with a broken elbow, were treated at a nearby hospital.[117]

In November 1996, five football players from Grambling State were arrested and charged with raping a teenager. The girl had wandered into their dormitory during a homecoming celebration.[118]

The roots of this violence may lie in precollege experiences, but it may also lie in the violent nature of the sport itself and the treatment the players receive from their coaches. A recent litigation by a football line coach against Notre Dame revealed physical fighting among coaches and coaches striking players.[119] Normal hard contact at practice and in games, coupled with the expectation that players always go all out and even play when hurt, contributes to the problem.[120]

Violence, crime, and gambling often go together. In 1995, five University of Maryland athletes, including the starting quarterback, were suspended for sports gambling.[121] Thirteen players from the Boston College football team during the 1996–97 academic year were involved with gamblers and organized crime.[122] At least two of the players bet against their own team in a contest with Syracuse University in October.[123] In December 1997, two players on the Arizona State University (ASU) basketball team pleaded guilty to point shaving. They were paid $20,000 per fixed game during the 1993–94 season.[124] Three months later another point scandal broke when two basketball players at Northwestern University were indicted for fixing games in 1994–95.[125] Further investigation of the incident by the FBI uncovered a gambling ring which involved the quarterback and others on the football team. Some players bet against their own team and others gave out inside information to the gamblers.[126] Four of the Wildcat football players were subsequently indicted for lying to a federal grand jury.

This list is hardly exhaustive. Back in 1951, 32 players from 7 universities were implicated in schemes to fix 86 games. In 1962, 37 players from 22 schools were involved in a major gambling scandal to fix basketball games. In 1981, a basketball player from Boston College and 4 others were convicted of shaving points during the 1978–79 season. Four years later, several members of the Tulane basketball team were accused of point shaving. In 1989, 4 football players from the University of Florida and 9 athletes at the University of Arkansas were suspended for betting on football games. Sadly, the number of detected incidents of student-athlete gambling has only gone up in the 1990s. In addition to the cases mentioned above, players from at least 7 other schools have been implicated in gambling on college games.[127]

A 1996 survey of 648 Division I football and basketball players revealed that 4 percent of the players admitted gambling on games in which they played and 25 percent admitted gambling on other college sporting events.[128] A 1998 survey of 765 Division I football and basketball players found that over 80 percent of the male student athletes had gambled in some way, 45 percent of them had gambled on sports, and 7.1 percent placed a bet with a bookie or on a sports card.[129]

Gambling and violence frequently go hand in hand. In 1995, 220 college athletes were involved in criminal proceedings, for alleged crimes from gambling to murder; 112 were charged with sexual assault or domestic violence. One study based on cases of university violence from 1991 through 1993 found that male athletes, who comprise less than 3 percent of all male students, accounted for 19 percent of the reported sexual assaults and 35 percent of the reported instances of domestic violence.[130]

Alcohol and drug abuse also are highly correlated with violent behavior. A 1993 survey of 17,251 college students found that in the two weeks prior to the survey 61 percent of the male athletes engaged in binge drinking, while only 43 percent of the nonathletes did so.[131] The male athletes were also more likely to ride in a car with an intoxicated driver, to engage in unprotected sex, and to have more sexual partners than the male nonathletes. The previously cited survey of Division I football and basketball players found that 50 percent admitted to driving while under the influence of alcohol, 45 percent admitted to hitting or threatening someone who was not a member of their own family, and almost 40 percent said they had thrown objects at cars or people.[132]

A 1990 study based on interviews with college athletes estimated that 20 percent of college football players used steroids.[133] The percentage of athletes at NCAA Championships who have tested positive for drugs has increased nearly sevenfold since 1991.[134]

PSYCHOSOCIAL DETRIMENTS

Stanford University psychiatry professor Hans Steiner conducted a study of 2,100 high school and college students and found that high school athletes earned better marks on various psychological tests than their nonathlete classmates, but among college students the athletes had inferior marks. In particular, Steiner found that the very attributes that may foster success in competitive sports placed the athletes at risk of alcohol or drug problems. Successful athletes are able to repress the fear of failure, Steiner reasons, but this repression causes other personal problems. Another hypothesis is that the additional pressure and time commitment required by big-time college sports may upset the balance between healthy exercise and release from sports, on the one hand, and tension and exhaustion, on the other.

In 1987 the NCAA commissioned a $1.75 million study on the psychological and social impact of college athletic participation. The results of the study were not sanguine, concluding that college athletes have lower GPAs, more psychological, physical, and alcohol and drug-related problems than other students involved in time-demanding extracurricular activities. It also found that athletes are less likely to accept leadership roles or assume responsibility for others.[135]

Joe Roberson, former AD at the University of Michigan, put the issue of proper proportions in different terms:

> In many respects, *arete* [Greek word meaning "striving for excellence in a balanced and unified physical, mental, and spiritual way"] provided much of the model for intercollegiate athletics . . . [there has been, however] a disturbing shift in balance that is moving us closer to the physical aspect of college sports and further from its mental and spiritual benefits. . . . [There is] a growing emphasis on success—that is, winning—and less emphasis on excellence, which is the maximization of potential.[136]

However one explains the phenomenon, it is apparent that there is a fine line between the psychosocial benefits and detriments that are engendered by college sports. Big-time sports certainly threaten to make the balance negative. Most of the positive aspects seem to be available in intramural sports and intercollegiate athletics in its less commercialized forms. As Title IX advances the interests and commercialism of women's sports, it may be important not to emulate the male model too closely.

The Value of the Overall Compensation Package

In his book *Keeping Score*, Richard Sheehan estimates the implicit hourly wage of an athlete on full scholarship at a Division IA school. His basic method is to value education at the tuition rate plus room and board,[137] adjust this number by the proportion of athletes who graduate at the school, and to divide this adjusted number by the estimated number of hours a student dedicates to his or her sport. The estimated median hourly wage is $6.82 in men's basketball and $7.69 in football.

To the extent that the athlete takes his classes seriously and earns a degree, then this is not bad remuneration for a "minor league" sport. In minor league baseball, salaries average between $850 and $2,500 per month (approximately $5.00 to $14.50 an hour), depending on the level of play.

Students who receive a full-ride scholarship in the "non-revenue" sports, such as swimming, volleyball, soccer, tennis, etc., receive a very handsome remuneration for their services given that their sports generate very little, if any, revenue for their schools. Moreover, male and female students in these sports would experience higher implicit hourly wages because they have higher rates of graduation and most dedicate fewer hours to their sport. Together with the coaches and ADs, these student athletes are the real beneficiaries of intercollegiate sports. Once again, there is a pattern for revenue to be produced by lower-income students and distributed to higher-income students, coaches, and administrators.

Another pattern is for nonathletes, and especially those who are not sports fans, to subsidize the athletes. This subvention occurs via the student fee, which has been creeping upward in recent years at most universities.[138]

Still, the star players are paid at the same implicit wage via the grant-in-aid as the reserves in basketball and football. Stars do not receive "market" wages, especially those who gain neither an education nor a credential from their college years. Thus, there is ongoing pressure to enrich their compensation packages. But the present NCAA Executive Director, Cedric Dempsey, himself the beneficiary of a private corporate jet, a salary exceeding $600,000, and untold perks, argues that it is not viable to increase the value of monetary scholarships because only sixty-five schools have surpluses in their athletics budgets.[139] And, as we shall see in chapter 7, even this is likely to be an optimistic assessment. Further, paying college athletes a wage not only means payroll taxes, workmen's compensation, and other expenses, but, most significantly, it means creating a labor market where players receive widely different salaries.

In the end, the number of Division IA student-athletes who are financially exploited by the current system is small. The players who produce the most revenue are likely bound for the pros where many will become instant millionaires. These players certainly are not exploited more than the minor league baseball players who become future stars.

Large numbers of student-athletes, however, are harmed by the system because they get neither an education nor a degree. These athletes are not the top stars and they never make it to the pros. Nor do they produce large revenues for their schools.

Some student-athletes benefit from the system. They fall into two groups. First, those who are well-qualified students upon entering college and who receive a valuable college education gratis. Second, those who are not well-qualified academically upon entering college but take their studies seriously and get a degree. For them, their athletic skills are not only a ticket to get into college but they also provide a full-ride, free education.

Finally, some studies have found that participation in college athletics provides greater social mobility for students from lower-class backgrounds, though the evidence is hardly robust.[140] Insofar as college athletes make better connections and develop better discipline or interpersonal skills, then one would expect them to earn higher incomes over time than nonathletes, other factors held constant.[141] Insofar as college athletes lag behind in the development of cognitive skills or career maturity, then one would expect them to earn less over time. One careful study, based on a survey of some 10,000 college freshmen from 1971 and their incomes in 1980, found that, other things being equal, male athletes had 4 percent higher incomes than male nonathletes. There was no differential gain for female athletes. The study, however, did not distinguish among different sports or among colleges in different NCAA divisions.[142]

Participants in big-time college sports are all unpaid professionals, but paying them directly for their work on the school team is neither economically feasible nor socially desirable. A reasonable argument, however, can be made that the NCAA places too many restrictions on the top athletes' ability to earn income off the playing fields. For instance, it makes little sense for schools to be able to sell memorabilia that exploit a student-athlete's likeness and for the player to receive no compensation from related royalties. Most U.S. Olympians are not paid for their performance in the Olympics, but they are permitted to sign remunerative advertising and endorsement deals. The NCAA has a proper role in limiting a student-athlete's time in such commercial activities during the school year, but if student-engineers can work in Silicon Valley during the summer months, then student-athletes should be allowed to pursue professional opportunities when school is not in session. That said, the real problems with intercollegiate athletics lie elsewhere.

CHAPTER THREE

Gender Equity I

EQUAL OPPORTUNITY FOR ATHLETES

The Olympic Games must be reserved for men.... [We] must continue to try to achieve the following definition: the solemn and periodic exaltation of male athleticism, with internationalism as a base, loyalty as a means, art for its setting, and female applause as its reward.
> —Pierre de Coubertin, founder of the modern Olympic Games

The costs of Title IX and the entry of women into the big time should not be blamed for today's highly publicized financial problems for college sports. At the heart of the problem is an addiction to lavish spending.
> —Walter Byers, Executive Director of the NCAA, 1951–87

JENNIFER Baldwin Cook played on the women's ice hockey team at Colgate University from 1987 through 1990.[1] In 1990, the women's team went to the national championship and made it to the finals. Yet the university did not believe that Jennifer's team was worthy of its support.

The women's hockey team at Colgate was organized in 1978 as a club, rather than a varsity sport. Club status meant that the team members had to self-finance the team, rather than receive funding from the athletic department budget. The twenty-eight women skaters did not receive athletic aid. They had to buy their own equipment, including skates, sticks, gloves, mouthguards, and tape. They had to pay to have their skates sharpened. Each paid a $25 club fee, plus an average of $400 for equipment.

The female hockey team was assigned a 20-square-foot area in a locker room which they had to share with two other women's teams. They were allowed to use the rink for an hour and a half four times a week to practice in the evening, unless the male team had a game or a local city team had a game.

When the team traveled, it had to rent a University-owned van at an average of $375 per trip. It was customary for the team to stay in relatives' or friends' houses and pay for their own meals. Jennifer was club president and it was her responsibility to devise the team schedule, make all travel plans, arrange for student referees, oversee the budget, and select a student coach.

Twenty-one of the twenty-two members of the male hockey team at Colgate were recruited and were on full athletic aid. Many were allowed to bypass the essay portion of their college application. The admissions office reserved ten slots yearly for the men's hockey team.

The team members received all their equipment from the school, and some members even resold the skates provided them by Colgate and used their own. The team was transported in commercial buses, stayed in expensive hotels (such as Boston's Copley Plaza), and received a $30-per-day meal allowance. The team practiced three hours a day, six days a week, in the school rink. The players had personal lockers, spread across three large locker rooms. The team had three full-time coaches and two trainers.

Jennifer and her teammates were not seeking equal status with the men when, in 1988, the women's hockey club applied for the fourth time to gain varsity status. Their proposed budget was only $16,000, less than 3 percent of what was spent on men's hockey. When they went to present their proposal to the designated committee, several members indicated that they had not read it. One committee member stated at the outset: "I had better get comfortable; this one puts me to sleep." The athletic director at Colgate said that he had only seen the women's team play for one-half hour during his 15-year tenure at the school. The committee asked few questions and, then, for the fourth time denied the team's request. The committee asserted that the proposed change was too costly, but the same year the stick budget for the men's team was increased by $12,000.

Jennifer and her teammates decided they had had enough. In 1990, they brought a Title IX discrimination suit against Colgate. On September 29, 1992, a Federal Magistrate Judge found Colgate to be in violation of Title IX. The University appealed and in April 1993 the U.S. Court of Appeals for the Second Circuit vacated the Magistrate's decision on grounds of mootness—the last two plaintiffs would have graduated by the 1993–94 season. New club members had to refile the suit. Finally, in February 1997, just three weeks before the case was scheduled to go to trial for a second time, Colgate capitulated, agreeing to grant varsity status to the women's team.

Amy Cohen began competing seriously in gymnastics at the age of eight. She trained three hours a day, five days a week. When she applied to

Brown University in 1987, she was led to believe that Brown was a progressive institution committed to women's gymnastics and women's sports in general. Her first semester, fall 1988, Amy learned differently.

The women's gymnastics team did not have its own trainer, despite the inherent danger in the sport. It did not have a laundry service for its workout uniforms. Women gymnasts had to schedule their use of the gym around the needs of men's basketball and wrestling. Men's teams frequently traveled to away games a day early to allow for rest and preparation; women made same-day trips.

Virtually all recruiting dollars were spent on men. Student hosts for football recruits, who were transported to the campus at Brown's expense, were given $50 to entertain them. The budget for women's recruiting covered only phone calls. While six cars were available for recruiting for men's football and three for men's basketball, none was available for women's sports. John Parry, who served as Brown's AD for eleven years, stated that he believed only 10 percent of Brown's male athletes would have been admitted to the school on the basis of academic merit.

In 1990–91 the coaches of the sixteen men's teams received a reported $932,227, while the coaches of the fifteen women's teams received only $360,862. Between 1988 and 1992 there was no effort by the school to promote attendance at any of the women's sports. The AD met with the captains of many of the men's teams to discuss how to improve them, but with no captains of the women's teams. The AD did not attend one single women's gymnastics event during the four years Amy Cohen was at Brown.

In Amy's first year at Brown, 1988–89, Brown hosted the Ivy League Gymnastics championships. The Brown women's team won the title for the first time in the school's history. Their recognition came in a meeting a few months later with Brown's new AD, Dave Roach. Roach had received instructions from Brown's president, Vartan Gregorian, to cut $78,000 from the athletic department's $5 million budget. This cut was part of a school-wide austerity program to deal with a projected budget deficit in excess of $1 million. Gregorian spared only student financial assistance and library acquisitions from his budgetary ax.

Roach decided to eliminate two men's teams (golf and water polo, with a budget of $15,295 together) and two women's teams (gymnastics and volleyball, with a budget of $62,028). Brown, however, upgraded men's squash from club to varsity status in 1989. AD Roach's perception that he was in a financial straightjacket notwithstanding, in the same year that he cut women's gymnastics and volleyball he increased athlete meal money for away trips from $15 to $22 per diem, bought out the contract of the men's soccer coach at a cost of $80,000, and left $62,000 of Brown Sports Foundation money unspent.

The women gymnasts were left with little alternative but to operate as a club, raising $15,000. The school's support services evaporated, scheduling facility use became more difficult, injuries went untreated, prospective gymnasts were no longer interested in Brown, and so on. The women gymnasts got together with the volleyball players and decided to take action. They contemplated filing a complaint with the Office of Civil Rights at the Department of Education, but they learned that the Office had insufficient resources to deal with the cases before it and the students needed a quick remedy. Instead, in April 1992 they brought a civil Title IX suit of sex discrimination against Brown.

The students obtained a preliminary injunction in U.S. District Court in December 1992, ordering Brown to restore the two women's teams until the case was decided in trial. Brown, however, appealed the order before the First Circuit U.S. Court of Appeals and obtained a stay on the decision (Brown did not have to reinstate the teams) until the Court considered the appeal. The students won the appeal in April 1993, but by this time the 1992–93 season had come and gone, as had recruiting time for the next year. This victory meant the temporary restoration of the two teams until the Title IX case itself went to trial.

The trial began in September 1994. Judge Pettine decided for the students and ordered Brown to prepare a plan to bring the school into compliance with Title IX. Brown appealed again. In November 1996 the First Circuit Appeals Court ruled in a 2-to-1 vote to uphold Judge Pettine's decision. Brown appealed yet again—this time to the U.S. Supreme Court.

Brown President Gregorian was indignant. He felt that the judges were wearing blinders; apparently, so were the presidents of the other Ivy League schools who chose not to come to Brown's defense on this issue. Gregorian believed that Title IX was a smokescreen for an affirmative action quota and, worse still, it elevated sports above the central academic functions of the university. How, Gregorian wondered, could the courts tell him that it was okay to cut the humanities budget but that it wasn't okay to cut athletics? The courts had said no such thing. Rather, the message was: athletics could be cut, but it was not all right to cut women's sports when women were already being discriminated against.

Why, Gregorian wondered, was Brown being picked on when Brown treated women athletes better than most schools? Amy Cohen answered this query when she testified before Congress in 1993: "If they were above average in preventing date rape yet date rape was still a problem on the campus would that mean that they are fine, that they do not need to make changes and improvements because other schools have a larger date rape problem? I don't think so."[2]

In April 1997 the Supreme Court refused to hear the Brown appeal. Now it was time for Gregorian to wonder why he had spent an estimated $1 million on legal expenses and faced a similar charge to cover expenses for the plaintiff, when he could have retained the two women's teams in perpetuity with an endowment that size. In July 1998 a federal court approved a settlement that Brown reached the month before which pledges to maintain women's athletics participation within 3.5 percentage points of women's enrollment at the school and to increase spending on four women's sports.

After being upheld in five previous Appeals Court rulings, Title IX and its implementation guidelines, as promulgated by the Office of Civil Rights, for the first time were sanctioned (if only indirectly) by the highest court in the land. Other challenges to Title IX may come in the future, but U.S. colleges and universities took the April 1997 decision as a clear message that they must act decisively to support gender equity. Still, gender equity generates sharp controversy and tension. What, then, is Title IX and what are the issues surrounding its implementation?

BRIEF HISTORY OF TITLE IX

In 1972, notwithstanding an aggressive NCAA lobbying effort against it, Congress passed Title IX of the Educational Amendments to the 1964 Civil Rights Act. Title IX, in its entirety, states: "No person in the United States shall, on the basis of sex, be excluded from participation in, be denied the benefits of, or be subjected to discrimination under any educational program or activity receiving federal financial assistance." The progress toward gender equity in school sports since 1972 has been remarkable, albeit not without its struggles, setbacks, and shortfalls.

Even though the original regulation regarding the implementation of Title IX was not published until June 1975 and high schools and colleges were given until July 1978 to comply, its passage sent an immediate signal to athletic programs throughout the country. The law of the land now unequivocally asserted that women cannot be discriminated against (must be treated equally) in any educational program or activity (such as intercollegiate sports) where the institution received federal assistance. Practically overnight, female athletic participation shot up: in 1971, 294,015 girls participated in high school sports; that number increased 2.8 times to 817,073 in 1973, and to 2.08 million in 1978.[3] At the college level, 31,852 took part in varsity sports in 1971, and by 1977 the number had more than doubled to 64,375.

This early momentum, however, was not sustained as an ineffectual enforcement apparatus and judicial impediments extracted most of the teeth from Title IX. Until the 1990s, the Office of Civil Rights of the U.S. Department of Education, the government agency charged with enforcing gender equity, played a minor role at best in advancing the cause of equal opportunity for women in college sports. In the judicial sphere, where few gender discrimination cases appeared until recently because the right for injured parties to receive monetary damages was not established until 1992, the Supreme Court dealt a major setback to the implementation of Title IX in February 1984. In *Grove City College v. Bell*, the Court ruled that Title IX applied only to those specific programs at an institution which received federal aid. Thus, if the athletic program did not directly receive federal funds, then gender equity within the athletic program was not required. In March 1988, however, in the Civil Rights Restoration Act the U.S. Congress reaffirmed Title IX's institution-wide protection against gender discrimination.

While women's position in intercollegiate sports has made significant gains in recent years, much remains to be accomplished before equity can be claimed. After doubling between 1971 and 1977, the number of female college athletes grew only at a modest 3 percent annually between 1977 and 1995 (the number of male athletes grew at 1.8 percent annually over this same period). In 1995–96, while women comprised over 50 percent of college students, they accounted for only 37.6 percent of college athletes. Further, women received less than 38 percent of athletic scholarships (male college athletes received almost $140 million more in scholarship dollars than their female counterparts), less than 28 percent of sport operating budgets, and just over 25 percent of athletics recruiting dollars.[4] Women's participation rose again in 1996–97 by 3.4 percent, lifting the female participation rate to 39 percent.

Interestingly, after failing to derail Title IX in Congress in 1972, the NCAA turned to supplementary political initiatives intended to negate or minimize the law's effect. First, in early 1974 the NCAA approached the former Department of Health, Education and Welfare to lobby for the exclusion of athletics from Title IX. Later in 1974 the Association organized a powerful campaign in support of the Tower Amendment which would have exempted "revenue" sports (i.e., men's football and basketball) from Title IX coverage. According to the *Kansas City Star*, the NCAA spent $300,000 on its lobbying efforts against Title IX during 1972–74.[5] Next in 1976, the NCAA challenged Title IX's constitutionality in the courts. All these efforts were rebuffed.

Failing to defeat Title IX, the NCAA turned its attention to gaining control over women's sports. Its target was the thriving Association of Intercollegiate Athletics for Women (AIAW), which was founded in

1971 and since had grown into the effective governing body for women's intercollegiate athletics. The AIAW was serving over 75,000 female athletes and 823 member colleges, and offering 17 national championships in 12 different sports.[6] In 1980, the NCAA established competing championships for women in several sports. To lure schools away from the AIAW, the NCAA provided special inducements to participate in its tournaments: free trips to the championships, free memberships for women's programs when the men's program already belonged to the NCAA, and, the decisive blow, including its women's basketball championships in the national television package and scheduling its final round to be at the same time as that of the AIAW. The AIAW was overwhelmed by the NCAA's superior resources and folded in 1982.

As the NCAA came to control women's sports, the leadership of women's programs was defeminized. While in 1972 more than 90 percent of women's college teams were coached by women, by 1996 only 47.7 percent were.[7] While in 1972 over 90 percent of women's athletic programs were directed by a woman, in 1996 only 18.5 percent were.[8] Title IX and NCAA control had brought some status back to women's sports and now, it seemed, the women's programs were too worthy for women's work.

Today, ADs no longer publicly challenge the goals of Title IX. The only issue is how rapidly full gender equity can be attained given the economic constraints faced by the schools. Yet, it is not clear that economic concerns have legal standing in deterring the march toward gender equity. Title IX has no clause that asserts discrimination protection shall be subject to a financial constraint, and the courts, accordingly, have dismissed defenses premised on budgetary inadequacy. For example, the immateriality of economic conditions to the fulfillment of Title IX provisions for gender equity was reaffirmed in the 1992 *Cook v. Colgate University* case discussed above.[9] An article in the *Seton Hall Journal of Sport Law* described the court's decision as follows:

> While the court acknowledged Colgate's argument that funding of the program would be expensive, it did not allow the finances to be a justification for refusing to allow the program to move forward. The court aptly observed that if financial concerns could justify disparate treatment, Title IX would become meaningless.[10]

Similarly, in *Favia v. Indiana University of Pennsylvania*, Judge Maurice Cohill Jr. wrote in his opinion:

> We are also sympathetic with the fact that the football team represents a large portion of the dominance of men's teams over female teams at IUP.

Football is a high profile sport; it generates money through ticket sales and undoubtedly heightens the interest of students, alumni and potential students in the university. As a dangerous sport, it is also expensive. Unfortunately, however, Title IX does not provide for any exception to its requirements simply because of a school's financial difficulties. In other words, a cash crunch is no excuse.[11]

In its 1991 report on Intercollegiate Athletics, the Knight Foundation Commission emphasized (p. 14): ". . . that continued inattention to the requirements of Title IX represents a major stain on institutional integrity. It is essential that presidents take the lead in this area. We recommend that presidents . . . develop procedures . . . to promote equity for women's teams in terms of schedules, facilities, travel arrangements and coaching." And in its 1993 report, the Commission concluded (p. 93): "Against the backdrop of the imperative for cost reduction, the unfinished agenda of equity for women also demands attention. . . . But the opportunity is not truly equal. On many campuses, fans would be outraged if revenue-generating teams were expected to make do with the resources available to women . . . the situation carries with it the threat of continued legal and Congressional scrutiny into when young women are denied the benefits of participating in college sports." Indeed, at the end of 1994 Congress passed the Equity in Athletics Disclosure Act which mandates colleges and universities to release detailed financial data on the operation of men's and women's sports programs.[12]

COMPLIANCE WITH OCR'S TITLE IX GUIDELINES

The Office of Civil Rights (OCR) of the Department of Education is encharged with implementing compliance with Title IX. The framework for compliance was established by the OCR in its 1979 policy interpretation which encompasses three major categories: accommodation of student interests and abilities, athletic financial assistance, and other program areas. Despite the abiding and substantial gender inequalities in the categories of financial assistance and other program areas, the greatest attention and most active litigation efforts by far have been concentrated on the category of accommodation of interests and abilities. The OCR has issued separate guidelines on compliance in this category. Basically, a school is deemed in compliance if it fulfills any one of the following three standards: (1) provides athletic participation opportunities for women and men that are substantially proportionate to their respective rates of enrollment; (2) demonstrates a history and continuing practice of program expansion for the underrepresented sex; or,

(3) fully and effectively accommodates the interests and abilities of the underrepresented sex. Each of these criteria leaves substantial room for interpretation.

The third criterion opens the Pandora's Box of quantifying women's interest in or demand for sports participation. It is theoretically possible, of course, that although women might be 50 percent of a student body, only 30 percent of them might be interested in participating in intercollegiate sports, and only half of those interested might have the requisite ability to compete. In such a case, it could be argued that the women's interests and abilities are accommodated when only 15 percent of the school's athletes are women.

Most Title IX proponents, however, argue Say's Law—that supply creates its own demand. That is, if a school offers an intercollegiate sport, the interest to participate will materialize and the ability will soon follow.[13] One might add the qualification that the school must not only offer the sport, but must endow the sport with the same support (recruitment, playing facilities, coaching staff, travel opportunities, promotion, etc.) enjoyed by the men's team. Absent equal levels of support, it is impossible to discern the potential demand for athletic participation by women. Available statistics on female participation in interscholastic and intercollegiate sports over the past 25 years provide some prima facie support for the Title IX proponents. In 1971, 294,015 girls participated in interscholastic sports nationwide in contrast to 3.67 million boys; that is, girls were 7.4 percent of the total number of participants. By 1994–95, 2.24 million girls participated and 3.54 million boys participated in interscholastic high school sports; girls represented 38.8 percent of total participants.[14] High school girls responded to the improved opportunity to participate in sports and the more supportive culture by increasing their participation at an annual average rate of 8.8 percent between 1971 and 1995. High school participation continued to increase in 1995–96, with the number of boy athletes growing by 2.7 percent to 3.63 million and the number of girl athletes growing by 5.7 percent to 2.37 million.[15]

Further, in 1994–95 there were 110,524 women participating in NCAA intercollegiate sports, fewer than one-twentieth the number of female participants in high school sports. Women represented only 36.9 percent of participants in intercollegiate sports, in contrast to 38.8 percent in high school. It would appear, then, that the interest and experience more than suffices to continue to increase women's participation in intercollegiate athletics. Naturally, women may have less time and interest to do sports competitively once in college, but so may men. Thus far, women have responded enthusiastically to increased opportunities, and this has been the case despite decidedly inferior levels of support.

The Brown University case turned on the court's interpretation of this third Title IX standard. Brown argued that it was meeting women's needs even though 51 percent of its students but only 38 percent of its athletes were women in 1993–94. Women were simply less interested in sports than men, Brown maintained. Many slots on women's teams were left unfilled due to apathy. But the U.S. Court of Appeals saw matters differently: "To assert that Title IX permits institutions to provide fewer athletics participation opportunities for women than for men, based upon the premise that women are less interested in sports than are men, is [among other things] to ignore the fact that Title IX was enacted in order to remedy discrimination that results from stereotyped notions of women's interests and abilities."

The second criterion is vague by its nature. Athletic directors have pored over OCR case histories to understand what constitutes sufficient continuing expansion. The OCR has issued clarifications which many complain are obfuscations. The ambiguity around this second criterion also surfaced in the Brown University case. Brown argued that there had been a significant expansion in the number of women's sports since the early 1970s. Yet it turns out that most of that growth had occurred when Brown merged with its sister school Pembroke. Since 1977 Brown had added only one women's team; further, many of the women's teams Brown was counting were clubs which received scant university support.

The first criterion of substantial proportionality (between varsity sports participation and enrollment rates) is also ambiguous because "substantial" is not defined by the OCR. Various court cases have established a judicial interpretation of "substantial"—more than a 10 percentage point differential between participation and enrollment rates is too large. OCR rulings suggest that a 5 percentage point differential is acceptable. Despite some remaining imprecision, the proportionality criterion is quantifiable by nature and has therefore been relied on more heavily than the other two standards in judging compliance.

Participation Rates

The record on proportionality shows appreciable improvement in recent years, with still a considerable distance to travel. *USA Today* conducted a survey of the 107 schools in Division IA for 1994–95. Only 9 of the 107 schools met the OCR proportionality test of a participation/enrollment spread below 5 points. According to the NCAA participation study for 1994–95, the percentage of women among all student-athletes rose from 30.8 percent in 1982–83 to 35.7 percent in 1993–94 and 36.9 percent in 1994–95.[16] Division I had the lowest female participation rate (35.4 percent) and Division III had the highest (39.3 percent) in 1994–95.[17] In the 1997 NCAA gender equity study only 27 of 305 Division I schools met the proportionality test in 1995–96.

What strategies are schools likely to pursue to meet the OCR participation standards? The most accessible short-term strategy would appear to be reducing participation in men's sports while increasing participation in women's sports. One method to accomplish this is to add women's sports and subtract men's. The record on adding women's sports is somewhat encouraging. According to the *USA Today* survey of the 107 Division IA schools, 30 schools had added a female sport in the previous 3 years and 7 schools added 2 sports. Fifty-six schools had plans to add at least 1 female sport in the next 3 years, and half of these planned to make the addition during 1995–96.[18] It is politically more difficult to drop sports, however. Between 1993–94 and 1994–95, the men's sport experiencing the largest reduction in sponsorship was wrestling, which fell by 7 from 264 to 257 across all 3 divisions. Men's gymnastics was dropped by 3 schools. Yet, between 1989 and 1993 the average number of varsity sports offered for men at Division IA schools stayed the same at 10, while the number of women's sports increased from 8 to 9.

The aggregate statistics for all Division I schools are shown in Table 3.1 and reveal a similar pattern. There has been a steady rise in the number of sponsored women's sports since the early 1980s, with an average growth of approximately 42 sports added per year in the 1990s. The number of sponsored men's sports has increased only incrementally since the early 1980s and has remained steady in the 1990s, with small year-to-year variations. While statistics for 1996–97 suggest a reduction in the average number of men's sports per Division IA school, most of this decrease can be attributed to the new practice of counting indoor track, outdoor track, and cross-country as one sport.

Another method, which is at once less expensive, politically less contentious, and less likely to provoke litigation, is either to reduce the number of athletes per men's sport or increase the number of athletes per women's sport. Participation numbers include both scholarship athletes as well as walk-ons. The latter generally play a peripheral role at best in a team's performance and coaches of male teams under OCR compliance pressure should find it relatively easy to reduce their number in certain sports. For instance, in 1993–94 one major Big Ten university had 28 athletes on its varsity men's basketball team, 13 of whom were on athletic scholarship, and 112 athletes on its football team, 88 of

TABLE 3.1

Number of Sponsored Sports Teams by Gender in Division I, 1981–95

	1981–82	1986–87	1991–92	1992–93	1993–94	1994–95
# Women's Teams	2,011	2,274	2,409	2,436	2,527	2,576
# Men's Teams	2,829	2,821	2,848	2,836	2,885	2,853

Source: NCAA, *Participation Statistics Report, 1982–95*, pp. 90–117.

whom were on scholarship.[19] Although the affected athletes would be disappointed, there are 39 walk-ons on these 2 teams who could be cut without seriously jeopardizing team success. As walk-ons are subtracted from men's teams, they can be added to women's teams. The University of Massachusetts in Amherst, for example, increased the size of its women's crew team from 71 during 1994–95 to 101 during 1995–96, while the average size of women's crew teams in all Division I schools was only 41 in 1994–95.[20] Manipulating walk-on athletes is easier in some sports, such as track or crew, and harder in others, such as basketball, but it presents a viable short-run option to meet OCR standards. It does not, however, represent a persuasive strategy to establish real gender balance. Further, reducing walk-ons in some sports is likely to have negative repercussions. If schools reduce the number of walk-ons in football, for instance, it will put pressure on the general policy to redshirt* freshman in that sport, and this, in turn, can be expected to lower graduation rates of football players.[21]

Another strategy to achieve gender equity is to play loose and fancy with the numbers. The number of participating athletes can be counted at the beginning, middle, or end of a season. Invariably, the earlier the count is taken, the higher will be the number of athletes participating. Indeed, some schools may even count the number showing up for tryouts. They can declare that they all made the team and then have them sit on the bench until they drop the sport. Oklahoma State University discovered another way to cook the numbers: OSU counted the women in indoor and outdoor track twice, even though they were the same athletes.[22]

Ultimately, actual resources will have to be committed to support change. In this regard it is instructive to consider the recent experience in the Big Ten conference with participation rates. In late 1992 the Presidents of the Big Ten universities agreed that by 1996 each program would have to present a gender equity plan based on at least 40 percent female participation rates. With a 50/50 enrollment balance between

---

* Not allow academically eligible students to play in their first year, giving them an additional year of eligibility at the end of their college career.

men and women, such a plan would entail a spread of 10 points and would fail the OCR participation criterion. Nonetheless, for the academic year 1993–94, no Big Ten school met this 40 percent threshold. The highest female participation rate was 37 percent at Michigan State, while the overall Big Ten average was 33.3 percent. For 1994–95, the highest female participation was 39.4 percent at Iowa and the Big Ten average had risen to 35.7 percent. The schools with the lowest female participation rate—Illinois and Purdue, each at 30.9 percent—were also among the lowest in Big Ten revenues. Yet, it is notable that the athletic department at Illinois reported a surplus of over three-quarters of a million dollars in 1994–95 and that Indiana with less total revenues than Illinois had a female participation rate 3.7 points higher. Further, the Big Ten had only three schools whose athletic departments ran a deficit (two of them were below $150,000) and surpluses at other schools ran as high as $2.7 million at Michigan. Michigan, with revenues in excess of $28.6 million and consistent surpluses in recent years, had a female participation rate of 38.9 percent. For 1995–96, the female participation at Illinois actually dropped to 30.3 percent, while the overall Big Ten average improved to 38.1 percent—still below the 40 percent target set for 1996 by the Big Ten Presidents in 1992. It appears, then, that progress toward gender equity is detained by more than just financial constraints.

Financial Assistance

After the Title IX victory in April 1997 when the Supreme Court refused to hear the Brown appeal, the National Women's Law Center in Washington, D.C., decided to strike when the iron was hot. The Center filed 25 Title IX suits against schools which dedicated the smallest shares of scholarship funds to their women athletes.

Women also lag significantly in the second category of overall OCR guidelines—financial assistance or scholarships. The financial aid lag roughly parallels the participation lag. Table 3.2 summarizes the unequal, yet improving, allocation of scholarship aid to male and female student-athletes. The first noteworthy fact from this table is that the NCAA did not keep data on women's athletic scholarships in 1985. Since this was prior to the Civil Rights Restoration Act of 1988 and Title IX was virtually moribund at the time, it is probably safe to surmise that grants-in-aid to female athletes were meager at best. Second, women constitute approximately the same percentage of participants and athletic scholarship aid. Yet, out of the 305 Division I schools, only at 10

TABLE 3.2
Scholarship Aid by Gender and Division
(figures in $thousands)

Program Averages	1985	1989	1993	Difference 1989– 1993	Pct. Change 1989– 1993	1995	Difference 1993– 1995	Pct. Change 1993– 1995
Division IA								
Men's Programs	$1,015	$1,248	$1,698	+$250	36.1%	$1,729	+$ 31	1.8%
Women's Programs		$ 447	$ 684	+$237	53.0%	$ 850	+$166	24.3%
Women/Total		.264	.287			.330		
Division IAA								
Men's Programs	$556	$667	$792	+$125	18.7%	$813	+$21	2.7%
Women's Programs		$236	$337	+$101	42.8%	$433	+$96	28.5%
Women/Total		.261	.298			.348		
Division IAAA								
Men's Programs	$255	$361	$449	+$ 88	24.4%	$501	+$ 52	11.6%
Women's Programs		$234	$354	+$120	51.3%	$471	+$117	33.1%
Women/Total		.393	.441			.485		
Division II w/football								
Men's Programs	$235	$254	$329	+$75	29.5%	$327	−$ 2	−0.7%
Women's Programs		$ 85	$125	+$40	47.1%	$144	+$19	15.2%
Women/Total		.251	.275			.306		
Division II w/o football								
Men's Programs	$135	$185	$160	−$15	−13.6%	$202	+$42	26.3%
Women's Programs		$110	$117	+$17	6.4%	$162	+$45	38.5%
Women/Total		.373	.422			.445		

Sources: Raiborn, 1990; Fulks, 1994; Ursula Walsh, Office of Research, NCAA.

colleges did female athletes receive within 5 percent of the amount of athletic aid awarded to the male athletes.

Third, there is a clear inverse correlation between the existence of a football program and the women's share in total scholarship aid. Division IAAA schools, which are without football, were virtually at parity in 1995 and those Division II schools without football were just 5 percentage points from parity. Divisions IA and IAA and Division II with football were each at least 15 percentage points below parity. It is striking that Division II schools without football had a women's share in scholarships of .445, almost 50 percent above the share of Division II schools with football. While the low women's share is understandable perhaps in Division IAA and Division II with football, where the football programs are not alleged to be money makers, in Division IA the claim is usually that football generates net income to support the other sports. Yet the women's share in Division IA was .330, below the share in Division IAA.

Interestingly, if we consider not the women's share in total aid, but the absolute magnitude of scholarship aid to women per school in each division, the results are more mixed. The amount spent on scholarships for female athletes in the average Division IA program ($850,000) is nearly double the amount spent in the average Division IAA program ($433,000). Yet the amount spent in Division IAAA, without football ($471,000), is greater than Division IAA, and the amount spent in Division II schools without football ($162,000) is greater than the amount spent in Division II schools with football.[23] Thus, it appears that only big-time Division IA football makes a contribution to the absolute level of women's athletic scholarships, but the relative scholarship standing of women in Division IA is still the second poorest of the five divisional categories considered—and it is the relative standing that is considered by Title IX.

Fourth, there has been a gradual improvement in the women's share since 1989, but a significant part of this must be attributable to the 1991 decision to decrease the maximum number of grants-in-aid to football players from 95 to 85 (which took full effect in 1994–95); suggesting that ongoing improvement may depend on a further reduction in football scholarships.

Fifth, many have expressed the concern that women's gains are coming at the expense of men. In only one of the five categories was the 1993–95 increase in scholarship aid for women accompanied by a decrease for men. This occurred at Division II schools with football and the average decrease was only $2,000 per school.

Complying with Title IX became still more complicated when on March 16, 1998, the Third Circuit Court of Appeals ruled that the NCAA is bound by Title IX, since its member schools receive federal financial aid. (The U.S. Supreme Court agreed to review this matter on January 20, 1999.) This ruling raised two pressing questions for the NCAA. First, does the present NCAA policy of spending nearly twice as much on the men's postseason basketball tournament ($16.4 million) as on the women's ($8.5 million) constitute a violation of Title IX? Second, do NCAA rules about grants-in-aid constitute a violation?

NCAA rules distinguish between two types of athletic scholarship sports: head-count sports and equivalency sports. In the former sports, each grant must provide a "full ride" to the student-athlete, covering 100 percent of tuition, fees, room and board, and books. In the latter, partial grants may be given. In Division I, the two head-count sports for men are football (limit of 85 full grants) and basketball (limit of 13 full grants), and for women they are basketball, tennis, gymnastics, and volleyball (total limit of 47 grants). Thus, women begin 41 scholarships in the hole.

At the University of Colorado, the school sponsors 9 varsity women's teams and 8 varsity men's teams and the school meets the OCR's gender participation guideline. However, because of the imbalance in scholarships from the head-count sports, the university offers the equivalent of 78 grants-in-aid to women and 125.9 grants-in-aid to men. Since the OCR stipulates that scholarship spending should be "substantially proportionate" to the percent of female athletes (defined in July 1998 to be a proportion of expenditures on women within 1 percent of the proportion of athletes that is female), Colorado is in clear violation of the Title IX scholarship guidelines.[24]

Many schools have similar problems and the NCAA's rules appear to be a major culprit. Either the number of full scholarships for men's football needs to be reduced, the number of full rides for women's head-count sports needs to be increased, or the number of women's head-count sports needs to be raised.

Other Areas

In the OCR's 1979 policy interpretation for the implementation of Title IX, the third major category for compliance review is "other program areas." This third category includes equipment and supplies, scheduling of games and practices, travel and per diem allowances, tutoring, coaching, locker rooms and playing facilities, medical services and training conditions, housing and dining services, publicity, support services, and recruitment of student-athletes. Despite substantial improvements in most of these areas, women still lag significantly. For instance, in the Big Ten in 1994–95, the reported operating expenses for all men's sports were $114.7 million and for all women's sports $36.3 million, or 24 percent of the total. Even if the entire reported budget for men's football ($66.8 million) is excluded, the amount spent on the men's sports still exceeded that spent on the women's sports by 32 percent. Reduced expenditures on coaching for women's teams is one of the more salient contributors to this deficit.

To comply fully with Title IX ultimately it will be necessary for schools to provide nearly equal support in all areas of intercollegiate athletics. For instance, similar sums will have to be spent on recruiting male and female athletes. According to the NCAA's 1997 Gender Equity study, the average Division I school spent 2.7 times the money on recruiting men than it did on recruiting women; and this ratio is almost certainly understated because off-budget recruiting expenditures (usually from booster monies and/or sneaker companies) are much greater for men. Similar sums also will have to be spent on coaches and trainers (see next chapter). Similar facilities will have to be provided. Similar support for lockers, travel, tutoring, and team promotion will have to be achieved.

Despite the significant gains in and the increased financial commitment to women's sports, the *absolute growth* in average operating expenditures (which includes lodging, meals, transportation, officials, uniforms, and equipment) per school on men's sports in Division I between 1990–91 and 1995–96 ($552,894) was 63 percent greater than the *total amount* of operating expenditures per school on women's sports in 1995–96 ($338,600). Total operating expenses for men's sports per institution were $1.17 million or 3.44 times those for women.[25] Total reported spending per school on Division I men's sports in 1995–96 was $2.81 million and on women's sports it was $1.37 million, less than half of the men's level.[26] Further, since men's sports receive healthy off-budget support from boosters and footwear companies, sometimes amounting to several million dollars annually, the total differential in practice is much larger than these figures suggest. Cedric Dempsey conceded the results from the Association's 1997 gender equity study were "disappointing." Christine Grant, director of women's athletics at Iowa University, reacted more emphatically, calling the results "pathetic." Both would agree that much remains to be done, but there are troublesome matters on the horizon.

As the commercialization of college sports has grown to parallel that of professional sports, the partial adherence to the standards of amateurism has come increasingly under attack. To the extent that the NCAA, or just Division I, recognizes economic reality and allows increased income for college athletes, financial resources will be strained further in two ways. There will be less overall to support new programs and athletic grants-in-aid. For instance, in 1994–95 the average Division I program maintained the equivalent of 128 full grants-in-aid for men and 64 for women. The new NCAA policy is to allow each of these athletes to earn $2,000 income during the school year. Although some or most of this income might not be charged to athletics, the additional annual cost per school can reach $384,000 to cover all of these student-athletes. To the extent that the $2,000 limit is further relaxed, financial resources will become more limited.[27]

In the Colgate and Brown cases, as well as many others, the schools maintained that the superior support for the men's teams was a function of the revenue they generated. In fact, the NCAA vernacular has a special category of "revenue sports" that it reserves for men's basketball and football. Taken literally, the phrase denotes that other sports, such as women's basketball, don't produce a dime of revenues. This, of course, is nonsense. But ADs will explain that by "revenue sports" they mean sports that generate *net* revenues (revenues greater than expenses). Yet of the 973 schools of the NCAA, there are maybe 30 or 40 schools where the men's football and basketball teams produce net revenue (i.e., revenues are greater than expenses), and we will discuss these special cases in chapter 7. There are, however, no men's teams at Brown that produce net revenue. They all lose money; and so does the men's hockey team at Colgate.

With sound management, most of the 30 or 40 schools that have made the big-time commercial scene have sufficient resources to push forward with Title IX compliance. It is probable that gender equity gains at these schools will become the models for other NCAA institutions. To some extent, this is already happening with Kansas, Georgia Tech, Stanford, Washington State, Wisconsin, and a few others. The problem is that the other 930 schools cannot internally generate the same level of resources to develop the women's programs, and this implies either that the institution (or the state government behind the institution) will have to allocate more resources to athletics or that cuts will have to be made in the men's program.

Eventually, as certain women's sports further develop their commercial potential, women's programs will be able to generate more of the resources to support their own activities. To be sure, the popularity of certain women's sports has grown remarkably over the past fifteen years.

A substantial issue for commercializing women's sports is inadequate media coverage. A 1996 study at Vanderbilt University found what we already know. After reviewing 66 sports sections and 3,529 articles from three newspapers (the *Tennessean, USA Today,* and the *New York Times*), the researchers found that only 11.1 percent of the articles covered women's sports. Further, the articles on men's sports were 4.9 times more likely to be accompanied by photos.

The media will only step out inches in front of perceptions of where the readership is. Attitudes must shift, but this is a gradual process. Modest successes must build upon themselves. Women's basketball seems to have already launched itself on a growth curve. After growing from 1.1 million in 1981–82 to 6.7 million in 1996–97, attendance at women's basketball games in 1997–98 rose by 653,194 to 7.4 million, an increase of 9.7 percent over the previous year and the seventeenth consecutive year an attendance record was set.[28] Several women's teams outdrew those of their male counterparts. Three women's teams averaged above 10,000 attendance per home game, 13 women's teams averaged above 5,000 attendance per home game, and 100 women's teams averaged above 1,000 attendance.

Meanwhile, attendance at men's games remained below its 1991–92 peak of 29.4 million. Attendance in 1997–98 reached only 28 million, 4.8 percent below the peak reached six years earlier.

The television appeal of women's games has experienced a steady ascent. The 1997 NCAA women's championship game between Old Dominion and Tennessee drew an ESPN record 4.0 rating (or 2.85 million households), above the previous year's record of 3.7. It was also the most watched NCAA basketball game—men's or women's—on ESPN since 1990. The rating of the 1998 championship game fell back to 3.7, which analysts attributed to the fact that Tennessee blew Louisiana Tech out of the game early on.[29]

The growth of intercollegiate female basketball has also fed off the women's Olympic team and promises to receive an important boost from the new professional leagues that began play in 1996–97. While the American Basketball League (ABL), launched in the winter of 1996, can be described as a qualified success during its first two years, insufficient financial resources and television exposure led to its demise halfway through its third season. The Women's National Basketball Association (WNBA), however, has been a smashing hit. The NBA put its media clout and significant promotional resources behind the league, and the response has been dazzling, with average attendance per game growing to 10,869 in its second season.[30]

The NCAA commissioned a survey in November 1997 of 2,000 randomly selected U.S. adults, aged 16 to 55. Forty-five percent stated that they were interested in men's college basketball and 29 percent stated they were interested in women's college basketball. The latter implies 44.4 million fans for the women's game. Not bad considering that Title IX did not actively engage elementary-school-aged girls in participating in competitive sports until the mid-1970s. What we are seeing now is first-generation talent. It will get better.

It is an imponderable whether or not the popularity of women's basketball will ever rise to the level of men's hoops. Certainly, most doubt that the level of physical prowess will ever be equal. Most fans, however, appear to want crisp play and sharp competition more than they want slam dunks or other acrobatic feats. When the college men's game lost practically all of its superstars to the NBA after the 1995–96 season, many television executives at CBS and ESPN were furrowing their brows, worried about viewership for 1996–97. But ratings for the 1997 men's championship game ended a 5-year slide, rising 3 percent above the previous year's level. The smiling executives explained that fans love the interschool rivalries. If this is true, women's basketball will likely continue upward along its growth curve as new rivalries develop. The quality of the play will increase as young girls become interested in the game, identify with role models, and perceive the promise of career options.[31]

Marx once said that success brings failure. As women's sports become more visible, commercial interests will intrude. ADs will be motivated to bend the rules, and agents, who play by their own rules, will become more prominent.[32] Women athletes' superior performance in the classroom (the graduation rate for women basketball players is 67 percent, compared to 41 percent for men) may be undone. Many hope that women stop short of fully emulating men—some for good reasons and some for bad reasons.[33]

But the vast majority of Americans support the goals of Title IX. A September 1997 CBS poll of 1,037 U.S. adults found that 86 percent believed that financial support for men's and women's college sports should be equal, and 77 percent said this should be so even if it meant cutting men's sports.[34] Popular opinion notwithstanding, gender equity will continue to be contested in the courtroom, in Congress, and in the locker room.

Gender Equity II

EQUAL PAY FOR COACHES

For someone to make $250,000 in the business world, he'd have to generate $60 million to $70 million in sales. When coaches say they're worth it, they don't know what's going on out there.
　　　—Bob Marcum, athletic director at the University of Massachusetts

Without question one of the biggest challenges and nuisances of a college marketer's job is producing and promoting a weekly coach's show.
　　　　　　　—Team Marketing Report, May 1998

There is no question we are overpaid.
　　　　　　　—Lute Olson, head men's basketball coach at the
　　　　　　　University of Arizona (1997 national champions)

I'd be the first guy to say coaches get paid too much.
　　　—DeLoss Dodds, athletic director at the University of Texas

Gentlemen, you're now going out to play football against Harvard. Never again in your whole life will you do anything so important.
　　　　　　　—Yale coach T.A.D. Jones in 1923

The rivalry is not a matter of life and death. It's a little more important than that.
　　　　　　　—UCLA coach Red Sanders (1949–57)

IN 1960, Marianne Crawford was six years old, old enough for her Uncle Jack to teach her how to reach a basket with an underhand toss. The basketball court was just across the street from the rowhouse where

Marianne lived with her six older siblings, her mother, and father, a Yellow Cab superintendent, just outside Philadelphia. She often tagged along with her brothers to neighborhood games after school.[1]

One afternoon when Marianne was thirteen her father came out to the court to find her straddling a boy and mercilessly pummeling his face. The unfortunate fellow had made the mistake of giving her a knee in a basketball game. That was not the last time that Marianne would fight to defend herself.

Five years later Marianne enrolled at Immaculata, then a tiny women's college of eight hundred students in Pennsylvania. The "Mighty Macs" won national titles in Marianne's freshman and sophomore years. Her team was headed toward another title in her junior year when Marianne discovered she was pregnant. Her game was off, but Marianne finished out the season.

Marianne and Rick Stanley got married and their daughter, Michelle, was born on October 22, 1975. Eleven days later, Marianne was back on the basketball court practicing with her team. In her four years at Immaculata, Marianne Stanley was a two-time all-American and played in four national championship games.

In 1977, with child but no longer with her husband, Marianne Stanley moved to Norfolk, Virginia, where, at twenty-three years of age, she became the head coach of the women's basketball team at Old Dominion. In her decade there, she guided the team to three national championships and a .820 winning percentage, earning the reputation of one of the very top female coaches in the country.

In 1987, Stanley stunned her colleagues when she left Old Dominion to take the head coaching job of the women's team at the University of Pennsylvania. There, she and her daughter Michelle would be close to her family and she would be able to broaden her interests, enrolling at the Wharton School of Business's continuing education program. But the basketball program at Penn was not competitive, there were no athletic scholarships, and her players were not committed to the game.

After two years at Penn, Stanley accepted a four-year job at the University of Southern California (USC). She once again compiled a sterling record of success. Coming off a strong 22 wins and 7 losses with PAC-10 coach of the year honors, in April 1993 Marianne Stanley went to the office of USC's new AD, Mike Garrett. They discussed bringing her base salary into the same range as her male counterpart's, George Raveling. Stanley at the time was earning $62,000 a year, Raveling's base was around $130,000. Marianne maintains that Garrett agreed in principle to such a salary increase, but when it came time to make a concrete offer, Garrett fell far short. His final offer was below $100,000. Stanley, holding out for an offer closer to parity, was summarily replaced by Cheryl Miller, a player Stanley herself had coached and one who had no college coaching experience.

Marianne Stanley brought a Title IX (and Equal Pay Act and Title VII) suit against USC. She sought first to get her job back. She failed. Then she sought monetary damages; the trial judge threw her case out and she appealed to the U.S. Ninth Circuit. In the meantime, Stanley needed money to survive. She worked in the back shop of a Los Angeles furniture store. She stripped furniture with steel wool until her hands bled. She applied for dozens of coaching jobs, but no school was interested. "Once you are labeled a troublemaker, it's like flypaper," Stanley said, "You can't shake it off." Stanley moved to live with a friend in South Carolina and worked part-time in a used book store.

With her case against USC still pending, Stanley's colleague and friend Tara VanDerveer, the head coach of the Stanford women's basketball team, persuaded her to take a part-time marketing job with the women's program at Stanford. The following year VanDerveer took a leave of absence to coach the women's Olympic team, and Stanley was appointed as the co-head coach of the Stanford team, ending her de facto blacklisting in college coaching.

Now Stanley is the head coach of the women's team at Cal-Berkeley. She gets the same base pay as her male counterpart. And she looks forward to the opportunity of arguing her Title IX case before a jury. The facts she will adduce are outlined in Table 4.1.

George Raveling's first year of coaching the men's basketball team at USC was 1986–87. The men's team had won the PAC-10 Conference two years earlier. Raveling's team performed abysmally during his first four years at USC. Each year the team's win percentage was well under .500. The overall record for his first four years was 38 wins and 78 losses, while the conference record was even worse, 17 wins and 55 losses (a .236 win percentage.) Needless to say, the team did not play in either the NIT or NCAA postseason tournaments in any of these years.

In Raveling's fifth year, 1990–91, Harold Miner joined the team and the team achieved a winning record, proceeding on to the NCAA tournament. The Trojans, however, lost in the first round. The next year the Trojans further improved on their regular season record, but they did not make it beyond the second round of the NCAA tournament. The following two years the Trojans attained an above .500 win percentage overall, but only .500 in their conference. The team did not receive a berth in the NCAA tournament, but settled for two undistinguished appearances in the NIT tournament, losing in the quarterfinals in 1992–93 and losing in the first round in 1993–94.

Raveling's eight-year record at USC was a mediocre 115 wins and 118 losses overall, while his eight-year conference record was a poor 60

TABLE 4.1
Comparative Coaching Records

Coach	Overall	Postseason Highlights
Raveling		
First Four Years at USC	38–78	No Record
Conference, Four Years	17–55	
First Eight Years at USC	115–118	1–2, 2 NCAAs; 2–2, 2 NITs
Conference, Eight Years	60–84	
Lifetime through 1994		
(22 years)	326–292	No Nat'l Championships
Stanley		
First Four Years at USC	71–46	3 NCAAs, 2d Round, Final 16, Final 8
Conference, Four Years	45–27	
Lifetime	347–146	3 Nat'l Championships; 1 Nat'l Women Invit. Tourn.

wins and 84 losses (a .417 win percentage). It is not surprising that Raveling's Trojans experienced dwindling attendance over this period.

Gate revenues were the largest single source of income for the men's basketball team, accounting for over 40 percent of total revenue. To the extent that other (non-gate) revenues grew during Raveling's tenure, this growth essentially was from the Pac-10 conference media contracts and general NCAA disbursements. That is, it had to do with the growing popularity of college basketball as a media event, rather than with any particular growth in popularity for the Trojan basketball team.

USC maintains that Raveling's lucrative contract was warranted by market forces. This is dubious. Perhaps an argument could be made that USC offered Raveling his first five-year deal, worth well over $300,000 annually when auxiliary income and special benefits are included, on the erroneous expectation he would contribute this much and more to the team's success and revenues.[2] What cannot be explained away, however, is the fact that, after five dismal years of declining performance and attendance, USC actually offered Raveling a larger contract, worth well in excess of $400,000 annually. Stanley, it should be recalled, wanted to be paid a sum equal to Raveling's base salary (around $130,000), not his total compensation (over $400,000).

Richard Sandomir, writing for the *New York Times* in 1995, stated that Raveling had grown weary of his coaching job: "Truth is, he [Raveling] said, he's been looking to get out for years. . . . He has looked for the right exit job for years, in television, college administration, pro scouting or teaching. . . ."[3] USC claimed that Raveling's long years of coaching experience made him a more valuable asset to the school. In fact, Raveling seemed to have grown tired of coaching and the team's performance reflected as much.

Raveling's contribution to team revenues was most probably negative during his first five or six years. Game attendance, which generated the revenue stream that was directly linked to team performance, went down appreciably, dropping from an average of 4,425 per game during the five years preceding Raveling at USC to 3,287 during Raveling's first five years (a drop of 25.7 percent). Thus, it appears indefensible to argue that the lofty compensation level in Raveling's second contract was a product of his economic contribution.

The coaching record of Marianne Stanley stands in sharp contrast to that of George Raveling. Stanley took a losing team at USC and brought it to the NCAA tournament in her second year, where it went to the second round. Each of the next two years Stanley brought her team to the NCAA tournament, where it advanced to the final 8 and final 16 in successive years. That is, during her four-year tenure as head coach at USC, Stanley's team went to the NCAA tournament three times; Raveling's team made it to the NCAA tournament in only two of his eight years. Of the two appearances, Raveling's Trojans lost once in the first round and once in the second. Stanley's team never lost in the first round, and twice made it to the "Sweet 16" or beyond. In Stanley's final year at USC, 1992–93, the team was beset with injuries at the end of the season.[4] Had she remained at USC, many believed that Stanley's team had an excellent opportunity to win the national championship in 1993–94.

Stanley's overall record at USC was 71 wins and 46 losses. Her conference record was 45 wins and 27 losses. That is, Stanley's overall win percentage at USC was .607, compared to Raveling's .494, and her conference win percentage was .625, compared to Raveling's .417.

The two coaches' career records parallel their performance at USC. Raveling's lifetime record is 326 wins and 292 losses (a .527 win percentage) with no national championships. Prior to taking on the co-head coach job for one year at Stanford in 1996, Stanley's lifetime record was 347 wins and 146 losses (a .704 win percentage), with three national championships.

In sum, it is apparent that Stanley's contribution far exceeded that of Raveling. The fact that the men's team generated substantially more revenue than the women's team was a product of the superior support and resource endowment it received from the university as well as historical circumstances. It was neither a product of Raveling's efforts, nor of his effectiveness.

Thus, Stanley should have a good case. But before she can win, she needs a hearing. Her case should be helped along by the successful Title IX equal pay suits brought by Sanya Tyler and Molly Perdue.

Tyler was the coach of the women's basketball team at Howard University. She sued Howard back in 1991 when she was being paid $62,000 for carrying out her double duties of coaching basketball and serving as Assistant Athletic Director. In contrast, the men's basketball coach was being paid $78,000 and was given free use of a car, and coaching the team was his exclusive duty. She argued that as coach she performed the same duties as her counterpart and had better results. She won her litigation at the trial level in June 1993 and was awarded over $2 million in damages by the jury. Although the damages were sharply reduced by the trial court judge in September 1995, the judge upheld the finding that Howard University had violated Title IX and was liable for damages.

Molly Perdue was the women's basketball coach at Brooklyn College from 1990 to 1992. Her salary was $65,000. In court she testified that she had to clean the locker room and gymnasium floors as well as launder the team's uniforms because there was no one else to do it. In June 1998, a U.S. District Court found Brooklyn College guilty of sex discrimination and awarded Perdue damages of $799,566.[5] Following Perdue, Tyler, and Stanley, several additional gender equity pay suits have been brought in recent years.

The Stanley/Raveling comparison is more common than many would anticipate. Consider the case of Jody Conradt, the women's basketball coach at the University of Texas. She was hired in 1976 at the then hefty salary of $19,000. In the last twenty-two years her teams have compiled a phenomenal win percentage of .771 and in recent years have had an average home attendance of between 7,000 and 8,000, always ranking in the top ten of women's teams nationally. Six years ago she was made the AD for women's sports at UT and has continued as basketball coach. Her total compensation package for 1998–99 is $237,235, making her one of the top-paid women in college sports. Not much to complain about—except in relative terms.

John Mackovic who was let go as head coach of the UT football program after the 1997–98 season is being paid $602,235 this year as a consultant to the athletics department. His main assignment is to find a new venue for the UT golf team.[6]

Rick Barnes is the new UT men's basketball coach. He brings a career win percentage of .601 to the job, .170 points below Conradt, and Conradt has coached more than twice as many games as Barnes. Barnes's compensation package is worth $700,000. And Auggie Garrido, the men's baseball coach, is paid $248,880, $11,645 more than Conradt even though baseball is considered a non-revenue sport and Conradt performs two jobs.[7]

DeLoss Dodds is the men's AD. In Dodds's seventeen years as AD, UT's men's teams have won a total of seven national championships. In Conradt's six years, UT's women's teams have won four national championships. The six-year graduation rate of female athletes from the entering classes of 1987–90 is 75 percent, while that of the male athletes is 45 percent. Yet Dodds's base salary is $19,000 above Conradt's, even though Conradt is also the coach of the women's basketball team.

SALARIES AND TITLE IX

In his last year of coaching the basketball team at UCLA and after leading his team to a record ten national championships, in 1975 John Wooden's salary was $32,500. He was offered a shoe company contract equal to his salary, but, said Wooden, "I didn't sign it because I didn't think that money belonged to me."[8]

Lou Henson did Wooden one better. Henson was the head basketball coach at the University of Illinois for 34 years. His teams won 663 games—only 6 coaches have won more games—and he took his teams to the NCAA tournament 18 times. He retired after the 1995–96 season. But then the basketball program at New Mexico State University, his alma mater, ran into trouble. Its team was hit with a grade-tampering scandal and the coach, Neil McCarthy, was forced to resign. Actually, McCarthy was simply reassigned to become the new assistant athletic director. But New Mexico State needed a coach for the 1997–98 season and Henson volunteered to do it for no pay. This would violate NCAA rules (whatever happened to amateurism?), so the university paid Henson $1 a month for his labor. Henson said that he wanted to pay back his alma mater for the wonderful education he received.

Wooden and Henson, of course, are anomalies. The NCAA's 1997 gender equity study found that at the Division IA level the average base salary was $99,283 for the head coach of the male basketball team and $60,603 for the head coach of the female basketball team. That is, the head coaches of the women's team received just over three-fifths (61 percent) the base salary received by the head coach of the men's team.[9] Moreover, the men's head coach often quintupled or more his base salary with other sources of compensation arranged through the college or its boosters, including: sponsorships, usually from sneaker companies; bonuses for team performance; appearances on radio and television talk shows; summer camps; and speaking engagements. It is not uncommon to hear of male coaches with compensation packages in excess of $1 million, and the *New York Times* reported Rick Pitino's income in his last years at Kentucky to be around $3 million.[10] Complementing this income, there are a flood of perquisites, such as free use of cars, downpayments and mortgage subsidies on a home, country club memberships, lavish severance provisions,[11] and much more. The head coach of the women's team rarely receives compensation beyond base salary and the job perquisites are diminutive relative to those of the men's head coach.

Consider the 1997 compensation packages of the following male coaches.[12]

- Steve Spurrier, head football coach at the University of Florida, earned a base salary of $168,850, plus $430,000 for radio and TV shows, $525,000 for deals with apparel and equipment companies (primarily Nike), $300,000 in forgiven loans, $125,000 in speaking engagements, and $500,000-plus in bonuses and other compensation. His total package was worth over $2 million for 1997, without the perks.
- Bobby Bowden, head football coach at Florida State, earned a base salary of $157,500, plus $275,00 for radio and TV shows, $225,000 from Nike, $200,000 for public relations work for the university, and $176,560 in other compensation, for a total of $1,034,060.
- Nolan Richardson, head basketball coach at the University of Arkansas, earns approximately $900,000 a year, plus club memberships worth about $5,500 annually.[13]
- Bob Huggins, head men's basketball coach at the University of Cincinnati, received a base salary of $126,400, deferred compensation of $130,000, $240,000 from Nike, $125,000 from radio and TV shows, and $87,500 in other compensation, for a total of $708,900.
- Rick Barnes, head men's basketball coach at Clemson University until 1998–99, received a base salary of $138,000, plus $225,000 for radio and TV shows, $150,000 from shoe contracts, $75,000 from basketball camps, and $87,900 in other compensation. He was lured away by the University of Texas for the 1998–99 season with a reported compensation package of $700,000 and a membership at the prestigious Barton Creek Country Club, which costs $38,000 for entry plus yearly dues.[14]

It seems redundant to observe that these coaches are paid to perform their duties as college coaches. These duties nominally include building a successful team and promoting a balanced pursuit of academics and sports for their team members. It is questionable whether many coaches are emotionally or intellectually equipped to support their athletes' academic endeavors.[15] Consider, for instance, the profile of ACC coaches by John Feinstein in his 1998 book, *A March to Madness*. Feinstein talks about the great motivational skills of the coaches and quotes the closing exhortation of one of Rick Barnes's pregame pep talks: "Be mother-fuckers, that's what it's all about."[16] Feinstein shares a few other interesting details about the backgrounds of the ACC coaches. Eight of the nine he discusses led their teams in pregame prayer sessions. Bobby Cremins, Georgia Tech coach, paid someone $50 to take his SAT test when he was applying to colleges. His midterm grades freshmen year included three F's and a D. Pat Kennedy, Florida State coach, had a combined SAT score below 800. Feinstein goes on to tell us that the standard coach's compensation package in the ACC for the 1996–97 season was in excess of $500,000.

Some coaches do considerably better than those in the list above. John Thompson, Georgetown basketball coach until 1999, for instance, not only earned nearly $400,000 per year from Nike to have his players wear Nike apparel, but Nike put Thompson on its Board of Directors. With this, Thompson has options on 80,000 shares of Nike stock, worth over $3.1 million in early October 1998.[17]

Perquisites and severance pay are nothing to sneeze at either. Ron Cooper, head football coach at the University of Louisville, enjoyed these perks in 1996: use of two Ford Explorers, a Dodge Stealth, and memberships to the Hurstbourne Country Club, the Oxmoor Country Club, the Wildwood Country Club, and the Caritas Health Fitness Club.[18] After his team had only thirteen wins in three seasons, Cooper was let go and given a golden handshake of $1 million.[19] Danny Ford resigned at Clemson in 1990 while under NCAA investigation and received an estimated $1.1 million. Jackie Sherrill left Texas A&M under similar circumstances with a $684,000 handshake plus a house.[20] Steve Fisher, who was fired as Michigan's basketball coach in the wake of an agent/player scandal, was awarded a $402,000 buyout.[21] Tom Penders lost his job as the head basketball coach at the University of Texas, but was given a going-away present of $643,000 and allowed to keep his membership at the Barton Creek Country Club. And so on.

Are men's college basketball coaches worth compensation packages approaching $1 million? It is certainly conceivable that a few exceptional coaches during certain years are worth this much. John Calipari at the University of Massachusetts, with the help of a new, state-of-the-art arena and strong institutional support, took a program from oblivion to national prominence.[22] But even in this case, in the year when the UMass Minutemen went to the NCAA Finals, in 1995–96, the team's gross revenues were only $3.1 million and their reported net income was but $0.5 million.[23]

Head coaches in the NBA in 1991–92, Marianne Stanley's penultimate year at USC, received salaries ranging from $187,500 to $1,250,000, and their teams had reported revenues (with actual revenues being considerably higher in many cases) ranging from $19 million to $56 million.[24] In 1994–95, the average revenue of basketball teams at Division IA schools was $2.5 million, with 51 percent of schools earning below $1.6 million and 69 percent earning below $3.2 million.[25]

Coaches' salaries in the NBA are set under competitive conditions by profit-maximizing firms. In Division I they are set under protected conditions with interlacing sponsorship contracts, booster contributions, and a well-oiled old boys' network of conference commissioners, athletic directors, and coaches. Dozens of men's head basketball coaches at Division I schools seem to earn compensation packages upwards of $500,000 whether or not their team is successful.

THE ECONOMICS OF PAY INEQUITY

Are these large compensation differentials between the coaches of men's and women's teams economically justifiable? In economic theory, a profit-maximizing firm in a competitive labor market will be compelled to pay a person a wage equal to the incremental value of what they produce (their marginal revenue product). When labor markets function in this way, they are functioning in the most efficient manner. Where competition is imperfect because of incomplete information, concentration of economic power, protection, or regulation, these wages or salaries may deviate from the marginal revenue product.[26]

College athletic programs are not subjected to normal market pressures. This enables their employment practices to deviate from paying their coaches according to market forces and, hence, according to their coaches' marginal revenue product or productivity. Instead, cultural or social norms seem to play a large role in determining remuneration. There is, in effect, a closed circle of male athletic directors and male basketball coaches who serve artificially to inflate and to validate each others' worth.[27] Walter Byers, executive director of the NCAA from 1951 to 1987, cites abundant evidence that conference commissioners, athletic directors, and coaches use each other's salaries to ratchet up their own. Base salaries for some conference commissioners have risen above $300,000.[28] The absence of normal market pressures has enabled this practice to be sustained.[29] This practice engenders salary discrimination in favor of male coaches and preserves the monopoly or near-monopoly that male coaches have over coaching Division IA male basketball teams.

The market is a social institution and as such reflects societal values. In a competitive market, economic pressures generally compel social discrimination to disappear. For instance, under competition, a professional basketball team that refused to hire a black coach, who was proven to be superior to a white coach and was willing to work for the same wage as the white coach, would not be maximizing its team's performance nor the franchise's profits.[30] Over time, the owner of this team would pay for his/her discriminatory attitude in lower profits. Under these circumstances, there would be compelling economic forces that worked to eliminate the prevailing discrimination.[31] But athletic directors in collegiate basketball are largely insulated from these competitive economic pressures. There is no private owner who has invested $150 million to buy the team and who stands to lose millions of dollars if his team does not perform to its potential.

What does it mean, then, to say that college coaches are paid according to market forces? It means that their salaries are determined by competition in the labor market for coaches among schools that experience little competitive pressure in the product market.[32] The apparent fact that Division I basketball coaches' salaries (where annual team revenues averaged $1.1 million in 1992–93)[33] have evolved in a way to parallel professional coaches' salaries in the NBA is a social, not an economic, artifact.[34]

The preservation of this artifact is in the interests of the male coaches and athletic directors. ADs at Division IA schools receive base salaries from $125,000 to $250,000 or higher with attractive benefits and perquisites, often worth an additional $100–150,000, in large part because of the higher base pay received by the head coaches of the men's basketball and football teams.[35]

Sometimes the reach of the old boys' club extends beyond the athletics department to the top university administrators. Consider, for instance, the University of Texas. When Tom Penders, former basketball coach, and John Mackovic, former football coach, were let go after the 1997–98 academic year, they were allowed to keep their $38,000 memberships at the exclusive Barton Creek Country Club. Joining them with university-paid memberships at the club were new basketball coach Rick Barnes; University of Texas President Larry Faulkner (who also held membership at the Headliners Country Club); University of Texas Vice Chancellor for Governmental Relations Mike Millsap; and University of Texas Chancellor William Cunningham (who also held memberships at six other clubs). Altogether fifty athletic department officials hold private club memberships provided by the university.[36]

These luxurious compensation packages are not, however, economically justifiable, either on grounds of the coaches' productivity or their reservation wage (see below). What determines the marginal revenue product or productivity of a coach? Notwithstanding the argument made by the University of Southern California in its equal-pay case against Marianne Stanley, it clearly is not determined by the total revenue of the organization or the activity for which the coach works. No economist would argue that a CEO who presides over and contributes to the stagnation of a Fortune 500 corporation has a greater productivity than a CEO who incubates a startup venture into a highly profitable, dynamic, rapidly growing, and important corporation.

A head coach's or manager's productivity is directly proportional to his/her impact on team performance. As team performance improves, the team sells more tickets and concessions, reaps higher media contracts, and garners more lucrative promotional deals.[37] In the case of professional sports teams this analysis is particularly complex because the talent of the team's players has to be controlled for before the coach's contribution to performance can be assessed properly. In the case of college sports teams, especially teams with small rosters such as basketball, the analysis is less complex because the head coach has a large responsibility for attracting or recruiting the player talent.

One way to justify high compensation to the coaches of men's basketball teams is by noting that the players go unpaid. The coach's compensation picks up the value of the players he recruits, which in normal labor markets would go to the players. But this formulation gives the coach all the credit for bringing particular players to a school. Other factors are also important, such as the school's reputation, its facilities, the conference it belongs to, the television exposure it receives, the size of its recruiting budget, its affiliation with particular sneaker companies, the effectiveness of assistant coaches in recruiting, the magnitude of support from booster organizations, the composition of a particular team, etc.

The reservation wage is the economist's term for the wage of the next-best paying job an individual could obtain. Apart from a handful of Division I coaches who might qualify for an NBA head coach's job (and history suggests that these would be the younger Division I coaches), the vast majority of these coaches' next-best opportunity would be to work as a Division I assistant coach or a Division II head coach. If no head or assistant coaching jobs were available, most Division I coaches would probably end up in average jobs earning average wages (approximately $25,000 a year in the United States in 1998).[38] All other things being equal, to induce an individual to take a new job, he must be paid at least his or her reservation wage.

In comparing the compensation of coaches for male and female teams, it is necessary to make a further adjustment to ascertain each coach's contribution. The standard formulation would be to estimate a coach's contribution to the number of team victories in a season and multiply that number by the estimated additional revenue per victory. The additional revenue per victory, however, will be strongly affected by the differential resources in promotion, marketing, facilities, equipment, support personnel and salaries, inter alia, invested in the men's and women's teams.

Consider, for instance, the circumstances of Marianne Stanley's team at USC in the early 1990s. The women's basketball team played its home games at the Lyon Center, an intramural gym with a seating capacity of 1,200. It had no concession stands and fans were not even allowed to bring their own snacks or drinks inside the building. The Lyon Center had no locker rooms, so the players had to change and shower at another site. The basketball floor was encumbered by the markings and lines for volleyball and other activities. The men's team, in contrast, played its games at the Sports Arena with a capacity of 15,509. All games at the Arena are automatically advertised on an electronic billboard above the Harbor Freeway. The official promotional budget of the men's team was 7.2 times that of the women's team. USC sponsored a weekly press conference and luncheon for Coach Raveling and the men's team, but not for the women's team. Tickets for the men's games were available at Ticketron and Ticketmaster outlets; for the women's games they were only sold on campus. When Marianne Stanley arrived at USC she shared one secretary with seven other sports people and a small office she had to partially furnish; Raveling had a full-time secretary, an administrative assistant, several clerical workers, and a much larger, fully furnished office. And so on. Even if the outside world treated men's and women's basketball equally, it would have been inconceivable that the USC women's team could have matched the men's team in revenues.

But the outside world does not treat the men's and women's games equally. It is clear that in the late-1990s the potential for incremental revenue from a successful men's basketball team is much greater than a successful women's team. Using assumptions favorable to the coaches, I estimate that the marginal revenue product range for an excellent Division I men's basketball coach is from $121,000 to $172,000.[39]

Yet, dozens of male coaches are receiving compensation packages three to six or more times even the highest MRP estimate of $172,000 for an excellent coach. Clearly, coaches' salaries are being inflated by the artificial NCAA restriction on paying the players. One researcher, Robert Brown, estimates that top college basketball players in the early 1990s produced revenues of $870,000 to $1 million each year.[40] The figure today would be considerably higher.

Since schools expect to gain significant sums by developing winning teams, they have an economic incentive to build for success. Since the most direct method for creating a strong team would be to attract strong players and since players are not allowed to receive money income, schools end up competing over other inputs (e.g., coaches' salaries, playing and practice facilities, etc.).[41] Thus, the surplus generated by the exploited top players is transferred to the coaches and ADs, who are paid in excess of the value they produce.[42]

THE FUTURE

In October 1997, the U.S. Equal Employment Opportunity Commission (EEOC) issued guidelines about pay equity for college coaches. These guidelines made it clear that the acute disparities prevailing at most schools are illegal. Consider two hypothetical examples offered in the EEOC report.[43] First, the male coach of the men's basketball team and the female coach of the women's team have similar education, experience, and responsibilities, but the school pays the male coach 50 percent more because the men's team generates more revenue. However, as is typical in Division I, the men's team has three assistant coaches and a staff to handle marketing and publicity, while the women's team has only two assistant coaches and no staff. In this case, the EEOC states that the pay disparity is not justifiable, because the two teams enjoy significantly different resources.

Second, a university hires a male coach for the men's team at a salary of $100,000 and a female coach for the women's team at $50,000. The two positions are substantially the same in their responsibilities, but the institution purports to defend the disparity on the grounds that they are simply paying the "going rates." The EEOC disagrees. The guidelines state that "sex discrimination in the marketplace which results in lower pay for jobs done by women" cannot be used as a justification for paying female coaches less than their male counterparts.

To be sure, under the watchful eye of the OCR, growing peer pressure, equal pay litigation, and the emergence of two professional women's basketball leagues in October 1996 and June 1997, base salaries of women coaches seem to be approaching gradually those of the men. The Women's Basketball Coaches Association did a 1994 study which found that in Division I the mean base salary was $52,593 for women's head coaches and $91,000 for men's. That is, women's base salaries had risen slightly to 57.8 percent of men's, up from 51.5 percent in 1991. And the 1997 NCAA gender equity study finds that this ratio rose further to 61.0 percent for the 1995–96 season.

The upward trend appears to have accelerated in the last two years. Marianne Stanley, for one, was hired for the 1996–97 season as the head women's basketball coach at the University of California, Berkeley, at the same base pay as the head coach of the men's team. The University of Kansas and Stanford University, among others, also have begun paying the same base salary to its men's and women's basketball coaches. And in July 1997, the University of Tennessee announced a new contract for its star coach, Pat Summit. Ms. Summit, who had led her team to five national championships during her time at the school, was awarded a compensation package worth an estimated $390,000 a year for five years. Summit's package includes a base salary of $135,000-plus, $50,000 from radio and television shows, $55,000 from a sneaker contract, $25,000 from a game ball contract, an undisclosed sum from summer basketball camp, public lectures, and other sources. Stanford University's women's basketball coach Tara VanDerveer also signed a five-year deal in 1997 worth a reported $450,000 annually. But Summit and VanDerveer are the two most prominent and successful women's coaches in the country, and their total compensation packages are still below those of their male counterparts.[44]

It is noteworthy that the pattern of salary and benefit discrimination persists, albeit at a considerably lesser scale, in Divisions II and III. According to the 1995 surveys of the Women's Basketball Coaches Association, in Division II, 48.7 percent of the head coaches of male basketball teams earned base salaries above $40,000, while only 24.4 percent of head coaches of women's teams do so. In Division III, the salary disparity was 15 percent between the head coaches of male and female teams. The men's teams' coaches also received decidedly superior benefit and support packages.

The largest source of compensation differentials in Division I is "outside" income (e.g., shoe deals, TV shows arranged by the schools or boosters, etc.). As yet, schools are doing little to address this. There has been, however, a strong trend toward schools gaining control over "outside" deals and arranging for all finances to be funneled through the college budget. As schools begin to pay coaches these larger sums directly, they will undoubtedly become part of the contested terrain in gender equity negotiations.

In 1995–96, women's basketball still generated less than one-fourth the revenues of men's basketball and, with only a handful of possible exceptions, women's programs ran in the red. Nevertheless, the sport is ascendant and the emergence of professional women's basketball will give the sport a further boost. In this sense, women's basketball might be likened to an emerging industry that still requires nurturing and patience, but whose potential returns are promising.

In the meantime, the drive toward gender equity in intercollegiate athletics has caught the NCAA in its ultimate contradiction. When the NCAA wants to protect its members from payroll taxes, unrelated business income taxes, and antitrust review as well as to preserve their tax-exempt bonding status, it raises the lofty banner proclaiming college sports, above all else, to be an integral part of the larger educational enterprise. Yet when women's demands for equal access to educational resources becomes too strident, the NCAA and its member schools are quick to point out the inherent commercial nature of big-time college sports. As long as the struggle for gender equity endures, intercollegiate sports will be confronted with this deepening identity crisis.

CHAPTER FIVE

The Media

COMMERCIALIZATION AND STRATIFICATION

Of course, athletics departments need money to operate and provide good athletic opportunities for student-athletes. But our desire to generate these needed revenues has gone wildly out of control, creating a financial and commercial "arms race" among schools that creates a never ending upward spiraling need for more revenues in order to beat the other guys.
—Gary Roberts, law professor at Tulane University and member of the Sugar Bowl Committee, testifying before the U.S. Senate on the College Bowl Alliance in May 1997

A postseason game draws the football season out over a large part of the regular academic year [and after the] strenuous . . . regular schedule [the players must focus on their studies.] But much as we need money and could use it here, it does not seem to us best for the boys [on the football team] and for the University to try to procure it in such a way. So far as we can see, a postseason game would be played at the sacrifice of many values, physical and academic, which properly belong to the students participating in football.
—Letter from John Cavanaugh, vice president of Notre Dame University, to Sugar Bowl Committee, 1941

WHEN THE NCAA was founded back in 1905, its primary purpose was to sanitize and standardize the playing rules for football in order to preserve it as an intercollegiate sport. The Association also articulated a philosophy of amateurism, but it had no pretensions to coordinate the economic policies of its membership. Rather, the explicit NCAA policy was known as "home rule," meaning that each institution was in control of its own athletics program. The "home rule" policy was not seriously

altered until the 1948 Sanity Code attempted to control financial aid
to, and recruitment of, athletes, which, in short order, was found to be
unworkable.

Thus, it is not surprising that, as radio technology advanced at the
beginning of the twentieth century, individual colleges struck their own
deals to broadcast games. The first college football games to be carried
on radio occurred at the University of Minnesota in the fall of 1912.
The university set up its own experimental station for this purpose.
Eight years later, on November 25, 1920, the first commercial radio
broadcast of a college game was heard on WTAW in College Station,
Texas. Historian Ronald Smith, however, calls the 1922 contest between Princeton and Chicago the "first significant" radio broadcast; the
game was carried by telephone from Chicago to New York City and
broadcast over WEAF.[1] The first network radio coverage, in 1926, was
initiated by NBC, which also broadcast the first Rose Bowl game on
January 1, 1927. By 1929, there were over ten million radios in the
United States and many colleges were poised to take advantage of this
potential new source of advertising and revenue.

Similar to the debates within Major League Baseball at the time, there
was a profound ambivalence about radio policy. In 1932 an NCAA
straw vote revealed that 90 percent of the membership believed that
radio hindered, rather than helped, football revenues. In the midst of
the Great Depression, at the 1936 annual NCAA meeting there was a
report on a survey of over four hundred schools which found that three-
quarters of the prominent football colleges thought that radio hurt gate
receipts. The small schools were more uniformly and adamantly opposed to radio, because they felt that big school broadcasts hurt attendance at their games and they were less likely to procure radio contracts.
On the other side, radio stations and alumni argued that radio broadcasting was the only free payback to the public for the subsidies received
by college teams; and, of course, many schools earned radio revenues
and felt that they benefitted from the publicity.

Under home rule, laissez-faire prevailed and each conference and college went its own way. The Pacific Coast Conference signed a contract with the West Coast NBC network. The Southwest Conference banned radio broadcasting of its games. The Southern Conference
banned broadcasting of conference games, but allowed interconference
games to be carried on the airwaves. The Big Ten adopted no confer-
ence-wide policy. The University of Michigan, still adhering to the
amateur model, allowed broadcasting at no charge but proscribed the
use of advertisements during the games. By 1935, however, Michigan
had a $20,000-a-year radio contract and opposed an effort by the Big
Ten to sign a conference radio contract for $100,000 which would have

been worth only $10,000 to Michigan. Yale University signed a 1936 pact worth $20,000, but was criticized by Harvard and Princeton which refused larger offers of $65,000 each for two years. Princeton President Harold Dodds criticized Yale's deal as "unfortunate" for submitting to the "commercial atmosphere which already surrounds intercollegiate athletics to a troublesome degree."[2]

Only Notre Dame adhered to the classical amateur model. The school allowed any radio station to broadcast its games without rights fee payment. Notre Dame believed that not only was this the proper policy for amateur sports and that it was congruent with the school's religious commitment, but serendipitously the policy would also allow more fans to follow Notre Dame games yielding positive publicity for the university.[3]

Such as it was, the first televised college contest was a baseball game between Columbia and Princeton in the summer of 1939. That fall, the first college football game was televised.[4] On October 5, 1940, the University of Pennsylvania's football team was televised for the first time;[5] Penn's games continued to be telecast throughout the decade. But by 1946 there were only seven thousand TV sets in the United States and few were worried about the impact of television on fan attendance or the economics of the game.

The following years, though, witnessed an explosion of the industry, as the number of sets grew to one million in 1948 and then to three million in 1949. Television's expanded reach and improved visual quality now commanded the attention of the colleges, conferences, and the NCAA. The Eastern College Athletic Conference (ECAC), a super conference composed of fourteen conferences in New England and the Mid-Atlantic, in 1948 declared that television would reduce gate receipts and requested that no college sign any TV deals beyond the 1948–49 season. Also in 1948 the NCAA conducted a study which found that 30 percent of those interviewed preferred watching a game on television to attending in person. But not all schools agreed with this finding: Penn did its own study that concluded television had only a negligible impact on attendance, and both Michigan and Notre Dame had their contests televised for two years with no impact on their attendance. The NCAA decided to do further study.[6]

It was also in 1948 that the NCAA's long-standing policy of home rule was disrupted by the introduction of the Sanity Code. Many wondered, if a national policy could be imposed for athletic scholarships, couldn't a national policy also be imposed for TV broadcasting? Meanwhile, other prominent football schools joined Penn and signed what were then lucrative TV deals. In 1949, Michigan signed a pact for

$2,000 a year plus reimbursement for any reduction in attendance; Wisconsin signed up for $10,000; Tulane for $7,500; Oklahoma for only $10 plus a percentage of broadcast profits; USC and UCLA for $34,500 each.[7] In 1950, Penn was offered $75,000 for its home games, and Penn president and future perennial presidential postulant, Harold Stassen, found it to be an offer he could not refuse. Nor could he refuse the offer of $850,000 over three years that he received in 1951 from the Du Mont Television network. Notre Dame came close to rivaling Penn as a TV attraction. For its game with Navy in 1948 it received $15,000 for radio rights and $6,600 for television rights. In 1949 Notre Dame signed a one-year contract for a guaranteed $36,000 plus incentives.

The National Opinion Research Center, hired by the NCAA and television networks to study TV's impact, reached the following conclusion in 1950: in areas where 30 percent or more of the homes had television sets, attendance at football games dropped 10 percent; in areas where less than 5 percent of the homes had sets, attendance rose by 10 percent. Based on these findings, the NCAA television committee recommended a moratorium on live telecasting during the 1951 season.

It is questionable whether the NCAA action was truly based on the NORC findings. On the one hand, the advent of television and suburbanization were shifting U.S. culture and leisure behavior. Attendance at major and minor league baseball games also dropped sharply in 1950. On the other hand, the NCAA moratorium set the stage for the Association's assertion of cartel control over the televising of college football—a more likely explanation for the NCAA policy.[8]

At its 1951 Convention, the NCAA voted 161–7 to end its home rule policy regarding television, and, then, moments later voted 130–60 to reinstate home rule regarding athletic scholarships. Harold Stassen of Penn asserted that the NCAA policy to restrict a college's right to broadcast its own games was a violation of the Sherman Antitrust Act and that Penn would go forward with its TV contract with Du Mont.

The NCAA Council declared that Penn was no longer a member in good standing and a group boycott of Penn commenced. First Cornell and then the other Ivy League schools announced that they would not play against Penn. Penn relented.

Notre Dame took no overt action against the new NCAA policy, but instead pursued an innovative policy that adumbrated many of the tensions to afflict the Association in coming decades. Notre Dame's president, John Cavanaugh, proposed a super conference of big-time football universities that would set its own rules regarding athletic aid, numbers of coaches, and television contracts. Although Cavanaugh's ideas would eventually come to life in the 1970s and 1980s with the

partition of the NCAA into divisions and subdivisions and the formation of the College Football Association, and in the 1990s with NCAA
restructuring and the Bowl Alliance, they were too radical for the early
1950s.

The NCAA, having successfully asserted its intention to centralize
college football television contracting, entered into an experimental deal
with the Westinghouse Electric Corporation in 1951. Westinghouse
paid $679,800 in rights fees to serve its network of fifty-two stations,
which covered approximately 58 percent of the U.S. population. The
plan included three nationally televised games and up to four regional
games on most Saturdays. On two Saturdays, however, there would be
no games televised and certain regions would be blacked out on rotating
Saturdays. The blackouts were intended as a control to test for the impact of TV on attendance.

The experiment of 1951 convinced the NCAA that it was desirable to
move forward with a national television plan (Table 5.1). In 1952 the
Association signed a contract with NBC worth $1.14 million. The new
Notre Dame president, Father Hesburgh, after having the school's call
for a super conference fall on deaf ears and observing no government
action against the NCAA TV policy on antitrust grounds, decried the
NCAA's cartelization of television as "socialistic in nature" and compared it to Huey Long's "Share the Wealth" program of the 1930s.[9] In
this heyday of McCarthyism, Notre Dame's AD Moose Krause took the
rhetoric to the next level: "Our stand is that it is Communistic."[10] The
Fighting Irish, though, had few allies; the NCAA voted overwhelmingly,
171 to 8, in favor of the 1952 accord with NBC.

After experiencing modest dips in 1952 and 1953, attendance at college football contests grew dramatically in the ensuing years. Television
became accepted as a vehicle to promote the sport and the colleges, but
there was still concern that excessive broadcasting of regional games
would hinder gate receipts.[11] There was also pressure, however, from
individual schools and conferences to televise their key games. One state
senator from Oklahoma, George Miskovsky, even introduced legislation
to compel the NCAA to add the annual Oklahoma vs. Oklahoma State
game to its broadcast schedule. After threats that the schools would be
kicked out of the Association, the state senate defeated the Miskovsky
bill. But the effort was personally worth it to the senator, whose seats at
the Oklahoma games were moved from the end zone to the 50-yard
line.[12]

Throughout the three decades of NCAA control of football telecasting, then, there was an abiding tension between general overexposure
and underexposure of particular schools. NCAA policy varied a bit
through the years, but the basic plan after 1951 was to permit one

TABLE 5.1
NCAA Football Television Contracts, 1951–83

Year	Network	Annual Rights Fees ($)	TV Rating	Attendance
1951	Westinghouse	679,800		17,500,000
1952	NBC	1,144,000		17,300,000
1953	NBC	1,723,366		16,700,000
1954	ABC	2,000,000		17,000,000
1955	NBC	1,250,000		17,300,000
1956	NBC	1,600,000		18,000,000
1957	NBC	1,720,000		18,300,000
1958	NBC	1,800,000		19,300,000
1959	NBC	2,200,000		19,600,000
1960	ABC	3,125,000		20,400,000
1961	ABC	3,125,000		20,700,000
1962	CBS	5,100,000		21,200,000
1963	CBS	5,100,000		22,200,000
1964	NBC	6,522,000		23,400,000
1965	NBC	6,522,000		24,700,000
1966	ABC	7,750,000		25,300,000
1967	ABC	7,750,000		26,400,000
1968	ABC	10,200,000	12.9	27,000,000
1969	ABC	10,200,000	13.9	27,600,000
1970	ABC	12,000,000	13.8	29,500,000
1971	ABC	12,000,000	14.0	30,500,000
1972	ABC	13,490,000	13.1	30,800,000
1973	ABC	13,490,000	12.1	31,300,000
1974	ABC	16,000,000	12.0	31,200,000
1975	ABC	16,000,000	12.9	31,700,000
1976	ABC	18,000,000	14.1	32,000,000
1977	ABC	18,000,000	12.4	32,900,000
1978	ABC	29,000,000	12.0	34,300,000
1979	ABC	29,000,000	11.5	35,000,000
1980	ABC	31,000,000	11.3	35,500,000
1981	ABC	31,000,000	12.0	35,800,000
1982	ABC, CBS, TBS	64,767,362	10.7	36,538,637
1983	ABC, CBS, TBS	74,195,155	9.8	36,301,877

Sources: Murray Sperber, *Onward to Victory*, 1998, pp. 79–80; Arthur Fleisher, Brian Goff, and Robert Tollison, *The NCAA: A Study in Cartel Behavior*, 1992, pp. 53–54; Paul R. Lawrence, *Unsportsmanlike Conduct: The National Collegiate Athletic Association*, 1987, p. 97; "1983 NCAA Football TV Committee Report," NCAA, p. 100.

Note: The 12.9 rating in 1968 meant that 7.4 million homes were watching the broadcasts. The number of homes rose steadily to its peak of 10.04 million in 1976 and fell gradually thereafter to 8.22 million in 1983, the lowest level since 1969.

national and several regional telecasts each week. Each particular school was limited to two television appearances per year, and the only schools receiving television revenue directly were those that appeared in broadcast contests.

The NCAA skimmed between 4 and 12 percent off the top, and the rest was distributed to the colleges whose games were televised, with appearances in the national game bringing around 30 percent more than regional games.[13] However effective this policy may have been in the aggregate, it left few satisfied customers. The big-time football programs wanted more exposure and the small programs wanted greater revenue sharing.

At a special summer convention in 1973, the Association moved to placate the big-time colleges by breaking into three divisions. Each division would operate with significant autonomy, setting its own policies with regard to scholarship limits or number of coaches per sport. The NCAA Council would now have eight representatives from Division I and only three each from Divisions II and III. The Association attempted to mollify Divisions II and III by giving each its own football championship, each of which would be televised by ABC. In recognition of this, the two lower divisions would be allocated $500,000 of the new $16 million TV contract.

Conspicuously omitted from the benefits of this juggling act were the weaker Division I institutions, such as California State University at Long Beach, which did not appear on television and in 1974 averaged fewer than six thousand spectators per game. In hindsight, then, it is not surprising that President Stephen Horn of Cal State at Long Beach had a few suggestions to make. In July 1975, Horn proposed that 50 percent of all television revenues (including bowl games) be divided equally among NCAA members not appearing on television. Cries of socialism again resounded throughout the Association, and Horn's plan, dubbed the "Robin Hood" proposal, was rejected. But its contemplation sufficiently discombobulated the big-time schools that the Horn plan stimulated new centrifugal forces within the Association.

Concerned and angered by the implications of the Horn plan, twenty-five individuals representing schools from seven major football conferences as well as Notre Dame and Penn State met in Chicago on October 15, 1975. A steering committee was formed that eventually recommended the partitioning of Division I into two echelons; the upper echelon would be composed of the top seventy or eighty football schools and these schools would be able largely to self-govern. When no such reorganization occurred at the NCAA's 1976 convention, the steering committee prepared the launch of the College Football Association (CFA).

The CFA's first meeting was held in June 1977 with sixty-one members. As little more than a lobbying bloc within the NCAA, the CFA had little to show for its efforts after two years of operation. The share of television appearances by CFA members dropped from 67 percent in 1977 to 55 percent in 1979; meanwhile, TV ratings for college football fell from 14.1 to 11.4.[14] CFA members naturally linked these two developments, arguing that fans were only interested in watching the top teams on television. The CFA stepped up its lobbying and initiated discussions with the networks for a separate TV contract.

In 1981 the CFA reached preliminary agreement with NBC for a four-year deal worth $180 million. The CFA hierarchy had only to persuade its rank and file to bolt the NCAA television structure. The prospective CFA deal was enough to wrest an important concession out of the NCAA at its 1981 convention—the Association voted to split Division I into two parts, A and AA, and to allow each to control its own television policy. To qualify for Division IA a college would have to average at least 17,000 paid spectators at its football games and to play in stadiums with at least a 30,000 capacity. The top level would now have 105 instead of 180 schools.

The CFA leadership, though, argued that this did not go far enough. The top football schools numbered no more than 80. Indeed, some ADs and coaches of CFA institutions went further. Oklahoma's head coach, Barry Switzer, stated that what was needed was an Association of the top 40 football colleges. Switzer explained:

> We could set our own rules. Maybe give the players $50 a day.[15] Get rid of the 95 [football grant-in-aid limit]. . . . I don't care how many coaches Missouri has. If they want 20, let them have 20. . . . If we're expelled from the NCAA it could enable us to do some things that are realistic.[16]

But the concession to subdivide Division I, the increase in the maximum number of yearly appearances per school to three, and the handsome new NCAA TV contract with ABC, CBS, and TBS (more than double the previous one with ABC) led a majority of the CFA members to stay with the NCAA. Some CFA schools, however, were not willing to go down without a fight. Oklahoma, despite being the preeminent power in college football during the seventies, was earning $228,035 from the NCAA in 1979, less than 1 percent of the NCAA's total contract with ABC. Oklahoma was not willing to accept the status quo. Neither was the University of Georgia. The two schools filed an antitrust suit against the NCAA at the end of 1981.

The trial was held in U.S. District Court in Oklahoma City during the late summer of 1982. The judge ruled that the NCAA's 1982–85 contract with ABC, CBS, and Turner Broadcasting violated Sections 1 and 2 of the Sherman Act and that the Association's controls were "unreasonable, naked restraints on competition" and exhibited "rank greed" and "a lust for power." The decision ruled the NCAA to be a naked cartel that limited production and fixed prices.

The NCAA asked the district court for a stay (allowing it to go forward with its prevailing TV contracts) while it appealed the decision. The stay was denied at the district court but then granted at the U.S. Court of Appeals. The Appeals Court, however, reaffirmed the lower court's ruling in May 1983. The NCAA then appealed to the U.S. Supreme Court and asked for another stay until the Court ruled. Supreme Court Justice Byron White, a former all-American football player at the University of Colorado in the 1930s and a recipient of the NCAA's highest honor (the Theodore Roosevelt Award) in 1969, granted the stay, so the Association was able to go forward for a second year with its contracts with ABC, CBS, and TBS.

THE NCAA AS CARTEL AND THE 1984
SUPREME COURT DECISION

While the basic structure of the NCAA television plan remained the same over the years, the restrictions grew less severe. Gradually more broadcasts and more exceptions were allowed. In the last four-year contract with ABC, CBS, and Turner, ABC and CBS would carry nationally 14 games each and Turner would show 19 evening games. With exceptions for regional and local games, in 1983 there were 242 games broadcast involving 173 different schools. The rights fees paid to the participating schools were set by the plan, and only those schools which were televised received a piece of the $74.2 million television revenues in 1983.[17]

The Supreme Court looked at this information and ruled in a 7-to-2 decision that the NCAA was behaving as a cartel, in illegal restraint of trade. This meant that through its television package the NCAA was artificially limiting the number and selection of games shown. Thus, if consumers wished to watch the Oklahoma Sooners play more than three times a year, they could not. This restriction lowered consumer welfare and was a violation of Section 1 of the Sherman Antitrust Act of 1890. In the free marketplace, perhaps there was a television station in Oklahoma that wanted to carry additional Sooner games and the Oklahoma athletic department was ready to strike a deal with this station. The NCAA policy did not allow this to happen; it thereby restrained trade and lowered welfare. (Presumably, the station wanted to carry the games, because they believed companies would buy advertising spots during the broadcasts, and these companies, in turn, expected a significant number of people wanted to watch the Sooners compete.)

Further, the Supreme Court charged the NCAA with price fixing. That is, the price or rights fee received by the producers (the televised football teams) was set ahead of time, largely independent of the quality of the teams or the popularity of the contest.[18] For instance, in the fall of 1981 there was a televised contest on ABC between USC and Oklahoma, each team was ranked in the top five nationally, and it was carried on over two hundred stations. On another weekend that fall, ABC televised a game between Appalachian State and the Citadel which was carried on only four stations. All four teams received the same rights fees.

The Court was endorsing the economic argument that such interference with the market price would encourage overproduction of football at inferior football schools and underproduction of football at superior schools. Finally, the Court argued that the NCAA TV package represented a group boycott; that is, once the pact with ABC, CBS, and Turner was signed, there was a de facto boycott by all NCAA members of NBC and other broadcast and cable stations.

The NCAA's defense was that (a) if it allowed too many football games to be broadcast on television, it would threaten live attendance at the games and (b) by spreading television appearances out among the majority of Division I football schools, it allowed television revenues to be distributed more equally among the schools.[19] The more even revenue distribution, in turn, promoted more equal playing strength among the teams and fostered the amateur spirit by reducing the financial reward received by a school having a top-flight football team.

The Supreme Court's response to the NCAA was, first, that it did not matter if broadcasts lowered live attendance. If fans had a choice, they would choose the option that gave them the most pleasure. The relevant datum was not whether or not fewer people were in attendance, but whether the sum of fans in attendance plus fans watching on television would be greater if the TV restrictions were lifted. Further, the Court noted that the NCAA already broadcast its national and regional games at the same time the live games were played. Second, the Court argued that it was not clear that the TV plan promoted competitive balance and suggested there would be more effective ways to do so that would have a less restrictive impact on the number and variety of television broadcasts:

> The interest in maintaining a competitive balance among amateur athletic teams that the NCAA asserts as a further justification for its television plan is not related to any neutral standard or to any readily identifiable

group of competitors. The television plan is not even arguably tailored to serve such an interest. It does not regulate the amount of money that any college may spend on its football program or the way the colleges may use their football program revenues, but simply imposes a restriction on one source of revenue that is more important to some colleges than to others. There is no evidence that such restriction produces any greater measure of equality throughout the NCAA than would a restriction on alumni donations, tuition rates, or any other revenue-producing activity. Moreover, the District Court's well-supported finding that many more games would be televised in a free market than under the NCAA plan, is a compelling demonstration that the plan's controls do not serve any legitimate procompetitive purpose.[20]

The Court, however, did not directly address the NCAA's professed concern to promote the values and institutions of amateurism. In the Court's dissenting opinion, written by Justice White, and joined by Justice Rehnquist, it is maintained that in supporting the more equal distribution of television exposure and revenues the NCAA plan reduced the incentive to win. A reduced financial incentive to win, in turn, supported the primacy of academic matters and discouraged commercialism, frenetic recruiting efforts, high salaries for coaches, and so on.

The division within the Supreme Court reflects the schizophrenia of intercollegiate athletics which is at once amateur in parts and intensely commercial. By applying normal standards of free enterprise, the majority of the Court was giving freer reign to the further commercialization of college sports. The resulting potential for heightened revenue, in turn, has led universities to devote ever greater resources to seeking athletic success and to the increasing prominence of sports in U.S. culture. And as the commercialization of college sports advances, the contradiction of not paying athletes cash income becomes more acute and pressing. This is part of the price that is paid because of the Supreme Court's decision. The gains are more television coverage of college football and coverage that better responds to demand.

Of course, had the Supreme Court upheld the NCAA policy it is likely that another, perhaps more commercialized, scenario would have ensued. The Universities of Oklahoma, Georgia, Notre Dame, and many others from the CFA would have seceded from the NCAA and signed their own television agreement. While this would have created a hypercommercialized sector within college sports, it might also have reduced the commercialization tendencies within the rest of the NCAA.

With the NCAA's TV policy struck down, schools and conferences were left to fend for themselves. The NCAA television cartel was broken. The leading football colleges and conferences were cut free and the weaker football colleges lost the protection of the NCAA plan. Meanwhile, the NCAA was left without football television revenue and with a legal bill of over $2.2 million.

MORE PRODUCT, GREATER INEQUALITY, AND INTENSIFIED COMMERCIALISM

What did happen in the wake of the Supreme Court decision was predictable. In the short run, disorder reigned. Oklahoma, Georgia, Nebraska, and USC put their football contests up for sale, but they were disappointed with the networks' offers. Notre Dame got the largest offer, $20 million, but turned it down. Scurrying about to arrange a deal in time for the 1984 season, the CFA managed to ink one-year deals with ABC and ESPN worth $35 million. In addition to the CFA pact, the Big Ten and Pac-10 signed their own contract with CBS for around $10 million. The combined value of the CFA and Big Ten/Pac-10 deals was still well below the value of the NCAA's 1983 contracts despite the fact that it involved roughly twice as many network games.

Some economists have viewed this outcome as a confirmation of monopoly theory: monopolists artificially lower output below and raise price above competitive levels. Thus, when the NCAA monopoly power in the television market was broken up, the resulting output was higher (almost double the number of televised games) and the price (TV revenue per game) was lower. While this dynamic probably explains part of the price drop in 1984, it is likely that a substantial portion of the drop is attributable to the inexperience and disorganization of the Division I football colleges in negotiating television deals as well as the shortness of time before the 1984 season. Indeed, for 1984 it was not only the revenue per game but the overall revenue from television that had fallen.[21] There was not, after all, very much competition in 1984—only two groups, the CFA and the Big Ten/Pac-10, existed.

The CFA, which had instigated and supported the suit against the NCAA's monopoly, was now part of a duopoly—and that was more competition than it wanted. The CFA had attempted to persuade the Big Ten/Pac-10 to join its elite group. When this effort proved futile, the CFA then refused to allow CBS to broadcast "crossover" games, involving contests between CFA and Big Ten/Pac-10 schools. CBS went to court in 1984 claiming restraint of trade (group boycott and price fixing) and won.

Ironically, it was not until the duopoly of the 1980s gave way to more competition in the 1990s that television revenue from college football began its next rapid ascent. In 1990, Notre Dame broke from the CFA and signed its own 5-year deal with NBC, worth $38 million. The new 5-year deal that the CFA had inked with ABC and ESPN was promptly reduced by $35 million, down to $300 million, which was still $25 million more per year than its previous 1987–90 contract.

Notre Dame's bolting from the CFA, however, had a larger significance. It revealed the fragility of the CFA cartel and the potential attractiveness for other schools or conferences to do their own negotiating. Conferences took this message to heart and began discussions with the networks. They were given a basic lesson in television economics. Their rights fees would grow in proportion to the size of their market. Further, the larger each conference, the fewer the number of conferences in Division IA and the lesser the competition.

Not surprisingly, the conferences began to realign and expand to extend their market coverage. The first step was taken by the Big Ten which voted in June 1990 to admit Penn State into its conference. The Atlantic Coast Conference (ACC) added previously independent Florida State. The Southeastern Conference (SEC) expanded to twelve teams and the Big 8 annexed four teams from the Southwest Conference.

Cosmetically enhanced, the conferences one by one broke off from the CFA cartel and signed their own TV deals. In February 1994 the SEC led the way with an $85 million deal with CBS, commencing after the last year (1995–96) of the CFA contract with ABC and ESPN. Three days later the ACC signed up with ABC and ESPN; the next day the Big East inked a deal with CBS and three weeks later the Big 8 entered into a contract with ABC and Liberty Sports (Table 5.2).

The revenue bonanza did not stop here, however. Network rights fees for postseason bowl games roughly doubled between 1985 and 1995. The payout to each team participating in the Rose Bowl, for instance, rose from $925,000 in 1969, to $1.42 million in 1974, $2.9 million in 1983, $5.75 million in 1992, $8.25 million in 1996, $9.5 million in 1997, and an expected $11 million in 1998. These payouts come from all revenues generated by the game (TV rights, ticket and concession sales, sponsorship fees, etc.). The bowl with the largest payout in 1996 was the Tostito Fiesta Bowl. Aided by a $12 million, 3-year sponsorship/naming rights deal with Frito-Lay, the minimum Fiesta Bowl payout in 1996 was reported at between $8.6 million and $13 million per team.[22] The Orange and Sugar Bowls also had per team payouts in excess of $8.2 million.

Meanwhile, corporate advertisers were tripping over each other trying to buy spots for the 1996 Fiesta Bowl. Thirty-second spots sold for $500,000, or 122 percent the rate for the "national championship" game (at the Orange Bowl) in 1995. This spot rate was approximately

TABLE 5.2
Major Division IA Football Conference
Television Deals, 1996–2000

Conference/ School	TV Network	Contract Amount (in $millions)
ACC	ABC/ESPN	70
Big East	CBS	65
Big Ten/Pac-10	ABC	115
SEC	CBS	85*
Notre Dame	NBC	38†

* Smith, 1994, p. 112. *New York Times*, February 15, 1994, reported the CBS deal with the Southeastern Conference to be worth $100 million, not the $85 million reported by Smith.

† Notre Dame began a new 7-year contract with NBC in 1998 worth $45 million.

half the going rate for NFL Super Bowl spots the same month. The 1996 Super Bowl was the top-rated sports event during the 1995–96 season, with a 46.0 rating (where each rating point represented 959,000 households watching the game), while the 1996 Fiesta Bowl tied for 29th place with game 6 of the NBA Finals and an 18.8 rating. These were heady times for college football.

THE BOWL ALLIANCE AND ANTITRUST

Like the rest of college football, bowl revenues have grown increasingly stratified in the 1990s. Bowl TV ratings had been lagging and network executives began to carp that quality control was next to impossible.

College bowl games generally are organized and controlled by local chambers of commerce, convention and tourist bureaus, and assorted businesses. The games' understood purpose is to generate business for the local economy which they usually do to some extent because the majority of attendees come from out of town.[23] The bowls have contracts with individual conferences that provide for conference champions, runner-ups, or other designated teams to participate in the bowl each year. On behalf of the conference, the participating school gets a share of the bowl revenue and, in turn, is obligated to purchase a substantial block of tickets for the game which it attempts to resell to its alumni, students, boosters, and others.

Under this system, each bowl did not know the quality of the teams it would be getting until the end of the season. The conference champion associated with a particular bowl may have had a relatively low national ranking and the opposing team may be no better. TV networks found themselves in the uncomfortable position of reserving a prime spot for a bowl and paying top rights fees, yet facing the possible prospect of two teams ranked below the top ten going against each other. In the best of circumstances, only one or at most two bowl games were relevant to determining the national champion; the audience for the other games was small.

David Downs, senior vice president of ABC Sports, explained: "All of the networks were souring on the bowl business. We couldn't go one more cycle where we wake up on the 1st of December and find out that we have a bad matchup and that we were going to get hammered in the ratings. How can we sell a college football game [to advertisers] when we don't know if we are going to have a 19 [in ratings points] or if we are going to have a 4?"[24]

The first step to rectifying this commercially threatening situation was taken in 1991 when the Atlantic Coast (ACC), Big East, Big Eight, Southeastern (SEC), and Southwestern conferences, along with Notre Dame, formed a bowl coalition with the prestigious college bowl committees of the IBM Fiesta Bowl, the Mobil Cotton Bowl, the USF&G Sugar Bowl, and the Federal Express Orange Bowl. Under the agreement, the Orange, Sugar, and Cotton Bowls continued to be hosted by their affiliated conference champions, while the Fiesta Bowl had two open slots. These four bowls agreed to choose teams in order and to fill their open slots from among the champions of the ACC and Big East, Notre Dame, and other highly ranked schools.

Although this coalition improved the chances of top, competitive matchups, it precluded contests between the teams ranked number one and two if they came from the Big East (champion obligated to play in the Orange Bowl), the SEC (obligated to play in the Sugar Bowl), or the Southwest (obligated to play in the Cotton Bowl). Nonetheless, this arrangement did manage to produce "national championships" between the teams ranked numbers one and two in both 1992 and 1993. The other problem from the networks' point of view was that there was no guarantee that any of the individual bowls would be host to the top matchup. Selling advertising under these circumstances remained problematic.

The next step was taken in 1994 with the formation of the Bowl Alliance. The Big East, ACC, Big 12 (a merger of the Big 8 with 4 teams from the Southwest), the SEC, and Notre Dame agreed to the following terms with the Orange, Sugar, and Fiesta Bowls: the champions of the four conferences plus Notre Dame (unless the team had a losing season) and one other top-ranked school either from within or outside the Alliance would play in these three bowls; the traditional conference/bowl ties would be severed in the interest of maximizing the possibility of having a national championship; and, the highest ranked game each year would rotate among the Orange, Sugar, and Fiesta Bowls. Since the bowls would share the championship game, advertisers were assured of the top matchup at least one out of every three years.

From the perspective of the Bowl Alliance conferences, there was still one missing piece. The champions of the Big Ten and Pac-10 conferences had been matched in the Rose Bowl for over fifty years. Moreover, teams from these conferences were often ranked either first or second in the nation. Without the Big Ten and Pac-10, the Alliance goal to offer a national championship game every year was elusive. In 1994, for instance, the No. 2 team was Penn State, from the Big Ten.

In June 1996, the Alliance struck a deal with the Big Ten, the Pac-10, the Rose Bowl, and ABC (which had broadcasting rights to the Rose Bowl). Beginning with the 1998–99 season, the national championship game would rotate among the four bowls and ABC would have broadcast rights for all four games over a seven-year period (for which the network paid the estimated modest sum of $700 million, or $25 million per game, which was roughly 2.5 times the average 1996 rights fees for the four games).[25] The teams for the national championship will be picked according to a new, computer-driven formula which will include the team record, difficulty of schedule, the average of the *USA Today/ ESPN* coaches' poll and the AP media poll, and the average of three computer rankings (*Seattle Times*, *New York Times*, and Jeff Sagarin).

Of course, what was good news for the Super Bowl Alliance or the Bowl Championship Series, as it is now called with the Rose Bowl brought into the fold, was bad news for virtually all the other bowl games. As these four bowl games came increasingly to be associated with a national championship, interest in the other bowls waned. Accordingly, TV ratings and attendance for the other bowl games have suffered. With one anointed championship game, ABC may even have difficulty sustaining interest in the three non-championship, runner-up games each year.

Although many fans welcomed the heightened prospect of a national championship game in college football, the Bowl Championship Series came under sharp attack and close scrutiny from many observers. Senator Mitch McConnell of Kentucky, for instance, was concerned that his home state school, the University of Louisville, was being excluded from a reasonable opportunity to participate in the most prestigious and lucrative bowl games. The University of Louisville belonged to the Conference USA (C-USA) which, along with three other Division IA conferences[26] and eleven independents, were not invited to join the Bowl

Alliance. Senator McConnell first raised the issue in 1993 when Louisville had a 7–1 record and a top ranking, but was automatically excluded from the leading bowls. The U.S. Justice Department commenced an inquiry and the Alliance agreed to open up two of the six Alliance bowl slots "to any team in the country with a minimum of eight wins *or* ranked higher than the lowest-ranked conference champion from among the champions of the ACC, Big East, Big 12 and SEC."

This new, "more open" policy was put to the test in 1996–97. Brigham Young University's football team, from the Western Athletic Conference (WAC), met *both* of the Alliance criteria, compiling a 13–1 record and earning a No. 5 ranking nationally, yet was not invited to any of the Alliance bowls. BYU's record and ranking was superior to nearly every Alliance team that went to an Alliance bowl that year, including Penn State, 11–2 record and No. 7 ranking; Texas, 8–5 and No. 20 ranking; Virginia Tech, 10–2 and No. 13 ranking; and Nebraska, 11–2 and No. 6 ranking.[27]

The Alliance, instead of promoting the highest level of postseason competition, seemed to be promoting the economic fortunes of its members and the college bowls, to the exclusion and detriment of other Division IA schools. The bowls themselves were originated in the 1930s to promote tourism in the host cities. The bowl committees continue to prefer to host universities with large, spendthrift student and alumni bodies. BYU is from the sparsely populated state of Utah (bad for TV ratings), and its students and alumni have the reputation of frugality and sobriety. Utah Senator Bob Bennett stated before the May 1997 U.S. Senate hearing on the Bowl Alliance: "BYU does not travel well. I'll be very blunt. There is a perception out there, and it may be true, that [BYU fans] do not drink and party the way the host city would prefer. Our football coach has been quoted as saying that BYU fans travel with a $50 bill and the Ten Commandments in their pocket, and they leave without breaking either one." Bowl host committees preferred teams from larger, wealthier, and wilder states.

The overall picture of bowl access in Division IA almost makes the income distribution in Haiti look equitable. The Big 12 is guaranteed an appearance in an Alliance bowl plus 5 additional bowls; the SEC is guaranteed an Alliance bowl plus 4 additional bowls; the Big Ten, an Alliance bowl plus 4 other bowls; the Pac-10, an Alliance bowl plus 3 bowls; the ACC an Alliance bowl plus 3 others; the Big East, an Alliance bowl plus 3 others; the WAC, 3 bowls; C-USA, 1 bowl; the Big West, 0 bowls; the Mid-American, 0 bowls; and 11 independents, 0 bowls.

The actual revenue earned per conference in 1996 bowl appearances is listed in Table 5.3.

The Alliance bowls, then, distributed approximately $68 million to its member conferences after the 1995–96 season. The new ABC contract

TABLE 5.3
1996 NCAA Division IA Bowl Revenues

Conference	No. of Schools in Conference	Alliance Bowl Revenue ($)	Minor Bowl Revenue ($)	Total Conference Bowl Revenue ($)
ACC	9	8,736,000	3,550,000	12,286,000
Big East	8	8,484,000	3,050,000	11,534,000
Big 12	12	16,972,000	4,400,000	21,372,000
SEC	12	8,736,000	6,600,000	15,336,000
Pac-10	10	8,250,000	3,150,000	11,400,000
Big 10	11	16,736,000	7,250,000	23,986,000
Alliance				
Total*	62	67,916,000	28,000,000	95,916,000
Big West	6	0	150,000	150,000
C-USA	6	0	800,000	800,000
WAC	16	0	2,750,000	2,750,000
Mid-American	10	0	150,000	150,000
Independents	11	0	1,550,000	1,550,000
Non-Alliance				
Total	49	0	5,400,000	5,400,000

Source: Testimony of Senator Craig Thomas, before the Senate Judiciary Committee, May 22, 1997.

* Excluding Notre Dame, an independent Alliance member. Although the Rose Bowl was not technically an Alliance Bowl in 1996, it is included here in this category. The above estimates may be conservative. At least one informed source, for instance, stated that the payoff to the Fiesta Bowl alone in 1996 was $13.6 million per team. From Website of *USA Today*, September 24, 1997.

promises that this figure will far exceed $100 million in 1998–99.[28] This gives the six commissioners of the Alliance conferences an enormous amount of influence in the world of college sports. These commissioners, unlike athletic directors, coaches, or university presidents, are not college employees, are not located on campus, and operate with a thicker veil of secrecy than the NCAA.

Schools with access only to the minor bowl games find that there is little, if any, financial payoff to bowl participation. Participating teams may receive $750,000 or $1 million from the bowl, but out of this they have to cover expenses, sometimes revenue-share with their conference, and must cover any shortfall in their obligation to sell a specified, large number of tickets. For instance, the Hall of Fame Bowl requires each school to sell 15,000 tickets and the Carquest Bowl requires 12,500 each, which at a minimum price of $30 a pop can set a school back hundreds of thousands of dollars.[29] Expenses include hauling approximately one hundred players, coaches, administrators, the school band, and cheerleaders, among others, considerable distances to warmer climes, then housing and wining and dining them for several days. In some cases, the free-ride contingent has risen to nearly five hundred people.[30] Stories about schools having to eat a large share of their tickets and losing money from their minor bowl participation are legion.[31]

Especially with the advent of the Alliance Bowl games, the eighteen minor bowls have less and less significance.[32] Fan interest in these games has plummeted, affecting both television rights fees and ticket sales. Nonetheless, the NCAA has increased the number of sanctioned bowl games by five over the last two years. Now 44 of the 112 Division IA schools play in postseason bowl games.

On May 22, 1997, the U.S. Senate Judiciary Committee held hearings on the antitrust issues raised by the Super Alliance. The practical effect of the Alliance is to create (or rigidify) two tiers within Division IA football (already a subdivision within Division I, itself the top of three NCAA athletic divisions). The bottom tier is effectively precluded from participating in the most prestigious, highest revenue bowls. The fans of the forty-nine football teams left out of the Alliance are thus deprived of the potential excitement associated with these bowls, and the schools are excluded from the revenue source and advertising value of playing in the top tier. This exclusion, many maintain, constitutes a restraint of trade and a group boycott.

The Alliance responds with two arguments. First, the national champion has almost always come from the Alliance conferences. Second, the Alliance allows for the development of a national championship game which is a procompetitive outcome for the consumer (it gives them an additional, desirable product), and offsets any anticompetitive trade restrictions.

While it is true that national champions have most frequently come from the Alliance conferences, it should be recalled that the Alliance conferences have been reformed through absorbing parts of other conferences and independents over the last ten years. Further, wherever national champions in the past came from, it is exclusionary (and not defensible on antitrust grounds) to prevent new champions from emerging.

While it is true that most consumers enjoy the prospect of a national championship, it is also true that there are less restrictive ways to provide the same other than the Alliance system. Although various alternatives have been suggested, the most obvious is to have the NCAA run a national championship tournament, as it does in basketball and in Division IAA, Division II, and Division III football. The Division III championship, for instance, began in 1973 as a single-elimination tournament for four teams. It became an eight-team, single-elimination tournament in 1975 and the current format has sixteen teams.

An eight-team format would involve three games to determine a national champion. The Alliance argues that three games in the postseason prolong the season two extra weeks and this would take up too much time for the student-athletes. Not a bad thought, but in the past decade three Alliance conferences have added conference championship games and two preseason games have been created. If those two weeks were used instead to support a championship tournament, sponsored by the NCAA, the selection of participants could be open and the distribution of revenues could be more equal, similar perhaps to the NCAA basketball tournament. If the regular season schedule could be tightened to save one additional week, the final tournament could include four rounds with sixteen teams. Furthermore, if the NCAA were to add games it would be far less disruptive for student-athletes to play during the first two or three weeks of January when school is not in session than is the scheduling of the March basketball tournament.

Many fans would prefer a playoff system for football, as in basketball, because it is more interesting to have real competition decide championships than to have it done by computer. Moreover, many writers have cited possible anomalies with the bowl championship formula that will result in the crowning of an ambiguous or disputed champion.[33]

In a playoff format, the greater the number of rounds included, the greater would be the financial bonanza to the NCAA. DeLoss Dodds, AD at the University of Texas, believes that a playoff system would be so popular that it would add at least an extra $1 million in revenue for every team playing Division IA football.[34] Schools clamoring for resources to meet the demands of Title IX might welcome such a financial windfall.

But the politics of change are not encouraging. The bowl committees would lose control if a playoff format were adopted, and, hence, resist such a change. The Alliance members would lose privileged access to their self-proclaimed championship games and they would be forced to share their postseason revenues with dozens, if not hundreds, of other NCAA schools. They too would also resist the change. Conference commissioners, ADs, coaches, and sometimes college presidents and trustees from the Alliance would lose the enticing perquisites provided by the bowl committees. Conference commissioners may also prefer to defer to the NFL wishes to have no intrusion of competition during its playoffs and Super Bowl.

Unfortunately, these groups are already sufficiently powerful to make such a reform unlikely. They seemed, for instance, to have been able to pull the necessary strings in 1996 to dislodge an investigation into the Alliance by the Antitrust Division of the Justice Department.

The Alliance is also cunning. In the aftermath of the Senate Judiciary Committee's hearings, the Alliance held out a carrot to the other

Division IA conferences. It would pay the WAC $1.6 million annually for making its sixteen teams available to play in an Alliance bowl; similarly, C-USA would receive $800,000 for its eight teams. Also, the Alliance would donate a total of $900,000 to the Big West and Mid-American Conferences and $150,000 to the six Division IAA football conferences whose members offer the maximum number of scholarships permitted by the NCAA.

Further, the Alliance pledged that if a WAC or C-USA team finished with a national ranking of No. 6 or better, the team would be nearly guaranteed a spot in an Alliance Bowl. The catch is that if other Alliance members are also ranked in the top six and do not receive an automatic Alliance bowl berth by winning their conference, then they may be chosen by one of the bowl committees instead of a WAC or C-USA team. For the moment anyway, the congressional inquiry has been derailed and an imperfect peace prevails.

Testifying before the Senate hearings on the Super Bowl Alliance, Tulane University Law School professor (as well as Tulane Athletic Representative and a member of the Sugar Bowl Committee) Gary Roberts argued that the real problem with the Alliance goes beyond legalistic matters of antitrust:

> Intercollegiate athletics is supposed to be about education and amateur student-athletes. We should run our programs with the primary emphasis on optimizing the welfare of the young men and women who play sports while they are getting their education. We should try to preserve the amateur nature of this enterprise and be always vigilant of the need to preserve the academic and moral integrity of the institutions of higher learning upon which our nation's future depends. To turn this amateur athletic enterprise designed to give students an extracurricular activity through which to broaden their horizons into a purely revenue driven commercial business that caters to the welfare of consumers is a perversion of the values for which it was founded and should stand. This is why the Alliance is so offensive—it accelerates and magnifies the perverse commercial motivations and values that have all too much corrupted intercollegiate athletics.

RATINGS, ATTENDANCE, AND THE FUTURE

Television rights fees for sports have experienced a protracted boom. But few industries rise forever and no industries rise without cycles. The 1980s and 1990s have witnessed unprecedented competition among the traditional and newer networks, as cable sport networks have been formed and over-the-air networks (FOX, WB, UPN) have been created. This competition has helped to bid up the rights fees.

But as rights fees and opportunities for television coverage have grown, new sports have appeared (e.g., professional soccer, women's professional basketball, beach volleyball) and others have augmented their visibility and popularity (e.g., car racing and golf). The proliferation of televised sports inevitably results in lower ratings. And lower ratings, especially once the network shakeout occurs and the economy slows down, will bring either stagnation or diminution in rights fees.

This danger is particularly problematic for college football because *(a)* the number of telecasts has skyrocketed since the 1984 Supreme Court decision and *(b)* the networks overbid in their initial effort to pry conferences loose from the CFA. The ratings trend for college football is not promising. Games televised on ABC had a rating of 9.9 in 1983 before the Court decision, falling to 8.3 in 1984 and continuing to decrease to an average 6.6 between 1991 and 1995, and an average of 5.1 during 1996 and 1997. Notre Dame's ratings on NBC averaged only 5.1 between 1991 and 1995, and 3.2 during 1996 and 1997. The combined ratings points for all New Year's Day bowl games fell from 92.1 in 1975, to 69.8 in 1994, and 50.7 in 1997.

Likewise, supersaturation of the airwaves with college football and other sporting events seems to have cut into the live fan base for intercollegiate games. Average attendance at Division IA games peaked in 1982 at 43,689, after which it has trailed off steadily to 41,471 in 1995 and to 41,337 in 1996 before recovering somewhat to 42,085 in 1997 and 42,510 in 1998. This decrease of 1,179 over the last sixteen years is hardly alarming, but it feeds an overall concern about rights and gate fees in the future, particularly for schools which find themselves outside the self-designated football elite.

TELEVISION AND COLLEGE BASKETBALL

Men's basketball has always played second fiddle to football as a revenue generator for colleges. In 1995, football accounted for 66 percent of all athletic revenues at Division IA schools while men's basketball accounted for 25 percent.[35] Basketball, however, has been catching up; that sport's contribution to total athletic revenues rose from 8 percent in 1960, to 9 percent in 1969, 12 percent in 1977, 13 percent in 1981, 15 percent in 1985, 18 percent in 1989, and 22 percent in 1993.[36]

And the fastest growing component of big-time basketball revenues has been income from the end-of-the-year NCAA Final Tournament.

Between 1985 and 1995 while postseason football TV revenues approximately doubled, postseason basketball TV revenues increased four and a half times.

The NCAA basketball tournament began in 1939 with eight teams, expanded to 24 teams in 1952, 32 teams in 1953, 48 teams in 1979, and to its present 64-team format in 1985. The NCAA lost $2,531 on the 1939 tournament. The following year the tournament champion was awarded $750. Prize money was modest for the next two decades.

As tournament hours televised more than quintupled from the late sixties to the mid-nineties, the television rights fees grew from $140,000 in 1966, to $28.3 million in 1985, and to $166.2 million in 1995 (accounting for 90 percent of total tournament receipts in 1995).

One of the NCAA's motives for expanding its tournament was competition with the National Invitational Tournament (NIT), which until the early 1960s was the preeminent postseason basketball championship. In 1960, the NCAA Executive Committee instructed its member schools and conferences that they had to prioritize participation in the NCAA tournament over the NIT. With the NCAA's increased television revenues and exposure, the NIT gradually receded in importance.[37]

In 1990 the NCAA signed a monster-contract with CBS for $1 billion over seven years to broadcast the tournament, almost double the annual value of the existing contract. The investment paid off for CBS, as ratings for the final game rose from 18.8 in 1988 to 22.7 in 1992, and then steadied at 22.2 in 1993 and 21.6 in 1994. In this latter year, CBS locked in the NCAA tournament by renegotiating its contract, this time for eight years (1995–2002) for $1.75 billion. Ratings have trailed off a bit, averaging 18.8 during 1995–97 (still considerably above the 15.1 average ratings for the NBA final game during 1991–96), but in the strong advertising market spot fees have continued to skyrocket, reaching a reported $600,000 for thirty seconds during the 1997 final game.[38]

The NCAA has gone out of its way to help CBS get a good return on its investment. During the first half of the 1997 final men's game there were 8 minutes of commercials and 20 minutes of playing time. "Coaches run out of advice to give players as timeout breaks drag past 2½ minutes. Teams like Kentucky and Kansas, noted for benches deep enough to wear down exhausted opponents, lose that advantage."[39] Not even the NBA allows commercial breaks to so disrupt the game's tempo and strategy.

Basketball's meteoric success created something of an embarrassment for the NCAA. Prior to the 1990 CBS contract, which took effect in 1991, the NCAA distributed 60 percent of the tournament revenues to

TABLE 5.4
Payouts to Teams in NCAA Tournament
($)

Team Reaching	1970	1974	1978	1982	1986	1989
1st Round	10,000	30,000	60,000	140,000	150,000	274,000
Regional Semis	30,000	60,000	120,000	375,000	560,000	822,000
Final Four	60,000	120,000	240,000	520,000	880,000	1,370,000

Source: Wilford Bailey and Taylor Littleton, *Athletes and Academe: An Anatomy of Abuses and Prescription of Reform*, 1991, p. 39.

the participating teams.[40] For each round a team advanced in the tournament up to the Final Four, their school would receive an additional share of that year's tournament income (Table 5.4).

The payout was increasingly handsome. Some worried that the incremental sums involved had grown too large and placed excessive pressure on the players to perform. The favorite metaphor was the $300,000 foul shot. Then, with television rights fees about to double in 1991, the NCAA decided to modify its revenue distribution practices in a way that putatively placed less emphasis on winning.

Here's what the NCAA did. First, they reduced the share of tournament receipts going to participants from approximately 60 percent down to 30 percent. The remaining 70 percent would now be distributed irrespective of a team's or a conference's performance. In 1990–91, the first year of the new CBS contract, the NCAA received $117 million; of this, $47 million covered NCAA costs and financed NCAA programs, such as catastrophic injury insurance for athletes, academic enhancement for athletes, emergency financial assistance for athletes, and the Division II and III national championships. The balance of $70 million was divided in half, with equal parts going to performance awards to the tournament teams and to broad-based distribution to schools according to the number of athletic teams and scholarships they sponsor. This was certainly a step away from performance incentives and toward a more equal sharing of the television booty.

Second, the NCAA changed the basis for the performance awards. Prior to the 1990–91 season team awards were proportional to the number of tournament games they played up to the Final Four. With the March 1991 tournament the awards were made proportional to the number of wins a team had over the previous six years in the postseason tournament. Thus, a tournament win in a particular year was worth only one-sixth as much as it had been in that year. That win, however, now would also be paid off in the subsequent five years and, hence, the present value of the win would be equal to roughly six times the first-year payoff. For example, in 1996–97 each tournament game played was worth $74,000 that year, so over the six-year period the present value of that game would be $74,000 × 6, or $444,000 (the payoff per game grew each year at roughly the same percentage as the discount rate).[41]

If a team made it to the Final Four in 1996–97, it would receive a payoff of $2.22 million. The payoff for making it to the Final Four in 1988–89 was $1.37 million. In both cases, the NCAA sends the payment to the team's conference where it is then subjected to redistribution among all conference schools, generally with the participating school receiving a larger share (see below).

The bottom line, then, is that the NCAA in stretching out payments over six years has done nothing whatsoever to lower the value of a foul shot; on the contrary, as the television package has grown richer, the foul shot has greater value than ever before. Even with the diminished share of TV revenues going to tournament participants (in 1996–97, participants shared $50 million out of total CBS and ESPN revenues of $191.1 million), the monetary incentive to win is greater than it has ever been. Overall, the distribution of the NCAA basketball fund among the major Division I conferences in 1997 (based on tournament success from 1991 through 1996) displayed the pattern of inequality in Table 5.5.

The spread between the maximum and minimum conference distributions from the basketball fund has widened from $3.96 million in 1991 to $6.06 million in 1997, while the spread for the total distribution increased from $7.16 million in 1991 to $12.86 million in 1997.[42] The conferences receiving more from the basketball fund are also receiving more from the other distributions.

The NCAA does not arrange TV packages for regular season games; those are handled by the individual schools and conferences.[43] There has been a veritable explosion of TV coverage of regular season games in the 1990s. In 1988–89, there were 2,078 college basketball games shown on cable or broadcast television; in 1995–96, there were 3,854. Ratings for regular season games have dropped 10 to 20 percent, depending on the carrier, but the number of televised games has increased 85 percent. Thus, the number of people watching the games has grown appreciably, and so have the TV rights fees.

Along with the glut of televised games, attendance at men's basketball contests fell from 29.4 million in 1991–92 to 27.7 million in 1996–97. Meanwhile, attendance at Division I women's games has increased from 3.1 million in 1991–92 to 4.9 million in 1996–97, compensating for the entire men's decrease.

TABLE 5.5
Conference Distribution of Basketball Tournament
Fund, 1997

Conference	Basketball Fund ($)	Total NCAA Distribution ($)*
Atlantic 10	2,964,959	6,660,061
Atlantic Coast	6,132,075	11,652,509
Big East	4,919,137	10,586,015
Big Ten	5,053,908	13,230,010
Big Twelve	5,053,908	11,525,292
Big West	1,010,782	3,818,752
Conference USA	4,110,512	7,614,248
Northeast	404,313	2,094,575
Pac-10	3,234,501	9,042,711
Patriot League	404,313	2,262,266
Southeastern	4,986,523	11,445,035
Western Athletic	1,752,021	7,956,565
Totals	**50,000,000**	**145,046,244**

Source: *The NCAA News*, September 29, 1997, p. 6.
* Includes basketball fund, academic enhancement fund, conference grants, special assistance fund, sports-sponsorship fund, grants-in-aid fund, and supplemental distribution.

PENALIZING THE IRS

Another interesting twist is NCAA treatment of schools that are found to have violated Association rules after their participation in the tournament. Consider, for instance, the peculiar case of former University of Massachusetts star Marcus Camby. Camby was the stellar center for the UMass team that went to the Final Four in 1995–96. Subsequent to UMass earning its five units in the tournament it was revealed that Camby had received tens of thousands of dollars in payments and gifts from an individual who was hoping to be Camby's agent when he turned professional. Thus, Camby was being paid as an amateur and he had broken NCAA rules. He was an illegal player and UMass's tournament performance was nullified.

A logical inference would be that, since UMass did not legally earn its way into the tournament and its tournament record was obliterated, the penalty would be the removal of all its revenue units. Far from it. Here's what happened.

Each tournament unit in 1995–96 was worth $67,385, so UMass earned five times that, or $336,927 in the first of six years. The NCAA levied a 45 percent penalty on the first-year payout only, or $151,617 had to be returned. UMass's five units in 1995–96, however, would also be counted for each of the next five years, so the total payout resulting from the school's performance in the 1995–96 tournament would be at least $2.02 million in present value terms. Thus, the NCAA penalty is not only not 100 percent, which might be presumed, it is not 45 percent either; rather, it is 7.5 percent of the total earnings from the tournament.

Now, the final twist is that Marcus Camby is making several million dollars a year playing in the NBA.[44] In search of exoneration, he made a $151,617 tax-deductible donation to UMass to cover the school's losses. So UMass loses nothing, and the only loser is the U.S. Treasury which receives approximately $60,000 less in income tax from Marcus Camby.[45]

REVENUE REDISTRIBUTION WITHIN CONFERENCES

When the NCAA stumbled upon its basketball gold mine with the $1 billion CBS contract commencing in 1991, idealism ran wild. Many believed that part of the funds would find their way into academic programs and others saw an opportunity to lift the financial fortunes of the low-revenue sports programs.

Neal Pilson, president of CBS sports when the NCAA deal was signed, offered some thoughts on how the NCAA might use its new-found riches:[46]

Besides being a television executive, I am a citizen, a taxpayer, and a father of three children, two currently in college. I would like to see this money used for broad educational purposes as well as athletic purposes.

Pilson went on to suggest one way such a balance of purposes might be achieved. He proposed that the television dollars be distributed to the NCAA schools in proportion to the graduation rate of their athletes rather than their success in the basketball tournament. Pilson reported that he had discussed his idea with Dick Schultz, NCAA Executive Director at the time, and that Schultz fully supported it.

Roy Kramer, longstanding and powerful commissioner of the Southeast Conference, also articulated some magnanimous ideals back in 1990:[47]

I believe that we can make a major statement in intercollegiate athletics by the way we distribute this money, if it is properly handled. I think that for the first time, we're really looking at positive ways to distribute the money, based not on the concept of winning in order to balance your

TABLE 5.6
Revenue Inequality among the Approximately Top 150
Athletic Programs, 1962–1997

Year	Top School/ Average School	Year	Top School/ Average School
1962	1.81	1985	3.38
1965	1.90	1989	3.04
1970	1.92	1993	2.88
1975	1.92	1995	3.29
1980	2.48	1997	3.48

Sources: Mitchell Raiborn, *Financial Analysis of Intercollegiate Athletics*, Kansas City: NCAA, 1970; M. Raiborn, *Revenues and Expenses of Intercollegiate Athletic Programs, 1970–1977, 1978–1981, 1981–1985, 1985–1989*, Overland Park, Kansas: NCAA, 1978, 1982, 1986, 1990; Daniel Fulks, *Revenues and Expenses of Intercollegiate Athletic Programs, 1993*, Overland Park, Kansas: NCAA, 1994; D. Fulks, *Revenues and Expenses of Division I and II Intercollegiate Athletic Programs, 1995, 1997*, Overland Park, Kansas: NCAA, 1996, 1998.

budget, but from the standpoint of a commitment to student-athletes across the board in your program.

We're making the statement that "We're going to play for the trophy." That's the real purpose of the types of championships we sponsor in the NCAA. We're not doing it in order to enhance the paycheck or the coach's position at the end of the year.

A few years later Roy Kramer was defending the elitism of the Bowl Alliance and the right of six Division IA conferences to share the TV rights of $25 million per premiere bowl game among themselves. In fact, as television rights fees have skyrocketed, intercollegiate athletic revenues have become more stratified, not more equal. The NCAA does not publish a detailed breakdown of revenue distribution among athletic programs, but a reasonably clear picture of growing inequality can be assembled from the scant data they do produce. For instance, if one considers the ratio of reported revenue from the top revenue program in the country to the average revenue of roughly the top 150 programs, one can discern a pattern for this ratio to grow consistently through 1985 and then to stabilize. Overall, by this measure, revenue inequality increased by 92.3 percent between 1962 and 1997 among the nation's top athletic colleges. A trend toward growing inequality is also apparent in the 1990s (see Table 5.6).[48]

Yet, it is axiomatic in the world of sports that in order to sustain fan interest a sports league must maintain a certain degree of competitive balance; meaning that there has to be substantial uncertainty as to the outcome of each contest as well as to the ultimate league or conference champion each year. If there was not such uncertainty, then, one presumes, fans would quickly lose interest.

Pious proclamations to the contrary, nobody really knows what is the optimal degree of competitive balance or interteam parity. In professional sports, Major League Baseball has experienced the greatest increase in competitive balance since the 1950s, but its popularity growth has certainly lagged behind that of the NBA, NFL, and NHL; and the team sport with the least competitive balance is the NBA, yet the NBA has seen its popularity grow more rapidly than the other sports.[49]

In professional sports, it is clear that the profit maximizing degree of competitive balance is not one where all the teams are of equal strength. A league will generate the most revenue when teams from larger metropolitan areas, with more modern stadiums or arenas, or where fans are willing and able to pay more to see their team win, are relatively stronger.

The same dynamic will apply, *mutatis mutandis*, for NCAA conferences. Most significantly, schools with historically strong teams will have an incentive to build larger and fancier facilities, and, once built, the same schools will experience a larger payoff to athletic success. For instance, the University of Tennessee plays in a stadium with a capacity of 102,544, while the University of Michigan stadium has a capacity of 108,001, UCLA's has 102,083, USC's 94,159, Penn State's 94,159, and Ohio State's 89,800. These schools are more likely to spend the largest sums on recruitment, coaching, training programs, academic tutoring, and so on, in order to attract the best athletes to matriculate. Other things being equal, these schools will also have sharper incentives to stretch NCAA rules.

To support competitive balance and deter rampant commercialism, then, conferences have cause to distribute their revenues in relatively equal fashion among member institutions. At the same time, for conferences to retain their stronger members they cannot be overly zealous in redistributing earnings from top bowl games, television appearances, the NCAA basketball tournament, and gate revenues.

Each conference is allowed to develop its own revenue distribution formula. Although the details differ, most conferences follow broadly similar patterns and these patterns have not changed much over time. Interestingly, though most conferences are composed largely of public, tax-supported institutions, many hold the specifics of their revenue distribution policies as closely guarded secrets. The tendency to regard such information as proprietary reinforces the view of big-time athletic programs as commercial enterprises, rather than as part of universities whose mission it is to promote open, intellectual discourse in pursuit of the truth.

From the information which is available, actual revenue distribution practices vary widely. The Big Ten appears to be the only major conference that shares gate revenues, with 35 percent going to the visiting conference team. The former Big 8 used to share the gate 50/50, but when it expanded into the Big 12 all ticket revenue sharing was terminated. Regular season television income sharing varies from 80 percent to participating team(s) and 20 percent to the conference in the Big 8 and Big East (for non-conference games), to 100 percent to the conference for subsequent equal distribution. Of course, some teams also have their own deal with a local television station and most have such deals with local radio stations. Revenue from the NCAA basketball tournament is shared relatively equally by most big-time conferences, with the participating school often receiving from one to several extra shares (roughly, an additional 10–30 percent).[50] The Atlantic 10 is an exception to the rule: in 1995–96 a conference team going to the semifinals would have earned the conference $336,925 in that year and would have received nearly half of that ($160,000) in conference revenue sharing payments.[51] There appears to have been a modest tendency for revenue sharing within conferences from postseason competition to have grown more equal over the last fifteen years.

The largest payoffs come from participation in the postseason football bowl games, particularly the Orange, Sugar, Fiesta, and Rose Bowl games associated with the Bowl Championship Series. When Notre Dame plays in one of these games, since it does not belong to any conference, the school retains the entire payoff plus any subsidiary income generated. When a school from a Bowl Championship Series conference plays, it has to share its payoff with the other members of the conference. Most conferences today allow the participating school an expense budget in the neighborhood of $1.2 to $1.6 million and then divide the balance of the $8 to $12 million payoff to the participant in the Orange, Sugar, Fiesta, or Rose Bowl among the conference schools (Tables 5.7, 5.8). The expense budget provides for team, band, cheerleader squad, top administrators, boosters, local politicians, and invited guests travel to and from the bowl as well as generous per diem and entertainment expenses. For instance, back in January 1996 the Pac-10 allocated $902,000 to crosstown USC to participate in the Rose Bowl. On this generous sum, the Trojans housed and fed about 150 players, coaches, trainers, equipment personnel, and others for about two weeks (school was out of session); bought Rose Bowl watches and rings for them; housed and fed the Trojan band for a week; shuttled everybody about for various bowl functions and practices; dealt with the cost of selling

TABLE 5.7
Distribution of Bowl Revenues to Colleges, 1995–96

School	Bowl	Expenses ($)*	Conference Share ($)*	Total ($)
USC	Rose	902,000	896,000	1,798,550
UCLA	Jeep Eagle Aloha	750,000	896,000	1,646,550
Oregon	Cotton	750,000	896,000	1,646,550
Washington	Sun	750,000	896,000	1,646,550
Stanford	St. Jude Liberty	750,000	896,000	1,646,550
Other Pac-10			896,000	896,000
Northwestern	Rose	1,100,000	770,833	1,870,833
Michigan	Builders' Sq. Alamo	1,000,000	770,833	1,770,833
Iowa	Sun	1,000,000	770,833	1,770,833
Penn St.	Outback	1,000,000	770,833	1,770,833
Ohio St.	CompUSA Citrus	1,000,000	770,833	1,770,833
Mich. St.	P/W Independence†	1,000,000	770,833	1,770,833
Other Big Ten			770,833	770,833
Florida St.	Fedex Orange	1,250,000	895,000	2,145,000
North Carolina	Carquest	750,000	895,000	1,645,000
Virginia	Peach	825,000	895,000	1,720,000
Clemson	Toyota Gator	900,000	895,000	1,795,000
Other ACC			895,000	895,000
Virginia Tech	Nokia Sugar	3,500,000	578,000	4,078,750
Syracuse	Toyota Gator	1,500,000	578,000	2,078,750
Other Big East			578,000	578,000
Nebraska	Tostitos Fiesta	1,500,000	1,103,750	2,603,750
Kansas	Jeep Eagle Aloha	1,000,000	1,103,750	2,103,750
Kansas St.	Plymouth Holiday	1,000,000	1,103,750	2,103,750
Colorado	Cotton	1,000,000	1,103,750	2,103,750
Other Big 8			1,103,750	1,103,750
Texas	Nokia Sugar	1,600,000	866,250	2,466,250
Texas Tech	Weiser Lock Copper	750,000	866,250	1,616,250
Texas A&M	Builders' Sq. Alamo	800,000	866,250	1,666,250
Other SWC			866,250	866,250
Florida	Tostitos Fiesta	2,173,600	268,667	2,442,266
LSU	P/W Independence†	630,000	792,553	1,142,533
Arkansas	Carquest	680,000	775,867	1,422,533
Georgia	Peach	826,000	777,200	1,603,200
Auburn	Outback	780,000	742,533	1,522,533
Tennessee	CompUSA Citrus	1,240,000	655,867	1,895,866
Other SEC			802,533	802,533
Notre Dame	Orange			8,330,000

Sources: Jim Hodges, "College Football Bowl Games," *Los Angeles Times*, Dec. 31, 1995, C1. *NCAA Football: The Official 1996 College Football Records Book*, pp. 248–50.

* "Expenses" is the amount paid to the team for the "cost" of playing in the bowl plus premium added by the conference. It does not always include additional allotments for transportation. "Share" is the total amount the team receives from conference revenue sharing practices during the year.

† Poulan/Weed Eater Independence Bowl.

TABLE 5.8
Shares of Bowl Payouts, 1998–99

School/Conference	Bowl	Payout per team ($)*	School Share ($)
Syracuse/Big East	Orange	12,000,000	4,681,250
Wisconsin/Big Ten	Rose	12,562,000	3,673,818
Ohio State/Big Ten	Sugar	12,000,000	3,673,818
Penn State/Big Ten	Outback	1,800,000	3,473,818
Michigan/Big Ten	Florida Citrus	3,750,000	3,473,818
Purdue/Big Ten	Alamo	1,100,000	3,273,818
Florida State/ACC	Fiesta	13,400,000	2,905,555
Tennessee/SEC	Fiesta	13,400,000	2,600,000
Florida/SEC	Orange	12,000,000	2,500,000
UCLA/Pac-10	Rose	12,562,000	2,313,300
Virginia/ACC	Peach	1,500,000	2,305,555
N.C. State/ACC	Micron PC	750,000	2,305,555
North Carolina/ACC	Las Vegas	800,000	2,305,555
Georgia Tech/ACC	Gator	1,400,000	2,305,555
West Virginia/Big East	Insight.com	750,000	2,281,250
Virginia Tech/Big East	Music City	750,000	2,281,250
Miami, Fla./Big East	Micron PC	750,000	2,281,250
Arizona/Pac-10	Holiday	1,800,000	2,178,300
Texas A&M/Big 12	Sugar	12,800,000	2,136,336
Washington/Pac-10	Oahu	750,000	2,128,300
Oregon/Pac-10	Aloha	750,000	2,128,300
Southern Cal/Pac-10	Sun	1,000,000	2,117,700
Texas Tech/Big 12	Independence	1,000,000	2,033,333
Texas/Big 12	Cotton	2,500,000	2,033,333
Nebraska/Big 12	Holiday	1,800,000	2,033,333
Missouri/Big 12	Insight.com	750,000	2,033,333
Kansas State/Big 12	Alamo	1,100,000	2,033,333
Colorado/Big 12	Aloha	750,000	2,033,333
Notre Dame/Ind.	Gator	1,400,000	1,400,000
Arkansas/SEC	Florida Citrus	3,750,000	1,390,000
Mississippi State/SEC	Cotton	2,500,000	1,140,000
Kentucky/SEC	Outback	1,800,000	840,000
Georgia/SEC	Peach	1,500,000	780,000
Texas Christian/WAC	Sun	1,000,000	750,000
San Diego State/WAC	Las Vegas	800,000	750,000
Brigham Young/WAC	Liberty	1,100,000	750,000
Air Force/WAC	Oahu	750,000	750,000
Mississippi/SEC	Independence	1,000,000	680,000
Alabama/SEC	Music City	750,000	680,000
Tulane/C-USA†	Liberty	1,100,000	325,000

continued on next page

TABLE 5.8 (*cont.*)

School/Conference	Bowl	Payout per Team ($)*	School Share ($)
Southern Miss/C-USA	Humanitarian	750,000	325,000
Louisville/C-USA	Motor City	750,000	325,000
Idaho/Big West	Humanitarian	750,000	291,667
Marshall/MAC†	Motor City	750,000	62,500

Source: USA Today, January 7, 1999, p. 8c.

Abbreviations: **ACC** - Atlantic Coast Conference; **C-USA** - Conference USA; **MAC** - Mid-American Conference; **SEC** - Southeastern Conference; **WAC** - Western Athletic Conference.

* All bowl payouts are early estimates provided by conference and bowl officials. Precise figures depend on ticket sales and other revenue sources at each bowl. Team shares reflect institutions' shares of total conference proceeds, not just payouts from the bowl in which an institution is playing.

† Conference USA and the Mid-American Conference do not disclose payout formulas. Team shares for those conferences are estimates taken by dividing total bowl proceeds for the conference by the number with football teams.

some 41,000 Rose Bowl tickets and bought a few extras for VIPs as well as for the players to give to their families or whomever; and threw elaborate parties for alumni and financial supporters.[52]

The expense budget always provides ample perquisites for those associated with the program and helps to set a basis for deepening the athletic department's endowment. Often, the "expense" budget is purposefully inflated to provide a bonus to the participating school. Other times, the idiosyncrasies of bowl management actually leave the school at a financial disadvantage for participating in the game. Consider, for instance, the case of the University of Nebraska and the Big 12 Conference in January 1997.

The Big 12 held its first conference championship game in December 1996. The game between the favored Nebraska Cornhuskers and the Texas Longhorns was certainly a financial bonanza for the conference, generating about $7.5 million in revenue. The Longhorns unexpectedly beat the Cornhuskers, so Nebraska went to the Orange Bowl, the second-ranked bowl game in January 1997, while Texas went to the "national championship" game at the Sugar Bowl. The Orange Bowl, however, required that each participating school purchase and resell 15,000 tickets at an average price of $80 each. The Cornhuskers fans already had spent money traveling to the St. Louis Trans World Dome for the Big 12 Championship and were disappointed that the team was no longer playing for the national championship. Further, it was estimated that some 10,000 Nebraska fans had purchased nonrefundable packages to the Sugar Bowl in New Orleans. The Orange Bowl in Miami was a tough sell; so tough that the university only sold 3,600 of the 15,000 tickets, taking a loss on the required seat sale of $912,000. They did receive $1.5 million in expense money for the Orange Bowl, but 60 percent of that was eaten up by the ticket deficit alone. Thus, other members of the Big 12 received $600,000 apiece from the Cornhuskers' appearance in the Orange Bowl, but the Cornhuskers, it seems, may have lost money.

Similarly, Michigan State seems to have generated some red ink by participating in the 1997–98 Aloha Bowl in Honolulu. They received a guarantee of $750,000, but the school chartered a plane to Hawaii for 97 players, 85 band members, the coaches and their families, and administrators and trustees which alone cost $300,000. Add to this the healthy per diem expense for this entourage and the school was $150,000 out of pocket. John Lewandowski, Michigan State's sports information director, claimed that the short-run cash drain would be more than made up for by the favorable publicity the school received: ". . . in terms of rebuilding our program, you can't assess the value of being in a bowl game just by the bottom line. It's a way to keep up our recruiting. It's great exposure for the program. There's no better marketing tool."[53] If any prospective students were among the few who were watching the Aloha Bowl on television, one wonders whether they might rather go to the University of Washington, which demolished Michigan State 51–23 in the game. Of course, Lewandowski and his bosses (and families) enjoyed an all-expenses-paid week in Hawaii, and nobody doubts that the bowl trip was worth it to these decisionmakers.

In the case of the Big East conference, the charade of the bowl "expense" allowance is magnified beyond all credibility as the $3.5 million expense allotment to Virginia Tech in 1995 makes manifest. In general, it appears that the expense category is a rather transparent subterfuge for providing a financial incentive to the school, or at least the school's top academic and athletic administrators as well as its benefactors, to perform at a top competitive level.

Bookkeeping legerdemain notwithstanding, the practices of conference revenue sharing are substantial and do support at least two worthy objectives of the athletic programs. First, revenue sharing guarantees a certain minimal revenue stream each year to allow for more even expenditures and more accurate budgeting. The Big Ten Conference, for instance, has contracts for appearances with five different bowl games and the possibility of additional invitations that guarantee a certain annual income flow. Second, revenue sharing supports competitive balance within conferences. Although most big-time conferences tend to have perennially dominant teams, this imbalance would presumably be more acute without revenue sharing. As conference revenue sharing has tended to become more nearly equal since the mid-1980s, there has been a modest, attendant equalization of win percentages of teams within most big-time conferences.[54]

Many, of course, would like to see the financial incentive to win entirely eradicated from college sports. Winning teams, however, benefit from larger sponsorship revenues, more largesse from the sneaker companies, greater ticket and concessions sales, and usually higher booster contributions. Coaches, athletic directors, and school administrators stand to gain financially as well as in perquisites if their team wins. The importance of these revenue sources, financial incentives, and centrifugal tendencies within the NCAA, discussed more fully in subsequent chapters, makes it unlikely that further revenue equalization will occur.

CHAPTER SIX

Commercial Connections

Nike hasn't called and told us when to start our games. Athletes don't miss classes because of Nike. If intercollegiate athletics has sold its soul, it wasn't to shoe and apparel companies. They sold it a long time ago, to television.
> —Joe Roberson, Athletic Director at the University of Michigan
> until August 1997

Yes, I fear for where this is going. If corporate America keeps involving itself with amateur athletics, if we keep allowing companies to own the schools, then you're going to be in trouble.
> —Sonny Vaccaro, the architect of Nike's
> recruitment/endorsement network

A tax-deductible donation to the MAC entitles a member to a long list of benefits. . . MAC accepts contributions by various methods: cash, securities, real estate, personal property, wills/trusts, life insurance, and matching gifts from employers. . . . Members of MAC receive priority on their purchase of football and basketball tickets. Seats are assigned according to the level of contribution. . . . A $3,000 contribution could earn a Director's Club status for one year, or a Gold Club for five years.
> —1996 Promotional Brochure of the Mountaineer Athletic Club
> [MAC] of the University of West Virginia

The Goal Line Club (GLC) is a service organization that exists for the sole purpose of promoting and supporting the University of Minnesota Football Program. . . . GLC members assist the University of Minnesota Football Program in securing summer jobs for student athletes. . . . GLC members organize a luncheon held prior to every

home game for club members and the general public. . . . The GLC is
responsible for the touchdown cannon that is fired at all home games
after the touchdowns and field goals. . . . The GLC has a special sec-
tion at the Metrodome where members sit together and cheer the
Golden Gophers to victory. . . . The GLC is a non-profit organization
and at the end of each fiscal year we allocate our funds on hand to the
head football coach to be used at his discretion.

—1997 Promotional Brochure of the University of Minnesota
Goal Line Club

EDWIN LOHN had been going to University of Southern California (USC) football games for sixty years, the last forty as a season ticket holder. In 1980, when USC established its "Cardinal and Gold Club," Edwin purchased a lifetime membership for $10,000. This membership entitled Edwin to buy season tickets every year on the 50-yard line. Edwin played rallying calls on his trumpet at the games and his car's license plate read "LOVESC." In 1995, USC informed Edwin and the other two thousand members of the Cardinal and Gold Club, which cost $20,000 for life or $2,000 a year to join, that they might be moved from their favorite seats to make room for members of a new club. The new club costs $18,000 a year or $100,000 for life to join.[1]

Sherry Boyles, the 1995–96 student body president at the University of Texas at Austin, took an aggressive stand during her campaign for office against the university's student seating plan for basketball games. In the 16,000-seat arena the school sets aside 5,000 seats for the students—4,000 in the upper deck and 1,000 in a corner section of the lower level. The seats are undesirable and student attendance at games had been low. Boyles credited her election to her position on basketball seats: "When I mentioned basketball seating, the response was, 'Oh, you have my vote.'" Boyles asked: "Is it our philosophy at U.T. that basketball games are for alumni or for students? We're arguing that part of the college experience is being able to enjoy games that your fellow students participate in."[2]

In November 1997, Marion Traub-Werner was a 20-year-old junior, crew team member, and Latin American Studies major at the University of North Carolina. Her school had a five-year, $11 million sponsorship deal with Nike that paid former basketball coach Dean Smith $300,000 a year as well as $500,000 up front for his assistance in negotiating the contract.[3] Traub-Werner, upset about the treatment of workers in Asian factories where Nike sneakers were produced, formed the Nike Awareness Committee. She, along with some fellow committee members, had a meeting with Coach Smith who tried to convince them of his view that Nike factories were as good as any in that part of the world. But Traub-Werner had done a lengthy research paper on the subject and found Smith's argument unpersuasive. The next day the school announced that Nike had invited a group of students and faculty at North Carolina to tour its factories in Asia. Traub-Werner knew of similar Nike tours, which she believed served only to whitewash the dim reality of Nike workshops. What she was doing at UNC other students were doing at Duke, Michigan, Illinois, Notre Dame, and elsewhere. Nike had its public relations department's hands full in 1997–98.[4]

Behind each of these vignettes there is an elaborate nexus of corporate connections that sustains big-time college athletics. Division IA athletic programs increasingly resemble corporate entities, directly employing 100 to 206 full-time staff with top-paid executives earning hundreds of thousands of dollars and handsome perquisites.[5] Whereas it might surprise few in the late 1990s to learn about sponsorship or licensing deals between universities and sneaker or beer companies, many may be astonished to realize the extent of Uncle Sam's complicity in this commercial nexus.

GOVERNMENT SUBSIDIES TO COLLEGE SPORTS

All Division I athletic programs benefit from a variety of federal government subsidies. First, when athletic programs build new sports facilities, the general practice is for the university to issue a tax-exempt bond. Such a bond would typically bear an interest rate in 1998 close to 5 percent, whereas a bond whose interest is taxable would yield around 8 percent. The tax-exemption saves the program around 3 percentage points on its debt service. If the facility cost and the bond value are $100 million, there is a saving (federal subsidy) of $3 million a year.

Since the athletic program is part of the university, the new basketball arena or football stadium enjoys the same tax exemption as would a new chemistry or social science building. But, unlike the academic buildings, the actual use of the arena or stadium nowadays is commercial. The $100 courtside seats or luxury boxes at the arena or the corporate advertisements on the jumbotron scoreboard are built or bought with tax-exempt funds.

Second, the revenue received by the athletic department from corporate advertisements and sponsorships benefits from preferential tax treatment. By long-standing policy, nonprofit organizations are exempt from corporate income tax.[6] The special treatment is intended to promote desirable social goals, but it also creates the potential for nonprofit organizations to compete unfairly with the private sector. That is, because it does not pay tax on its net income, the nonprofit entity can afford to offer its goods or services at a lower price. Thus, a hotel run by a college could charge lower room fees than a private hotel down the street or a college-run bookstore could sell books at lower prices than a private bookstore in town.

The unrelated business income tax (UBIT) is designed to curb such unfair competition. The UBIT is levied on nonprofit organization revenues garnered from activities that are not substantially related to the exempt purpose for which the organization was formed.

After corporate sponsorship of college bowl games began, the IRS in 1991 ruled that the income from such sponsorships should be taxed as unrelated income. In particular, when the Cotton Bowl Classic was renamed the Mobil Cotton Bowl Classic and the Mobil Corporation was allowed to display its name on the football field along with promotional materials, the IRS maintained that this arrangement was tantamount to the sale of advertising to Mobil. And since the sale of advertising was not the exempt purpose for which the Cotton Bowl Athletic Association was established, the IRS contended that the revenue from this sponsorship should be taxed. If it were not taxed, not only would the government be deprived of tax revenue but Mobil would benefit from receiving cheaper advertising.

Two years later, following an aggressive lobbying campaign by various corporate sponsors, the NCAA, the College Football Bowl Association, and the Professional Golfers' Association, among others, the IRS amended its proposed regulations. Under the new guidelines sponsorships and advertisements would remain exempt as long as the displays did not contain any comparative or qualitative description of the company's products. That is, Nike could have a sign with a swoosh and the slogan "Just Do It," but the company could not have a sign stating "We Do It Better." When a Senate bill was crafted to support this new IRS approach, President Clinton said it would cost the Treasury $67 million and he would veto it.

More lobbying and the passage of time led the president—of all things—to change his mind, and in August 1997 he signed into law H.R. 2014. This law exempts from taxation payments made to nonprofit organizations for advertising where comparative or qualitative description is absent. The guiding principle of this exemption is that such advertising does not substantially benefit the sponsoring corporation.

Thus, the president and the Congress would have us believe that Nike spends tens of millions of dollars a year on dozens of Division I sports programs out of charitable instinct, and that Phil Knight, Nike's founder and CEO, does not believe having a swoosh appear prominently on Ohio State football and basketball uniforms provides any substantial benefit to the company. If the absurdity of this proposition does not appear patent, then read the promotional material written by the Fiesta Bowl: "All sponsorship packages are tailored for sponsors so that they receive tangible returns on their sponsorship dollars."[7] And listen to a John Hancock senior executive whose company paid $1.6 million for sponsorship of the Sun Bowl in 1990: "The bowl is an extraordinarily efficient media buy. It would cost us a great deal more money to help influence sales by normal advertising." The executive estimated that the company received the equivalent of $5.1 million from its $1.6 million payment.[8]

The implicit subsidy here is substantial. For instance, Nike presently spends approximately $3 million a year on its sponsorship deal with Ohio State University athletics. Using the methodology of the Congressional Research Service, 25 percent of this sum is assumed to be the advertising expenses of the corporation. If the balance were taxed as UBIT at the normal corporate tax rate of 35 percent, then Ohio State University would pay $787,500 to the U.S. Treasury each year from its Nike contract. If this procedure were used to value the exemption for all tax-exempt college sports revenue, it would amount to an annual subsidy to colleges of tens of millions of dollars.

The third significant subsidy comes from the practice of allowing booster donations to college athletic programs also to be treated as tax-exempt. The general practice in big-time college sports today is to require large donations to the athletic program as a prerequisite to purchasing choice season tickets. Most schools even calibrate the size of the donation with the desirability of the seat. Some large donors not only buy an ability to purchase good seats with their contributions, they also buy an invitation to special dinners or events with the coach and/or players. That is, what is called a tax-exempt contribution is, in fact, the purchase of desirable products.

Sports fans may note a similarity between such booster donations in college sports and Personal Seat Licenses (PSLs) in professional sports. In professional football, for instance, a dozen or so teams require fans to buy the right to purchase season tickets at a price ranging from several hundred to several thousand dollars, depending on the desirability of the seat. Once the right is purchased, then the seat itself must be bought. It is rather like paying to see the menu in a restaurant, then paying for the meal.

One difference in college sports is that the upfront fee is expected annually as a contribution to the booster organization, whereas in pro sports it is a one-time payment that lasts from ten years to a lifetime. Another difference is that when one buys a PSL for an NFL team it is not tax-deductible. In practice, the IRS found it too distasteful to allow a 100 percent deduction for such college booster contributions, so in December 1996 it issued a new regulation allowing only 80 percent to be considered a tax-deductible gift when the donor receives the benefit of a ticket-purchase option. If the donor receives no explicit benefit, then the entire gift remains deductible. The implicit subsidy here again rises into the tens of millions of dollars annually.[9]

BOOSTERS

Back in 1965 recorded booster donations provided 5 percent of athletic department revenues at the major football schools. In 1996 they accounted for 15.3 percent, averaging $2.6 million per school.[10] Actual booster contributions are larger than the official figure, since many gifts go unreported.

A fascinating glimpse at the unreported activities of boosters was provided in an internal audit at the University of Wisconsin in March 1998. The audit was provoked by the discovery of over 630 booster payments between 1994 and 1997 that violated NCAA regulations either because they were not approved by the Chancellor's office or because they were unreported. The payments were for items such as plane travel, hotels, drinks, meals, golfing outings, rental cars, real estate purchases, moving allowances, health insurance, Super Bowl tickets and rings, pottery, neckties, and cellular telephone calls for coaches, athletic department personnel, and their spouses. Spouses received free trips to Hawaii courtesy of the boosters, administrators enjoyed regular golfing outings, coaches were given up to $5,000 for personal appearances, and some individual expenditures went above $15,000. Football coach Barry Alvarez alone received 99 booster payments and AD Pat Richter received 84 payments, just counting the ones that constituted NCAA infractions. One of the payments to Richter was for travel from Madison to Green Bay to attend a meeting of the Board of Directors of the NFL's Packers. The payment covered his mileage as well as lodging, meals, and personal cell phone calls for him, his wife, and son. One wonders why such expenses were not picked up by the Packers, since Richter serves on their Board.[11]

University of Nebraska boosters are reportedly behind another unreported activity, and this one deftly sidesteps the NCAA limit on 85 football scholarships for IA schools. Counties in Nebraska offer an "academic scholarship" to the University of Nebraska for the best graduating high school football player in the county, reportedly financed by booster organizations. The athlete then attends the university as a walk-on (without an athletic scholarship) and does not count toward the school's limit of 85 football grants-in-aid. Since there are 94 counties in Nebraska and each county might give one such "academic scholarship" per year, the total number of such outstanding scholarships at any point in time could theoretically reach as high as 376. Undoubtedly, such scholarships are only awarded to true football prospects, so the number awarded is considerably smaller than this upper limit. But Nebraska football is notorious for having a large, strong walk-on squad and the 85 official grants-in-aid can be saved for out-of-state prospects.[12]

Booster clubs at Division IA schools typically have 7,000 to 20,000 members, each contributing anywhere from $50 to $20,000 or more a year. Club membership entitles one to a panoply of perquisites and seat purchase options, depending on the level of one's contribution and other factors. Many clubs, such as the Fighting Illini Club at the University of Illinois or the Victors Club at the University of Michigan, provide a direct, unabashed link between one's yearly contribution and one's privileges. At Illinois, for instance, the following linkage schedule applies:

Yearly Gift	*Privilege*
$100–250	Option for 4 Seats in 6th Preferred Area
$250–499	Option for 4 Seats in 5th Preferred Area
$500–999	Option for 4 Seats in 4th Preferred Area
$1,000–2,999	Option for 6 Seats in 3rd Preferred Area
$3,000–9,999	Option for 8 Seats in 2nd Preferred Area
$10,000 +	Option for 8 Seats in 1st Preferred Area

At Michigan, seat options are more expensive:

Yearly Gift	*Privilege*
$100–500	No Seat Option
$500–1,000	No Seat Option
$1,000–1,500	Option for 2 Seats
$1,500–2,500	Option for 4 Seats
$2,500–5,000	Option for 4 Seats
$5,000–10,000	Option for 6 Seats
$10,000–20,000	Option for 8 Seats
$20,000 +	Option for 10 Seats

Along with the seat options, Michigan offers an escalating list of benefits, with the top category receiving free parking, VIP meals with coaches, and participation in golf tournaments—among many other privileges. Some schools use seemingly complex point systems, where the number of points determines the number and attractiveness of season ticket options. The program at Florida State is reasonably typical. It offers 2 points to those who were season ticket holders the previous year, 1 point for each consecutive year of being a season ticket holder, 2 points for members of the faculty and staff, 2 points for "varsity lettermen" [sic], 2 points for members of the state legislature, 2 points for members of the Florida State alumni association, 4 points for members of the President's club, and the schedule of points below according to the size of one's annual gift. The same point schedule applies to the total of one's gifts during the previous five-year period.

Yearly Gift	Privilege
$50–109	2 points
$110–249	4 points
$250–499	5 points
$500–999	7 points
$1,000–2,499	10 points
$2,500–4,999	15 points
$5,000–9,999	20 points
$10,000–19,999	25 points
Each addit'l $10,000	5 points

The actual schedule used by Florida State goes up to $110,000 (70 points) and then designates 5 points for each additional $10,000. Thus, a person who gave, say, $1,000 in a given year would earn 10 points, plus if he also gave $1,000 in each of the previous four years he would earn an additional 20 points for a total of 30 points. This total would overwhelm the points allocated for varsity lettermen, members of the alumni association, history of season ticket ownership, etc. In the end, even with a point system, what really counts is one's monetary contribution to the booster club.

Although the average booster club of Division IA schools contributed $2.6 million over the table in 1996, many of the more successful clubs raise over $5 million a year and contribute even more to special capital project fund drives.[13] The boosters of the Stanford University athletic department give $14–15 million in a typical year. The department now has an endowment of over $170 million.[14] The "Educational Foundation" at the University of North Carolina (UNC), for instance, has 13,000 members. Together these members had raised over $35 million toward a new football stadium as well as $4.8 million for athletic grants-in-aid during 1997–98, plus other support for athletic operations. The promotional material from the UNC booster club states: "We urge everyone with any affiliation to the University to be a part of this project." To the extent that the boosters appeal is persuasive, it can be inferred that raising athletic funds will detract from raising general educational funds.

STADIUMS

There's a sports facility construction boom going on in this country. Industry experts conservatively estimate that between 1996 and 2006 over $8 billion will have been spent on sports facilities.[15] New sports facilities for professional teams costing at least $180 million each have been built or are under construction in Atlanta, Baltimore, Charlotte, Chicago, Cincinnati, Cleveland, Ft. Lauderdale, Houston, Milwaukee, Nashville, Phoenix, Portland, St. Louis, San Francisco, Seattle, Tampa, and Washington, D.C., and more are in the planning stages in Boston, Dallas, Denver, Indianapolis, Los Angeles, Miami, Minneapolis, New York, Pittsburgh, and San Diego.

Being shown the way to greater revenues, colleges have followed in the pros' footsteps. As of early 1993, there were 106 stadiums or arenas in Division IA that contained luxury suites.[16] Since then, the construction boom in college sports facilities has accelerated. A sample of 25 major-college athletic programs found that since 1996 these schools had spent or committed over $1.2 billion on sports facilities.[17]

Item. The football stadium at the University of Texas underwent a $90 million facelift in 1998, raising capacity to 82,000, including 66 new luxury suites which are expected to generate $3 million a year. Other upgrades include a new Sony Jumbotron video system, a modern concessions plaza, and a 132,000-square-foot hospitality center.

Item. The Buckeyes of Ohio State University will be playing in a renovated facility in 2001, which is receiving a $150 million upgrade, boosting capacity to 96,000 including 82 luxury suites, 2,600 club seats, a club lounge, and new Marriott concession areas. Ohio State is also finishing construction of a new 20,000-seat basketball arena for the 1998–99 season at a cost of $110 million, including 46 suites, 3,950 premium seats, club lounges, banquet rooms, and the Ohio State Hall of Fame.[18] The Buckeye faithful purchased 4,100 personal seat licenses at prices between $4,000 and $15,000, giving them the right to buy season tickets over forty years. For the 1998–99 season all 46 suites sold at prices from $75,000 to $250,000.[19]

Item. Joe Paterno's roost at Penn State is adding 10,000 seats, lifting capacity to 103,500, plus 58 suites and 4,000 club seats complete with a 28,000-square-foot luxury lounge. The price tag for this renovation is estimated at $84 million.[20] Cost overruns in stadium construction and renovation projects of 20 percent or more are not uncommon.

Item. The Arizona State U. team plays in a stadium with the modest capacity of 73,379, but boasts 68 suites and a jumbo, color electronic scoreboard (increasingly *de rigueur* at Division IA stadiums) 54 feet high by 40 feet wide. Not to be outdone across the state at the University of Arizona facility, a four-story skybox section was added that includes 319 loge seats (priced at around $300 each per game), 24 suites (leasing at approximately $5,000 a game and requiring a five-year commitment), and a new media center.

Item. The University of Maryland Cole Arena added a row of courtside seats for the Terrapins basketball games, which go for $250 a night. The school has plans for a new, $106 million arena.[21]

Item. Seafirst Bank acquired the naming rights for the University of Washington's arena from 2000 to 2009 for $5.1 million. The bank also will pay $3.9 million for signage at the arena and the school's football stadium.[22]

Item. The University of Kansas is spending over $30 million to renovate its memorial stadium and add 36 luxury suites as well as a new press box.

Item. Elsewhere in the Big 12 Conference, not to be outdone, the University of Nebraska is spending $32 million to update its football stadium by adding 36 suites, elevators, escalators, concession stands, and a new press box for the 1999 season.

Item. After the 1997–98 season the University of Houston hired its alumnus and former NBA star Clyde Drexler to coach its basketball team. The school is adding between 16 and 28 luxury suites to its arena for the 1998–99 season, which are renting for $80,000 per suite, plus the cost of tickets.[23]

Item. In Lubbock, Texas, a new 15,020-seat, $53 million arena is being constructed at Texas Tech University. Funding for the project will come in significant measure from the sale of 24 luxury suites at $30–40,000 annually and 3,000 personal seat licenses at $1,250 a year. Texas Tech is also putting $47 million into an overhaul of its football stadium, and, not to be outdone, state rivals Texas A&M and Southern Methodist are planning $33 million and $43 million upgrades on their football facilities, respectively.

Item. For $5 million over ten years Wells Fargo purchased naming rights to the refurbished arena at Arizona State University. In addition to naming rights to the arena, Wells Fargo gets an on-court logo, courtside rotating signage, title sponsorship of one football game per year, and an option to open a banking center or ATM at the arena.[24]

Item. Ryder System, Inc., purchased naming rights to the new $35 million arena at the University of Miami for $9 million.[25]

Item. The eight schools that are withdrawing from the Western Athletic Conference to form their own more high-powered league announced in June 1998 that they are considering selling naming rights to their new conference.[26] That is, instead of being called something like the Great Western Conference, it might be called the Microsoft Conference of the West.

Item. More than 340 professors at the University of Kentucky signed a petition opposing both the construction of a new 23,000-seat arena and the retrofitting of luxury boxes to the existing Rupp arena.

The trick for college as well as pro teams is to get someone else to pay for the new facility. Spending $250–400 million for a new stadium, which might generate an extra $15–$40 million annually in revenue (at the professional level and probably about one-quarter to one-half of this at the college level due *inter alia* to fewer games) but also might cost an additional $1–3 million a year in operations and maintenance, is not likely to attract many private investors. But if the pro teams can get the municipalities and the colleges can get the states or boosters to foot most of the bill, then having a new arena or stadium is an opportunity too good to refuse.

Well, too good to refuse for everyone except Temple's basketball coach John Chaney and St. Joseph's coach Phil Martelli. The Temple team began its 1997–98 season at the new $110 million Apollo complex. Chaney claims to have mixed feelings. First, he now has the responsibility to fill the 10,224-seat arena. Second, he says: "It brings in what I call the corporate fan, you know the guy who sits on his hands and is more concerned about reading the stock reports than watching the game. You attract vagabond fans who are there to be seen at the Apollo. At the higher prices, you can't expect to attract the old fans, the students and alumni who clap their hands and enjoy themselves. You lose a lot of the loyal, rah-rah fans."[27]

Martelli's team plays in a 3,200-seat fieldhouse, and likes it: "I don't want a bigger place. The recruits know they can win at St. Joe's because St. Joe's has a tradition of winning." Martelli dismisses the alleged recruiting advantage of a new facility, arguing that recruits care first about the opportunity to play right away, and then about the level of a team's competition and TV exposure.

If a new arena is supposed to make a better team, then somebody should tell UMass, Villanova, Penn State, and Duquesne. Their basketball teams each got new arenas after seasons when the team registered a top-flight performance. Of the four, only the UMass team continued to play as well after the new arena was built as before. A new facility, then, makes financial sense if someone else pays for it, but it hardly guarantees championship teams.

SPONSORSHIPS AND LICENSING

According to the biannual NCAA survey, the average Division IA school earned $459,000 in sponsorship and signage income in 1995, $96,000 in program advertising and sales, and $833,000 in miscellaneous (which includes licensing income). As always, the top schools did much better than this.

After going to the regional finals in the NCAA basketball tournament in 1994, Michigan earned $6 million in licensing revenue.[28] Notre Dame has also hit this lofty level. Other schools, depending on the cachet and historical records of their football and basketball teams as well as the aesthetic appeal of their logos, make less. When Nebraska won back-to-back national football titles its licensing revenue reached above $3 million. Miami peaked at $4.6 million in 1993 and hovers around $1 million today. Ohio State has yet to surpass $2.2 million. After Wisconsin went to the Rose Bowl in 1994, its licensing increased from $300,000 to $1.3 million, and has since settled back down to several hundred thousand a year. It is estimated that approximately two dozen schools today have annual licensing income above $1 million.[29]

These large sums for licensing are unique to the 1990s. In previous decades, most schools would sell sweatshirts, T-shirts, etc., with the university logo only in the local bookstores and perhaps a few other retail outlets. In 1983, nationwide sales of university logo products was just $250,000. In the early 1980s, the principal connection was to the school, not the football or basketball team. These sales rose gradually to $1 billion in 1989, $2.1 billion in 1993, and $2.5 billion in 1994. Sales of products with university logos remained at $2.5 billion during 1995 and 1996 before dipping slightly in 1997 and 1998.[30]

The modest income from these sales (schools generally get about 8 percent of the wholesale price) went to the school's general budget, not athletics. As logo use was commercialized on the basis of a school's athletic success, the practice of sharing licensing income between the general budget and athletics emerged. While some sharing still prevails at most schools, there has been a clear trend for greater and greater shares of licensing income to go to athletics.

Schools license their logos for a dizzying array of products: hats, shirts, pants, shorts, sweatshirts, jackets, socks, underwear, pizza, Barbie dolls, jewelry, softdrinks, mugs, cups, birdhouses, pasta, spring water, popcorn, flags, bumper stickers, etc. The University of Wisconsin has 280-odd licensed vendors. Several schools even license their logo for use on caskets—some fans apparently really do live and die for their alma mater!

The Collegiate Licensing Company (CLC) in Atlanta handles the business end of licensing for 150 schools and takes a healthy cut (15–20 percent) out of the school's share. It assists in the design, selection, and registration of a logo, promotes its use to national vendors, and patrols the streets to curtail counterfeit marketers. University logo product sales reached around $2 billion in 1995 and has stayed at this level in the late 1990s.[31]

Back in 1996 when Kentucky still had a sponsorship agreement with Converse (they're now with Nike), the local Lexington, Kentucky, daily estimated the following breakdowns of the cost for Kentucky basketball jerseys and denim sneakers.[32] The Wildcat jersey retailed for $80; of this, $4–6 went to production labor in Los Angeles,[33] $20–25 to materials and fixed costs, $3.20 went to Converse as a licensing fee for the appearance of the Converse logo on the jersey,[34] and $3.00 went to Kentucky (of which, 60 cents was paid to CLC) for the use of the Kentucky logo and design. The Wildcat sneakers carried a suggested retail price of $75; of this, between 75 cents and $1.75 went to production labor in Asia, $9 to materials, $13 went to profits and marketing costs at Converse, and $2.81 went to Kentucky as a licensing fee (with 42 cents going to CLC).

The sponsorship deal between Kentucky and Converse is typical for the top several dozen athletic schools in the country. Usually, Nike, Adidas, Reebok, Converse, or Fila signs a multiyear deal with a school, worth between $1 and $3 million a year to the college.[35] The college receives free uniforms, athletic shoes, warmups, and equipment for the players on all of its teams and its staff, as well as cash to serve as bonus money for the coaches and athletic director.

Converse inked the first sneaker sponsorship of a college program in 1977 with Jerry Tarkanian, then head basketball coach of the University of Nevada, Las Vegas. In exchange for having the team wear sneakers with its logo, Converse gave Tarkanian a two-for-one deal. For every pair he bought for the team, Converse gave him a pair free. Therein Nike saw a competitive opportunity. In 1978 Nike offered Tarkanian free shoes and warmups for the whole team, plus $2,500 for himself. The terms of these sponsorships escalated rapidly thereafter. By the early 1990s it was commonplace for coaches to have deals with sneaker companies that paid them over $100,000 a year. The most successful or charismatic coaches (e.g., Duke's Mike Krzyzewski, Georgetown's John

Thompson, Utah's Rick Majerus) were getting four or five times that amount, plus stock options, a variety of perquisites, and assistance in their recruiting efforts.[36] John Thompson's options reportedly have led to his acquiring $4 million of Nike stock.[37]

Nike is said to spend nearly $1 billion a year on advertising, $300–400 million of which is spent on marketing.[38] Nike marketing consists of some 50 or 60 college sponsorships (though perhaps only half of these involve significant cash beyond the free outfitting), scores of individual athletes under promotional contracts, free sneaker deals with over 150 high school and AAU (American Amateur Union) teams, summer sports camps for promising athletes, and sponsorships with professional teams in various sports. Adidas, the only other sneaker company battling Nike in the recruitment trenches, supports about 75 high school programs, gives free sneakers to 150–200, and sponsors 60–75 all-star teams.[39]

Nike has been involved in its share of controversy through the years. In two areas, however, the controversy is raging: Nike's amateur recruitment networks and working conditions and wages in Nike's Asian factories.

Recruitment Networks

In order to level the recruitment playing field and lower costs, the AAU in coordination with the NCAA set up the first youth summer basketball camps around 1980.[40] Top high school athletes would congregate in one place and play against each other at the highest competitive level. College coaches could save time and money with one-stop, quality-controlled shopping. In 1984, Nike's Sonny Vaccaro got the idea that if Nike sponsored these camps it would be a wonderful, cost-effective way to promote its sneakers.

Vaccaro's strategy had two prongs. First, by running these summer camps Nike would develop links to the top high school basketball players in the country. Nike would provide shoes to the players on the summer teams and to the high school teams where the players were enrolled. Vaccaro viewed this as a direct link to the rank-and-file youth in the neighborhoods across America. If the star high school players and their teams were wearing Nike shoes, then this was compelling advertising for the company. Second, by identifying and developing relationships with the top prospects, their coaches, and their schools, Nike could build a lasting bond with tomorrow's superstars. When the next Michael Jordan comes along, Nike will have a better chance of signing him to an endorsement contract.

George Raveling, erstwhile unsuccessful basketball coach at USC and today a Nike consultant, describes Nike's penetration into youth basketball as Nike giving back to the community. Sonny Vaccaro has different words: "It's a cesspool, and we start the process. . . . We cater to 120 kids. I know these kids . . . and I see the harm that's done."[41] Vaccaro was fired by Nike in 1991 and now does the same work for Adidas. He has strong feelings:

> What I'm doing is morally wrong. But it's not in my power to stop it, and if I quit, they [Nike] get everything. . . . Am I missing something? Millions are being made, and the kids get nothing. They are turned into gladiators and tossed aside when they get hurt. When something goes wrong they are stigmatized for life; they suffer every punishment there is under the auspices of corporate America. They take a few dollars for some clothes they need, to go home to see a sick mother, take a girl out, thank you, and they are the bad guys. . . . Now we're paying high school coaches so we can tie up their kids, so we capture the minds and souls of the people. Look, I play by the rules. What I am saying is, for God's sake, go change the rules.[42]

Nike and Adidas are fighting it out in the playgrounds and schoolyards. Competition breeds innovation, but in this business innovation takes the form of carrying the recruitment wars to more neighborhoods and younger kids. Street agents stalk the playgrounds and begin offering promising junior high school kids free sneakers. Kids from poor neighborhoods are enticed at an early age to believe that basketball is their ticket to success. Never mind the odds of one chance in several thousand that a high school basketball player makes it to the NBA. Never mind the nightmarish stories portrayed in movies like *Hoop Dreams* and *He Got Game*.[43] Innovation continues. Players are bought off. High school coaches are bought off. College coaches are bought off.

Not only are coaches remunerated, some very handsomely, but affiliating with Nike or Adidas will help them recruit. Consider the case of 6′8″ Korleone Young, one of the most talented high school basketball players in the country. Korleone played at his hometown high school in Wichita, Kansas, through the 1996–97 season. During the summer of 1997 he played for an AAU team outfitted by Nike and coached by a Nike "consultant."[44] At the end of the summer Korleone announced that he was transferring to Hargrave Military Academy in Chatham, Virginia. Coincidentally, Hargrave Academy is outfitted by Nike. Next time around maybe the coach at Wichita East High School will consider a relationship with Nike.

It would not be unusual if Nike's next step is to send Korleone on several all-expenses-paid trips to visit different colleges under contract with the company. The coaches at these colleges would get a recruiting leg up on Korleone, not only because Nike is promoting them to the player but because *(a)* such visits do not count toward the limit each school is allowed under NCAA rules and *(b)* the school does not have to use its recruitment budget to pay for the trip. So, there's a nexus and one can only opt out at one's own risk. Either that, or as Vaccaro says, change the rules.

Indiana University men's basketball coach Bobby Knight had this to say on the subject: "I see lots of high school sophomores and juniors who don't have money taking visits to college campuses. They're given a choice, a list of four or five schools they can visit, all expenses paid, and what a coincidence: They're all schools that wear the same brand of shoe."[45]

Robert Gibbons, the national recruiting analyst who worked as Nike's All-America camp selection chief until 1995, worries: "The frightening thing is the control. Public schools are literally being stripped of the best players to go to Nike- or Adidas-sponsored schools. And there is a strong correlation of what shoes these kids wear and where they go to college." Dan Ruffin, a high school basketball coach in Slidell, Louisiana, echoes: "I'm afraid of sending my kids off to these shoe company camps or these AAU teams because I've seen a couple from around our area go to them and never come back. Some AAU coach, paid by some shoe company, tells the kid he'll be better off playing for one of these nationally ranked high school teams, and off they go."[46]

The payoff to the top dozen recruits is surreal. Nike pays Michael Jordan over $20 million a year, plus stock options and a lifetime executive position. Nike also makes it its business to sign as many of the first-round NBA and NFL draft picks as it can. The top ones get anywhere from several hundred thousand to several million dollars a year. With Adidas, Reebok, and Fila also competing to sign the best players with the most charisma, some superstars do even better. Grant Hill, who was first signed by Fila in 1994 and is largely credited with helping raise the company's sneaker sales from $617 million in 1994 to $1.3 billion in 1996, was signed again by Fila to a 7-year, $80 million deal in 1997.[47]

Sometimes the top picks are high school prospects who are choosing between turning pro and going to college. With the NBA rookie salary cap, the top ten picks stand to make between $1.17 million and $2.68 million a year in salary.[48] Often, the licensing deal that awaits them is richer than their salary. Eighteen-year-old Tracy McGrady from Auburndale, Florida, was the sixth pick in the 1997 NBA draft. He signed a three-year deal with the Toronto Raptors for $4.68 million.

Sonny Vaccaro signed him up to endorse Adidas products for $12 million over six years.[49] Some say McGrady would have gone to college were it not for the more attractive and longer term Adidas deal.

In the end, the bonanza endorsement contracts from the sneaker companies perpetuate the insidious circle of temptation. The pot at the end of the rainbow only looms larger and the basketball ticket becomes yet more irresistible.

Nike's Factories

During the third shift one evening in 1996 at the Garuda factory in Tangerang, Indonesia, there was a large explosion in the chemical storage room. A 25-year-old worker in the nearby outsole press room named Kusnadi left his station and ran to the storage room. Kusnadi burst through the door to find two immobilized women who had been cleaning Nike air bags. The exit door was engulfed in flames, but Kusnadi and the two women knocked out an air conditioner and escaped through the resulting hole in the wall. Kusnadi's arms were burned and his nose badly blistered. The building was destroyed by the fire. After his hospitalization, Kusnadi returned to the company only to be reprimanded by his supervisor and eventually laid off. Nike at first claimed that no one was injured in the fire, then the Kusnadi story became known.[50]

The Garuda factory is one of 20-odd companies that subcontracts with Nike in Indonesia, a country that produces approximately one-third of Nike's shoes. Nike also subcontracts with factories in China, Vietnam, Taiwan, and Pakistan. Lower sneaker sales in the U.S. and abroad reduced Nike's worldwide workforce from a peak of 550,000 in 1997 to around 470,000 in June 1998.

Nike has been well connected in Indonesia. One of its largest subcontractors is Astra International, a company controlled by billionaire and former president Suharto crony Mohamed "Bob" Hasan.[51] With Suharto's resignation in May 1998, political instability, and the Indonesian economic collapse, Nike cut back faster in Indonesia than elsewhere. The workforce in factories subcontracting for Nike in Indonesia had been reduced from a peak of 227,248 in 1997 to 120,000 in June 1998.

Eighty percent of Nike's Asian workers are female and most are between 17 and 22; some are younger.[52] The typical work week during busy season seems to be 6 or 7 days and 10 hours or more per day. With the Asian economic crisis in 1997–98 and local currency depreciation, the dollar value of a day's pay in Indonesia is under $1. In Vietnam and

China, the daily wage approaches $2. In many factories, workers must pay for water. Frequently, workers must offer a month's wages as a bribe to the personnel director who hires them. It is commonplace to hear of military discipline and corporal punishment in Nike's Asian factories.[53]

Nike, like Adidas and Reebok, subcontracts out virtually all of its Asian production. Some factories are owned by the Chinese government, some are privately owned by local entrepreneurs or politicians, some are owned by companies from other Asian countries. When Nike's Asian factories first came under public scrutiny, Nike was quick to point out that they did not own the factories and had little control over what happened inside of them. This excuse washed thin. First, if Nike cared about work conditions and really had no control over subcontractors, then they could establish their own factories. Second, Nike and the other sneaker companies wielded significant influence by virtue of the large business they brought the subcontractors. Many subcontractors worked solely for Nike, or for Nike and the other sneaker companies.

Nike's next line of defense was to establish a Code of Conduct in 1992. Among other things, the Code pledged all workers in Nike factories would be paid at least the local minimum wage, such as it was. Evidence suggests that this pledge has largely been adhered to, but there are loopholes. Most countries permit a "training wage" for the first three months or so, which is substantially below the minimum wage. Subcontractors have been known to turn over their workforce intentionally in order to maintain a higher proportion of workers on the training wage.

In August 1996, Nike joined President Clinton's Apparel Industry Partnership, intended to set minimum standards in the workplace. Two months later, Nike formed its own labor practice department, and in 1997 Nike sent several high-profile, purportedly independent groups to tour some of its Asian factories. Andrew Young, former U.S. Ambassador to the United Nations, led one group. Young's report was positive and naïve. The factories he visited were clean. The workers he interviewed did not report abuse. Indeed, they felt lucky to have steady jobs. Young did make one critical suggestion to Nike. They needed better communication in their factories. Sometimes supervisors did not speak the same language as the workers, and most workers seemed unaware of the principles of Nike's Code of Conduct.

Another "independent" monitor hired by Nike was the accounting/consulting firm Ernst and Young. Unlike the Young report which Nike intended for public dissemination, the Ernst and Young report was for company use, but it was leaked to an NGO (non-governmental organization) which made it public. Ernst and Young's report was quite critical, but still appeared to whitewash actual conditions. The report, for instance, found severe environmental conditions in one shoe factory outside Ho Chi Minh City in Vietnam where workers were exposed to carcinogens (primarily from the glue used in making sneakers) that exceeded local legal standards by 177 times in certain parts of the plant, and 78 percent of the workforce suffered from respiratory problems. The report also stated that workers at this factory, which is owned and operated by a Korean subcontractor, were forced to work 65 hours a week, far more than allowed by Vietnamese law, for $10 a week.

Still, Ernst and Young followed the methodology prescribed to them by Nike. They did no air sampling of their own. Their health and safety information came from secondary sources. No workers were interviewed outside the factory gates. Thus, many problems that had been reported by previous investigators (such as physical abuse or sexual harassment) were not detected by Ernst and Young.

Nevertheless, with Nike's reputation badly tarnished and its sneaker sales waning, founder and CEO Phil Knight called a press conference in early May 1998 and made some new promises. Hereafter, Nike would apply U.S. air quality standards in all its Asian factories, it would increase the minimum age for its workers, it would expand educational and loan programs, and it would increase independent monitoring of factory conditions. This latter point has been the focus of much criticism. At least until Knight's press conference, Nike's version of independent monitoring had been that it hired third parties to make reports. Critics have said that this was like the fox hiring another fox to watch the hens. The alternative is to have truly independent groups, such as NGOs, send trained monitors to make periodic, unannounced plant visits. Knight did not spell out how Nike planned to increase independent monitoring. He also said that Nike's wage policy would continue unaltered.

Knight also announced that Nike would be terminating its relationship with four subcontractors for code violations. Nike had made a similar announcement the previous September. Magnanimous perhaps, but also convenient given the drop in sneaker sales (new orders for March through July 1998 were down 13 percent overall and 34 percent in Asia).[54]

Nike's failings notwithstanding, the company has been unfairly singled out among multinational sneaker and apparel companies. There is little evidence that Adidas or Reebok factories in Asia pay higher wages or offer better working conditions than those of Nike. Indeed, it seems that the production of Adidas World Cup soccer balls in China has been performed in part by prison labor, working as long as 15 hours a day and paid $15 a month.[55] Many of these prisoners committed the "crime" of being involved in human rights activities. There are also dozens of non-shoe companies, including Liz Claiborne, Ann Taylor,

Ralph Lauren, Disney, JC Penny, and Walmart that contract in Asia. Nearly 50 percent of the apparel sold in the United States is produced in low-wage countries.

When Nike and these other companies employ labor in Vietnam, China, or Indonesia for $1 or $2 a day, the workers are receiving a market wage. Most of the workers are anxious to get these jobs; this is why many pay bribes. As hideously low as these wages are, the alternatives for these workers are worse. While it seems unreasonable to expect the sneaker subcontractors to go much above the market wage, it seems entirely reasonable for Nike to provide decent, non-abusive, fair working conditions. The great irony here is not that the production labor is only 1 or 2 percent of the cost of the shoe. It is that the cheap labor costs are not passed on to the consumer in the form of lower prices. Instead, they are passed on to Michael Jordan, Allen Iverson, Kobe Bryant, et al. in the form of multimillion-dollar endorsement contracts.

Nike is singled out because it is a company that tells the world to "Just Do It." And Nike doesn't do it. But the problem of underdevelopment in the Third World was not invented by Nike and it will not be solved by Nike.

Controversy on Campus

Back in 1995 when the University of Michigan signed its $7.3 million deal with Nike, the school's Board of Governors protested that they were not consulted—perhaps a face-saving cry of protest in the wilderness to calm their consciences. They were told that the athletics department's own Board in Control of Intercollegiate Athletics had been consulted and sanctioned the contract. However, one Control Board member wrote: "We received hell over this Nike contract even though we weren't consulted. But, they had to pass the buck onto someone and we were that someone. It was a deal between the president, the AD and Nike. We were rather surprised to read in the newspapers that we had approved it."[56]

Another Big Ten school, the University of Wisconsin (UW), ran into a different sort of problem with its June 1996 deal with Reebok. The contract draft had a clause which read: "University will take all reasonable steps necessary to address any remark by any University employee, agent or representative, including a coach, that [sic] disparages Reebok. . . ."[57] In other words, if someone at the University of Wisconsin didn't like what was going on in Reebok's Asia factories, the university was supposed to try to prevent them from expressing their views. So much for free inquiry and free speech, supposed hallowed tenets of academic life.

The UW Board of Regents approved the contract by a vote of 12 to 4, but State Senator Marlon Schneider noticed the Reebok image-protection clause. Schneider convinced the state's Attorney General to investigate whether the clause violated the university employee's right to free speech. An uproar ensued on campus and Reebok finally consented to remove it.

But for many the Wisconsin incident is merely the tip of the moral iceberg. Should schools allow Nike's swoosh logo to appear on team uniforms and other university products? Should Nike be allowed unrestricted use of its logo on campus? Do these sponsorship contracts transform colleges into little more than corporate subsidiaries? A faculty petition circulated at Wisconsin argued: "If the University of Wisconsin advertises a firm like Reebok, it accepts the conditions under which Reebok profits."[58]

College presidents respond that the sneaker companies do not place restrictions on university policy and that corporate logos regularly appear on all types of clothing. Maybe this is the justification for the provision in the Nike contract with the University of North Carolina which doesn't allow the players to conceal the swoosh on their uniforms. The athletics programs need the financial support of these sponsorships.

The University of Arizona (UA) has developed a new PR approach to dealing with Nike contracts. In August 1998, UA signed a five-year, $7 million contract with Nike with the provision that the university "can call off the deal if an outside monitor finds fault with Nike's labor practices in overseas plants and the company fails to fix them."[59] This clause is perhaps a step forward, but the devil is in the details. The substance of the arrangement depends on: (a) the outside monitor selected jointly by Nike and UA; (b) the budget assigned to the monitor; (c) once a problem is identified, how long Nike is given to rectify it; (d) how rectification is interpreted; and (e) whether UA interprets "can call off the deal" as "will call off the deal."

Sneaker companies have no monopoly on moral controversies on campus. In 1994 the University of Minnesota signed a three-year, $150,000 contract with Miller Brewing Company that allowed the brewer to advertise at college sports facilities and to use the school's mascot.[60] In 1997 a new three-year deal was negotiated, this time for $225,000; only this time the school administration vetoed it. Fourteen students from the school had entered an alcohol rehabilitation program, and students at Louisiana State and MIT died from alcohol abuse during the fall 1997 semester. Minnesota followed the lead of Baylor, Brigham Young, and North Carolina in abjuring alcohol advertising at sporting events. Luckily for the Golden Gophers, Minnesota replaced the Miller deal with a three-year deal with Land O'Lakes dairy company for $242,000.

The rest of the college sports community continues to accept beer and wine advertising. Mr. Becker of the Beer Institute is pleased by this ongoing relationship: "If you had to choose the best audience in the world for a beer advertiser, it is 21-to-34-year-old men who participate in sports and are avid sports fans."[61] So the money is too good for Fresno State which allows arena advertising and whose coach, Jerry Tarkanian, appears in ads for Budweiser. The money is also too good for the NCAA which allows beer and wine advertising on telecasts of NCAA championships for up to one minute per hour and in up to 14 percent of its programs and scorecards at these championships. The money is too good for Northwestern University which boasts Miller as one of its top five advertisers and too good for the Heisman Trophy which licenses its trophy image to Coors.

Schools decry the abuse of alcohol on their campuses, yet tolerate or encourage tailgating parties and enter business relations with beer companies. Experts say that the beer signs at arenas and stadiums and beer advertising on television promote beer consumption among the students. The schools' sanctimonious exhortations to control consumption are not taken seriously because the schools send out a louder message that money is more important than moderation, and bucks more important than books. The advertising further reinforces the view that it is normal to consume beer and abnormal not to do so. Donna Shalala, former chancellor at the University of Wisconsin and present Secretary of Health and Human Services, spoke at the January 1988 NCAA Convention and had this to say about the subject: "We need to sever the tie between college sports and drinking. Completely. Absolutely. And forever. . . . No turning a blind eye to underage drinking at tailgate parties—and on campus. And no to alcohol sponsorship of intercollegiate sporting events."[62]

She might have added that it may wax disingenuous and hypocritical to conduct an antigambling campaign on college campuses and allow the National Association of Collegiate Directors of Athletics (NACDA) to hold their 1999 convention in Reno, Nevada. The NACDA has also held recent conventions in Las Vegas.

The Economic Return to the Sneaker Companies

Is Nike engaging in the most cost-effective form of promotion by signing college sponsorship deals and creating player/coach recruiting networks? It is hard to argue with success. Few would claim that there is anything superior about Nike footwear. To be sure, Nike spends only $73.2 million yearly on new product development, compared with $300–400 million on marketing.[63]

Nike's aggressiveness and success in signing top athletes has paid off big time. Michael Jordan's shoe line accounts for hundreds of millions of dollars in sales annually. Nike's golf product sales have soared from $30 to over $200 million since signing up Tiger Woods. Part of this is Nike's good fortune. If Nike had landed Shaq O'Neal instead of Jordan, they would have lost millions of dollars. But Nike agents are told to sign everyone they can and in this pursuit their vast recruiting network gives them a leg up on competitors. One former Nike executive says that Nike agents "have never gotten in trouble for signing an athlete. They've gotten in trouble for not signing people."[64] Nike is known frequently to outbid its rivals by two or three times.

College sponsorships, while a bit risky, can be very effective advertising vehicles. Joyce Julius and Associates, a sports-marketing analyst, estimated that Nike, Champion, Starter, and Adidas each received over $1 million worth of television exposure from having their logos displayed on the jerseys of the athletes who played in the 1996 Fiesta and Orange Bowls. Nike, with its swoosh on the Florida State uniforms, got the most exposure, estimated at $2.6 million.[65] The trick is to sign up with the right schools.

It's a bit like playing the lottery. Sign the right player or school, and you win. All the sneaker companies are trying to sign the next Michael Jordan. Nike with its saturation bombing strategy has the best odds, but it also has the most financial exposure. Several companies have decided that there may never be another Jordan and, in any case, they were overinvesting in trying to sign him.

Reebok chairman Paul Fireman affirms that the hero shoe model has been overused and is increasingly ineffective. His marketing vice president, John Frascotti admits: "We're in the heart of a major change. . . . We sort of lost track of the reason for doing these deals." Commenting on Reebok being outbid by Nike for the UCLA contract in August 1998, Frascotti remarked: "The cost of these deals has grown out of proportion to the value they convey."[66] And Howie Birch, vice president of advertising at Fila, argues: "Kids just aren't as inspired by athletes a) because there are too many of them, and b) because of their behavior. It's contributed to the overall cynicism and distrust of sports personalities." Rob Erb, marketing director at Adidas, says that his disenchantment with endorsements reflects the "huge inventory risk involved if an athlete is injured or cut from a team."[67] Reebok has reduced its stable of NBA player endorsers from over 70 down to 20.[68] New Balance has begun an ad campaign, calling itself a grassroots company—no big stars, just shoes for the people.

Other companies are also cutting back, though not as drastically, and endorsement contract fees are drifting lower.[69] Several months after the rest of the industry, in early October 1998 Nike announced that it would reduce its commitment to endorsements for star athletes by some $100 million a year. For 1998, trendy boots seem to have more cachet than Nike sneakers.

Indirect Sponsorship Income

Schools also receive sponsorship income indirectly via the NCAA and bowl games. As discussed in the last chapter, corporations have invested millions of dollars to have their names associated with the postseason bowl games. The latest corporate moniker was attached in 1998: "The Rose Bowl presented by AT&T." This money filters down through the conferences to the participating schools.

The NCAA has also increased the commercialization of its name. The biggest step is a five-year deal with Host Communications which guarantees the Association $75 million from 21 corporate sponsorships. Host acts as the NCAA agent in signing up the corporate partners. The base fee is $1.6 million per year. Sponsors include American Express, Gillette, Marriott, Pepsi, Rawling, Champion, GTE, Pizza Hut, KFC, Taco Bell, Oldsmobile, RCA, Compaq, Hershey's, Ocean Spray, Nabisco, Phoenix, and Sears. Host trumpets the size of the student market. Students will spend an estimated $80 billion on goods and services in 1998.[70] College sports fans are an appealing demographic with a $55,000 average income. In 1997, 37 million attended college football games, 28 million men's basketball games, and 7.4 million women's basketball games. Attendance at NFL and NBA games during 1997–98 was below 25 million each. NCAA corporate sponsors are buying a lot of potential exposure for their $1.6 million. The Association also has numerous foreign deals, including a licensing contract with a Japanese company named Descente to market apparel worth more than $20 million a year.[71]

The NCAA's recent success in signing up corporate sponsors comes in part from its relaxation of restrictions on the use of corporate logos. NCAA championships used to prohibit corporate advertising on-site. For now, no advertising is allowed courtside, but it is permitted in the rest of the arena. Don't be surprised to see the commercialization imperative clear away any remaining hurdles in short order.

CHAPTER SEVEN

The Bottom Line

DEFICIT OR SURPLUS?

The accounting variables in college athletics make it difficult if not impossible to know whether a big-time sport pays for itself, much less whether it generates net receipts to finance the deficit sports. Actual cost accounting, in the sense of a hard-nosed business analysis, isn't done.
—Walter Byers, Executive Director of the NCAA, 1951–87

Even the best and most regularly collected of the data we examined (the NCAA Surveys) are fraught with problems of definition of elements, response bias, lack of weighting, and misleading interpretations.
—Report submitted to the U.S. Congress by Lamar Alexander, Secretary of Education, October 1992

DO INTERCOLLEGIATE athletics drain or support university budgets? The answer depends on whom one talks to and the occasion. University athletic directors trying to persuade a school to build a new sports facility or upgrade to Division I or IA (in football) invariably talk about the expected financial payoff to big-time college athletics. Academic economists, arguing that the NCAA is a cartel (independent producers joining together to form an effective monopoly), seem to feel compelled also to assert that big-time athletic programs are profitable. Why? Because monopolies, economic theory tells us, generate higher profits than competitive firms. Yet critics, such as Murray Sperber, James Thelin, or Francis Dealy, insist that intercollegiate athletics are a serious financial burden to the university.

While reality, not surprisingly, is more complex and lies somewhere in between these extreme views, there are certain truths that can be unequivocally asserted. First, of the six hundred–plus athletic programs in Divisions II and III, none generates more revenues than expenses. That is, they all run deficits—one might add, just as do the departments of economics, history, English, government, and so on in any university. If the athletic programs at these schools are an integral part of the educational curriculum, as opposed to a commercial appendage to the university, then there is presumably nothing wrong with an athletic department deficit as long as it is within manageable proportions. Second, of the two hundred–odd schools in Division IAA and IAAA, it is a near certainty that none have athletic programs with a surplus.[1] Third, of the 110 colleges in the top level of Division I (IA), 43 percent (down from 46 percent in 1994–95) reported operating with a surplus in 1996–97 when institutional subsidies are excluded.[2] However, without institutional support, the average Division IA school in 1996–97 reported an operating deficit of $823,000 (up from $237,000 in 1994–95).[3]

Yet from these numbers ensues a great polemic. The cartel-theorizing economists claim that these reported figures deceive.[4] The NCAA Division I is a cartel that restricts membership by setting various commercial standards (such as minimum stadium capacity and attendance averages) and artificially depresses costs by prohibiting payment to the athletes, limiting recruiting expenses, and other regulations. A cartel, after all, functions as a monopoly, and monopolies earn above normal rates of return. Ergo, intercollegiate sports programs at Division I schools must be profitable, whether or not they are willing to trumpet their financial success to the public.

As the argument goes, these athletic programs are too embarrassed by their riches to come clean. If they were to show their true net income, boosters would be loathe to contribute, student fees would diminish, state legislatures would cut subsidies, federal tax preferences would be curtailed, and fundraising would be impaired. Pressure to pay the athletes would also increase. Instead, the program accountants devise clever ways to hide their profitability, including: shifting revenue to other university departments (e.g., concession income at the arena attributed to food and dining services), or counting grants-in-aid at their listed price rather than actual cost. Further, since college athletic departments function in nonprofit environments and have no stockholders to answer to, the cartel economists argue that any surplus generated by sports programs is diverted to benefit administrators and coaches in the department via above-market salaries, handsome perquisites, fancy office facilities, and so on.

Most of these arguments are sharply contested by the sports critics.[5] They claim that intercollegiate sports programs, with perhaps a handful of exceptions, lose money and drain university finances. Sports programs, in an effort to deflect criticism, engage in creative accounting to make their finances appear rosier than they in fact are. First, they shift costs to other university departments. For instance, grants for athletes might be attributed to the general financial aid budget rather than the athletic budget. Telephone and travel costs connected to recruitment might be assigned to general university overhead or to admissions. Salaries and benefits of administrators and coaches in the athletics department may be allocated to the general faculty salary pool. Expenditures for the construction and maintenance of sports facilities, as well as for security, sanitation, and infrastructure, may be allocated to buildings and grounds, general debt service, campus security, and so on. Legal expenses and program review costs connected to NCAA violations may be attributed to the legal budget, or not allocated at all if the time of other faculty and administrative staff who serve on such review committees is not separately compensated.

Second, some of the revenue received by the athletics department may come in the form of subsidies from student fees, transfers from the university budget, or appropriations from the state budget. Third, as discussed in the last chapter, all Division I intercollegiate athletic programs benefit from substantial subsidies from the federal government, without which their financial fortunes would be diminished. Fourth, athletic departments benefit from large (often up to eight-figure) donations from local booster organizations which help to defray basic athletic department expenses. They also benefit from alumni gifts that may come at the expense of giving to the general fund.

Sorting out these arguments is more difficult than it ought to be. As we shall see, the major problem is that there is virtually no uniformity in the application of accounting practices. Thus, one university's athletic program in exactly the same financial condition as another university's may report a substantial surplus while the other may report a sizable deficit.

One matter, however, should be set straight at the outset. Whether or not economic cartel theory applies to individual sports in an athletic program, there is absolutely no reason to believe that an overall program including fifteen or sixteen sports should generate positive net income. Indeed, with few exceptions, it is clear that only Division IA football and Division I basketball ever run surpluses; the other sports are all supported by any net income from football and basketball and any other institutional subventions or outside support.

Of course, one might also question whether or not it matters if intercollegiate athletics generates surpluses or losses. Universities certainly don't hold up their academic departments to such standards. Does the economics or history department run a surplus that in turn benefits other programs at the school? Of course not. But academic departments do not conduct independent accounting for their services and do not attempt to justify their existence, as do big-time college athletic departments, on the basis of their financial contribution.

Naturally, it is possible that a superlative economics or history department at a university may benefit the school economically, but any such benefit would not be directly measurable in terms of the financial performance of the particular department. Rather, the teaching or scholarly excellence of the department may attract more and better students to apply to the school or it may inspire large gifts from wealthy alumni or others.

Similarly, an athletic program, whether or not it runs a surplus, may benefit a school economically by attracting additional applicants, by encouraging donations to the general academic fund, or by arousing legislative largesse among sports-crazed representatives. Therefore, any consideration of the athletic department's academic impact should look at both the direct as well as indirect financial results of its activities. We shall consider both direct and indirect results after taking a detour on the availability and reliability of financial performance statistics.

For now, we shall tentatively conclude that the cartel economists have far overstated their case. Financial troubles are far more prevalent than their analysis allows, and athletic programs are more enthusiastic about heralding their occasional, reported financial successes than they are about pleading poverty. One need look no further than the *NCAA News*, the official publication of the Association, report on the penultimate biannual study of college athletics finances to discern this manifest bias. The page-one headline of the November 18, 1996, issue read: "Study: Typical IA Program Is $1.2 Million in the Black."[6] If the Association wanted to leave a different impression, the headline could have read accurately: "Study: Excluding Institutional Subsidies Typical Program Is $237,000 in the Red."

ACCOUNTING CONUNDRUMS

While some colleges release data on the financial performance of their intercollegiate athletic programs, generally the details of this operation are considered to be proprietary. However, since 1960 the NCAA has published summary reports of school financial performance. These reports have become more detailed over time, but they provide little more than averages and frequency distributions with some breakdown by sport. The former College Football Association (CFA) conducted its own annual financial survey of the top Division IA schools during 1986–96. Further, beginning in October 1996, under the requirement imposed by the Equity in Athletics Disclosure Act (EADA), universities must release each year general financial and operations information on their athletics programs. Unfortunately, the usefulness of these data from the NCAA, the CFA, and the EADA is limited by the absence of common accounting conventions.

A few years ago Major League Baseball executive Paul Beeston described the chimerical nature of income reports for baseball franchises: "Anyone who quotes profits of a baseball club is missing the point. Under generally accepted accounting principles, I can turn a $4 million profit into a $2 million loss, and I can get every national accounting firm to agree with me."[7] The same point applies to college athletics with one exception. There are no generally accepted accounting principles.

One of the favorite ploys of professional sports teams' accountants is to use related party transactions to diminish the apparent profits of the team. If the same individual or entity owns the franchise and related business entities (e.g., the stadium or arena, the local television station, facility or concession management firm, beer company, etc.), the owner can alter the prices that one entity charges another in order to shift costs and revenues among them. Thus, Time Warner can pay its subsidiary, the Atlanta Braves, a below-market price for the right to broadcast the Braves games on another subsidiary, WTBS, thereby lowering the Braves revenues and WTBS costs. The Braves profits will shrink and those of WTBS will grow. For Time Warner, it is money in one pocket or the other.

College athletic departments have built-in related party transactions for almost all of their costs. Grants-in-aid (scholarships) for athletes can appear as an expense to the athletic department or the college financial aid office. Salaries for coaches can be assigned to the athletics budget, the faculty salary pool, or sometimes considered as an off-budget item covered by the booster club. Debt service on facilities construction can be paid by athletics, by the college's facilities budget, or by the state. Maintenance, utilities, sanitation, and security for the sports facilities can go to athletics or the general budget. Expenses for the college band (uniforms, travel, conductor salary, maintenance of and rent for practice rooms, etc.) can be attributed to athletics or the music department, or considered off-budget and defrayed by booster funds.[8] So may expenses for rent and utilities for athletic offices, tutoring and special course sections for athletes (the budget for tutoring athletes at USC was $800,000 in 1997),[9] extra medical and health insurance expenses for athletes, facilities insurance, film and video costs, special meal preparation and scheduling for athletes, laundry for uniforms, phone, mail, traveling expenses of athletic department personnel, and much more.[10]

The problem here is twofold. First, often expenses which are properly identified with athletics are placed elsewhere, yielding a misleading view of a program's financial status. Second, different programs include different items, making comparative judgments problematic.

In September 1991, the Arkansas State Legislature, after experiencing years of dubious and variable accounting practices in the athletic departments of its various state campuses, passed a law mandating uniform procedures. One such procedure was to require all sports programs to take on a facility maintenance expense equal to 10.65 percent of its budget (the average maintenance share at state colleges for all facilities). This change alone tripled the athletic department facility expenses at one school and engendered a sevenfold rise at another. The law also limited the annual state athletic subsidy per school to $450,000.[11]

Unlike many other Division I universities where facilities use is not charged to athletics, at the University of Massachusetts in Amherst some of the facilities expense is absorbed by the athletic department in the form of modest rental payments for the use of the Mullins Center arena. Yet when the direct operating costs of the facility are put against the rental and other revenues, the facility incurred an annual operating loss that ran between $356,000 and $537,000 during 1994–96. Moreover, the university annually sets aside $408,000 in its facility maintenance budget for the Mullins Center, so that the total net cost of the facility to the university has averaged over $800,000 a year. This is an athletic expense that is covered outside the athletic budget. Yet the true subsidy for the Mullins Center is even greater, because the facility cost $50 million to build for which yearly debt service and opportunity cost of capital is in the neighborhood of $4 to $5 million.[12]

The athletics program at Vanderbilt University has been suffering a long-standing malaise. Attendance at football games is waning, booster club membership dropped from 5,600 in 1991 to 3,700 in 1996, and the program ran an estimated $4 million deficit during 1995–96. Part of the solution was found in card shuffling: the university decided to pick up the cost of 150 athletics scholarships on its budget (worth about $3 million for the 1996–97 year) as well as take over the operation of two money-losing enterprises (the parking garage and the eating and social club at the stadium) from the athletics program.[13]

Similar strokes of the financial wand were employed at the University of Wisconsin in 1990 when its athletics program was reported to be nearly $6 million in the hole. The state legislature agreed to refinance the debt on the new McClain Center with tax-exempt bonds, lowering the debt service by $370,000 a year. The legislature also agreed to increase its share of maintenance costs and to increase the university's share of parking revenues by $500,000 annually. Meanwhile, the university administration imposed a $20-a-year student fee, which generated $760,000 yearly for athletics.[14]

Further, the University of Wisconsin, like the majority of big-time college sports schools, receives generous yearly contributions from its booster organizations. As discussed in the last chapter, many of those contributions are recorded in the athletic department budget, but many are not. The 1998 self-audit at Wisconsin revealed some $200,000 of unrecorded booster gifts. That is, costs of $200,000 were incurred by athletics that did not appear in the budget.[15]

Yet another indication of irregular accounting practices is provided by the huge disparities among Big Ten Conference schools for the 1994–95 year. Maintenance expenses on athletic facilities went from a low of $18,092 for Illinois to a high of $1.05 million for Purdue. Physical plant costs were zero for Iowa, Michigan State, and Minnesota, but $883,123 for Northwestern and $878,320 for Penn State. Debt service varied from zero for Indiana and Purdue to $1.98 million for Ohio State and $2.95 million for Penn State. Medical expenses went from zero at Ohio State to $370,831 at Purdue.[16]

Reporting irregularities were also evident in a 1992–93 survey of the eight members of the Big East football conference.[17] Home gate receipts went from a reported high of $5.4 million to a reported low of $158,000; team travel expenses varied from $87,000 to $477,000; football telephone expenses went from a low of $9,300 to a high of $80,000; team meals on campus from $85,000 to $592,000; and recruiting postage from $8,000 to $90,000.

The periodic NCAA survey of college sports finances suffers from the same irregular accounting practices of the reporting institutions. In addition, these surveys exclude certain revenue and expense categories in their accounting guidelines altogether, such as amortization expenses on capital, guarantee payments (assured shares of gate receipts to or from the opposing team), and income from corporate sponsorships.[18] Lastly, these surveys are weakened by response rates that have varied roughly between 40 and 85 percent of member colleges, though the response rates have been near the upper end for Division IA institutions.

Within an athletic program there is the problem of identifying which parts contribute most to the deficit and which, if any, contribute to a surplus. It is commonplace to hear the claim that men's football and basketball earn large surpluses which go to finance the "non-revenue" men's and women's sports. As we shall see, this is probably true at 50-odd schools, but the extent to which it is so may be substantially less than is reported in the NCAA surveys.[19] The principal reason for this is that the NCAA does not ask the schools to apportion non-sport specific costs among the sports themselves. Thus, if there is a facilities maintenance expense, it is considered to be general to the entire program and is not charged to basketball, even if 60 or 70 percent of its use and 80 or

90 percent of its revenues might be from the men's basketball team. Or, the overhead expenses of the athletics program, such as administrative salaries and benefits, travel, entertainment, advertising, utilities, phone, etc., may not be allocated to specific sports, even though the lion's share of these expenses are due to men's basketball and football.[20] Were such costs to be reasonably allocated to the different sports, the "profitability" of football and basketball at most big-time schools would be substantially diminished, and, in some cases, it would be reversed.

For instance, the only sport that ran a surplus at the University of Massachusetts between 1995 and 1997 was men's basketball, but department figures do not attribute any costs for film and video, advertising, insurance, maintenance, utilities, medical expense,[21] or telephone to the sport. Further, neither the annual operating deficit of the Mullins Center, in excess of $800,000, nor the debt service/capital cost on the facility appears anywhere in the athletic department budget. If only half of these expenses were attributed to men's basketball, what is a reported surplus of $1.78 million in fiscal 1997 would become a deficit of approximately $1.1 million.

In general, reporting by sport is muddled by all the standard irregularities plus inconsistent allocation of expenses and revenues between sport-specific and administrative budgets. The University of Wisconsin, for example, reported to the 1994–95 Big Ten survey that its football operations expenses were $5.88 million, yet it reported to the 1995–96 Equity in Athletics Disclosure Act (EADA) survey of the U.S. Department of Education that its football expenses were only $3.47 million. The discrepancy for Penn State was even larger, reporting $7.11 million to the 1994–95 Big Ten survey and only $2.33 million to the EADA survey the following year.[22]

Finally, there is the issue that the existing surveys about college athletic finances are all subject to sampling bias. That is, when the NCAA (or the CFA or the Division IA Coaches Association) does its periodic survey, they send out a questionnaire to all the member schools in a particular category. For the 1994–95 NCAA survey roughly 50 percent of Division II and III schools responded, 58 percent of Division IAAA schools, 61 percent of Division IAA schools, and 82 percent of Division IA. Division IA clearly responded with greater reliability than the other divisions, but missing almost 20 percent of the surveyed population can create serious distortions, especially if those not responding are systematically the ones which performed more poorly and do not want to share their results.

There is some evidence that this is the case. The Equity in Athletics Disclosure Act (EADA) went into effect on October 1, 1996. This act requires each college to submit to the U.S. Department of Education an annual report which details the school's compliance with the gender equity provisions of Title IX. Among other things, each school must indicate its total revenues and costs from men's and women's sports, the total spent on recruiting and scholarships for each gender, with some additional breakdowns by sport. Each school is also required to make the report available to the public. These reports, unlike the NCAA surveys, are mandated by law and, hence, the response rate is 100 percent.

The first time the EADA reports were made was in October 1996, referring to the academic year 1995–96. When the 109 Division IA schools' responses were collated, the average total athletic revenue per school was $10.43 million. In contrast, the NCAA study reported average athletic revenue per Division IA school to be $15.48 million in 1994–95 (based on 89 schools responding), and the Division IA Athletic Directors' survey reported average revenue to be $16.97 million in 1995–96 (based on 87 schools responding). That is, when the 22 schools not responding to the Athletic Directors' survey are included (as they are in the EADA data), the reported average athletic revenue per school falls by $6.54 million or by 38.5 percent. This is clear evidence that the schools not responding to the NCAA and Athletic Director surveys are the ones with lower athletic revenues. Either that or the schools are providing different numbers to the different surveys.

BIG-TIME ATHLETIC BUDGETS

Speaking before an NCAA football forum in February 1991, former NCAA Executive Director Dick Schultz addressed the financial perfor mance of Division IA athletic programs this way: "Now we're in a position where over 70 percent of Division IA schools operate in the red. We can count on both hands, or maybe one hand and one finger, the number of IA schools and athletic directors who can look you in the eye and say they don't have financial problems."[23]

A sobering assessment! Six schools out of over one hundred that do not have financial problems. Fortunately for big-time college athletics matters have improved a bit during the 1990s. Rising television, sponsorship, licensing, and facility revenues, as discussed in the last two chapters, have tilted financial outcomes a bit in favor of the more successful programs. This effect was reinforced by NCAA cost-cutting measures implemented at the 1991 Convention, where it was decided to cut team size by 10 percent in several sports, reduce the number of allowed coaches for certain teams, and restrict the earnings of the lowest-ranking assistant coaches. The latter action has since been found in violation of the nation's antitrust laws and has been rescinded. The effect, however,

TABLE 7.1

Trends in Class A* Institutions' Athletics Revenues and Expenses, 1960–81
(in $thousands)

	1960	1970	1974	1978	1981	Annual Growth Rate 1960–81
Avg Revenues	672	1263	1708	2368	3391	8.0%
Avg Costs	635	1263	1761	2238	3243	8.1%
Avg Net Income	37	0	–53	130	148	
Highest Revenues	1337	2400	NA	6616	11,678	10.9%
Football Share of Total Revenues	72%	68%	66%	62%	56%	
Basketball Share of Total Revenues	8%	9%	9%	12%	13%	

Source: NCAA. *Revenues and Expenses of Divisions I and II Intercollegiate Athletic Programs*, various years.

* Class A corresponds roughly to what is Division IA and IAA today.

was offset by rising tuition and room and board fees (and, hence, high costs associated with grants-in-aid).

Cognizant of the data limitations discussed above, we can now proceed to evaluate the available information on the finances of college athletics. We shall begin by considering what the data tell us about trends and then move on to an assessment of the present situation (Table 7.1).

The most obvious trend is that intercollegiate athletics has experienced steady and strong revenue growth since 1960. The annual revenue growth rate was 8 percent during 1960–81 and 8.9 percent during 1982–97. Since the data for the earlier period refer to a different and larger subset of schools, the two series are not linkable and the small difference in the growth rates may not be significant. It is likely, however, that there was some acceleration in growth, as the numbers suggest, after the early 1980s with the greater commercialization of college sports. This more extensive commercialization, in turn, is a result of the 1984 Supreme Court decision finding the NCAA's football television package to be an antitrust violation as well as the general trend in professional sports following the introduction of free agency in Major League Baseball in 1976.

Although average revenue growth accelerated during the 1980s, it slowed in the 1990s (Table 7.2). Average school athletic revenue in Division IA grew at a 10.3 percent yearly rate between 1982 and 1989, and at an 8.7 percent rate between 1989 and 1993, with still slower annual growth of 6.8 percent between 1993 and 1997. The net income with institutional subsidies in Division IA for the average athletic program fell from $1,146,000 in 1995 to $437,000 in 1997, and the average net income without subsidies fell from −$237,000 to −$823,000.

Slower *average* revenue growth, however, has been accompanied by faster growth of *highest* revenue. The highest school total revenue growth rate increased from 7.4 percent during 1989–93 to 12.1 percent during 1993–97.[24] Thus, median program income has grown more slowly than mean income, which is particularly troublesome given the fact that average costs have begun to grow more rapidly than average revenues.

One sterling example of a top-end program that turned itself around in the 1990s is the University of Michigan. The Michigan athletics program ran reported deficits of $1.4 million in 1988–89 and $2.5 million in 1989–90.[25] But Michigan's revenue increased from $16.5 million in 1988–89 to $35.9 million in 1994–95. With reported operating expenses of $33.2 million, Michigan's athletic program was able to record a $2.7 million net income in 1994–95.

This net income is almost entirely due to a surplus from its football team of around $10 million. The football team took in around $2.1 million for television rights, nearly $1 million for radio, $13.5 million for ticket sales at home games, $450,000 in food concessions, $125,000 in program sales, $65,000 in merchandise concessions, and $950,000 in postseason bowl games, yielding a gross football revenue of $21.3 million in 1996–97.[26]

Of course, Michigan is not a normal Division IA athletic program. It regularly enjoys football and men's basketball teams ranked in the top 10 nationally. With standing room, attendance at Wolverine games has averaged over 105,000 in recent years and the last time there were fewer than 100,000 fans in attendance was October 25, 1975, for a game against Indiana.[27] Indeed, in 1997–98 just 200 of the 90,000 season tickets became available and for the first time ever seats were rationed to students.[28] Excess demand for tickets should be slightly alleviated for the 1998–99 season when a $6 million expansion of the stadium will boost capacity to 108,001. Michigan has also led the NCAA in licensing revenues, averaging over $5 million annually in recent years. When you're hot, you're hot.

Thus, revenue opportunities for the top athletic colleges are growing more rapidly than they are for the average school. The increased inequality among Division IA schools, in turn, means that more colleges fall below the average and financial difficulties affect a greater number of schools than the average figures suggest (Table 7.2).

Table 7.3 depicts the number of CFA and Division I schools that have shown financial surpluses or deficits in the athletic programs since 1985.

TABLE 7.2
Trends in Division IA Institutions' Revenues and Expenses, 1982–97
(in $thousands)

	1982	1985	1989	1993	1995	1997	*Annual Growth Rates*			
							1982– 89	*1989– 93*	*1993– 97*	*1982– 97*
Avg Revenues	4916	6833	9765	13,632	15,482	17,734	10.3%	8.7%	6.8%	8.9%
Avg Costs	5054	6894	9687	12,972	14,336	17,297	9.7%	7.6%	7.5%	8.6%
Avg Net Income	−138	−61	78	660	1146	437				
Avg Net Income without Institutional Support					−174	−237	−823			
Highest Total Revenue	12,700	17,803	22,717	30,215	39,323	47,629	8.7%	7.4%	12.1%	9.2%
Avg Football Revenue*	2682	3735	4340	6300	6439	7629				
Highest Football Revenue*	6674	10,700	14,931	20,322	21,959	26,352				
Avg Basketball Revenue (men)*	578	995	1640	2117	2503	2847				
Highest Basketball Revenue (men)*	1800	3482	9174	6370	8527	10,960				
Share of Total Rev from Football*	56%	53%	44%	46%	42%	43%				
Share of Total Rev from Basketball (men)*	13%	15%	17%	16%	16%	16%				

Source: NCAA. *Revenues and Expenses of Divisions I and II Intercollegiate Athletic Programs*, various years.

* Data in 1982 column refer to 1981. All years are fiscal years; hence 1981 is academic year 1980–81.

Since average revenues grew at a yearly rate of 8.5 percent between 1985 and 1995 while average costs increased by 7.6 percent per year, it is to be expected that the proportion of schools reporting a deficit would fall during this period. The share of CFA schools reporting a surplus rose from 43.4 percent (23 of 53 schools) in 1989 to 63 percent (34 of 54) in 1995, and the share of Division IA schools reporting a surplus rose from 41.6 percent (37 of 89) in 1985, to 55.2 percent (48 of 87) in 1989, to 75.3 percent (67 of 89) in 1995. However, with costs increasing at an average annual rate of 9.8 percent between 1995 and 1997 and revenues growing at only a 7 percent rate, the proportion of Division IA athletic programs experiencing a surplus fell sharply in 1997 to 59.6 percent (59 out of 99).

TABLE 7.3

Trends in Number of Athletic Programs with Financial Surplus or Deficit, College Football Association (CFA) and Division IA, 1985–97

	Category	1985	1989	1991	1993	1994	1995	1997
Number in Balance	CFA	NA	7	9	8	9	5	NA
Number in Surplus	CFA	NA	23	31	28	28	34	NA
Number in Deficit	CFA	NA	23	19	17	17	15	NA
Number in Deficit without Institutional Support	CFA	NA	NA	NA	34	35	NA	NA
Number in Balance	Div IA	2	4	NA	4	NA	10	9
Number in Surplus	Div IA	37	8	NA	61	NA	67	59
Number in Deficit	Div IA	50	35	NA	20	NA	12	31
Number in Deficit without Institutional Support	Div IA	NA	NA	NA	42	NA	46	55

Sources: NCAA. *Revenues and Expenses of Divisions I and II Intercollegiate Athletic Programs,* various years. CFA, *Sidelines,* July/August 1992, July/August 1993, July/August 1994, September 1995, July/August 1996.

Note: NA = not available.

But there is more bad news. First, these reported results are suspect. The CFA was formed in the early 1980s as an organization of elite football schools within Division IA. It included 60 to 63 members until its demise in 1997.[29] As an organization of the elite within the elite of Division IA, on average CFA schools had higher revenues than Division IA schools overall. For instance, in 1995 the average CFA school earned $16.38 million in total athletic revenues, while the average Division IA school (for those responding to the NCAA survey) earned $15.48 million. The differential in 1993 was $14.38 million to $13.63 million. It is, then, somewhat peculiar for the CFA to be reporting 63 percent of its schools with a surplus, while Division IA reports 75.3 percent in 1995. This disparity may be due to more spendthrift tendencies among CFA schools, but it is more likely a function of irregular reporting practices and/or sample distortion.[30]

Second, the data in Table 7.3 reveal that when institutional support (read: subsidies from the university and state budgets) is excluded more than half of the CFA and Division IA schools operate in deficit. Further, the number of schools experiencing deficits without such subsidies increased from 42 (out of 85 responding) in 1993, to 46 (out of 89 responding) in 1995, to 55 (out of 99 responding) in 1997 for Division IA, and from 34 (out of 53 responding) in 1993 to 35 (out of 54 responding) in 1995 for the CFA. (No other years are reported.) That is, the trend toward improved performance disappears.

Let us now consider a detailed budget for the average Division IA school in fiscal year 1996 (Table 7.4a and b).[31]

TABLE 7.4a
Revenue for Division IA Schools, 1996
(in $thousands)

1996 Revenues	Number of Responding Institutions	Mean	Median
Football	87	5072	3763
Men's Basketball	87	1899	1502
Other Men's Sports	78	173	60
Women's Sports	85	112	38
Gifts	83	2607	2281
Institutional Support	54	2167	1751
Student Fees	65	1542	1220
State Aid	24	1332	839
Radio/TV	79	2004	2010
Auxiliary Income	86	1255	813
Investment Income	66	440	253
Other Income	80	1032	581
Total Income	**87**	**16,966**	**15,138**

Source: Division IA Athletic Directors' Association Financial Survey, 1995–96.

Note: Revenue from Football, Men's Basketball, Other Men's Sports, and Women's Sports includes gate receipts, away game guarantees, and postseason compensation. TV, radio, and other income is not segregated by sport. Since not all institutions reported income in each category, the average and median totals do not equal the sum of the categories.

The reported average revenue for 1996 of $16.966 million is 9.6 percent above the average revenue reported in the NCAA survey for 1995, indicating continued strong growth. However, a comparison of average total costs indicates that they increased by 15.5 percent and average net income fell from $1.15 million to $414,000 between 1995 and 1996. Football receipts from stadium revenue alone contributes 30 percent of total revenues on average and men's basketball contributes 11.2 percent.

The large size of institutional support, student fees, and state aid stands out. As a share of total income for the 87 responding schools, institutional support accounts for 7.93 percent, student fees for 6.79 percent, and state aid for 2.17 percent. If subsidies from these sources are added up and a proportionate share of investment income is included,[32] then the total subsidy to Division IA athletic program revenues is 17.23 percent. There may be additional subsidies on the cost side, such as university or state monies used for facility construction.

TABLE 7.4b
Cost Analysis for Division IA Schools, 1996
(in $thousands)

1996 Costs	Number of Responding Institutions	Mean	Median
Salaries/Benefits	87	5008	4574
Gate Sharing	87	1044	913
Equipment/Supplies	87	866	683
Operations	84	1363	978
Debt Service	54	902	526
Insurance	84	151	125
Team Travel	87	1102	977
Recruiting	86	361	351
Grants	84	2742	2358
Fundraising	62	311	233
Publicity	83	377	253
Capital Expenditures	57	965	354
Other Costs	58	2761	1740
Total Costs	**87**	**16,552**	**15,047**

Source: *Division IA Athletic Directors' Association Financial Survey, 1995–96.*

Debt service costs appear to include interest payments, but not amortization.[33] If the revenue side subsidies alone are adjusted for, then total revenue generated by the average Division IA athletic program is $14.47 million, and the average deficit is $2.08 million in 1996.[34] And this despite the substantial tax subsidies provided by the federal government (see chapter 6).

Furthermore, the average program reported $2.6 million in gift income in 1996 (14.7 percent of average program revenues).[35] Although such monies do not constitute direct subsidies from the university, they may represent indirect subsidies if gifts to athletics are in lieu of gifts to academic activities. Most gift money to athletics, though, comes from booster groups, not alumni, and it is unlikely that such substitution of giving is very prevalent.

The cartel economists will point to examples where costs might be artificially inflated, such as grants-in-aid or scholarships to athletes which are valued at the official college tuition rates. The claim here is that the *marginal* cost to the college of educating these athletes is substantially below the stated tuition. (The *average* cost of educating a student is usually considerably above tuition at both public and private schools, with the difference being made up by income from the endowment or government appropriations.) Even though the marginal cost in an accounting sense may be below tuition, the relevant concept is marginal economic cost and this includes opportunity cost. That is, if the school fills up one of its slots for the entering class with an athlete on full scholarship, then the slot cannot be filled by a tuition-paying student. In such a case, the tuition or tuition plus room-and-board is lost by the university and it is the appropriate measurement of cost. To the extent that the school has empty dormitory rooms or student slots, then the opportunity cost of the grant-in-aid would be lower. But even making the favorable assumption that only half of the average grant-in-aid budget for Division IA schools in 1996 is real cost, the reduction in costs would be half of $2.74 million or $1.37 million and the average program would still be $710,000 in deficit (and does not adjust for the failure to include certain costs in the athletic budget).[36] Of course, this deficit might reflect in part artificially inflated salaries and perquisites for coaches and top athletic administrators.

It is important to underscore that the above discussion applies to the *average* program. The most successful programs (perhaps a dozen top schools, such as Michigan, Notre Dame, Florida, Washington, Alabama, Nebraska, Oklahoma, and Tennessee) are generating real surpluses year after year. Another group of programs (perhaps two to three dozen schools) generates an occasional surplus when their teams perform well in postseason tournaments (see chapters 5 and 6).

But what happens to the top programs is not what happens to the median program. And, of course, half of the programs perform below the median. Division IA schools, which support the high expenses of football scholarships, large facilities, recruiting, travel, etc., but have not enjoyed on-field success, can lose large sums of money. Just ask Mitch Barnhart, athletic director at Oregon State University, who inherited a department budget deficit of more than $8 million.[37] Nonetheless, it is this vision of success at the top that tempts many schools to address their athletic department's financial woes by considering an upgrade to Division IA status.

Differences among the financial results at Division I schools can be further elucidated by reference to the possibility of empty dormitory rooms. To the extent that certain schools do not operate at their capacity constraint (have empty rooms), then the actual marginal cost to the school of a grant-in-aid is much lower than the reported cost. As such, the real costs of their athletic program are lower. These schools, likely to be both state and private universities which are weak academically, will have smaller net losses (or higher net gains) from their athletic programs than schools that do operate at their capacity constraint. Further, the weaker academic schools rely more heavily on the advertising function of their athletic programs (more on this below). In addition, some schools may see their athletic program as a way to increase their proportion of minority students and, thereby, relieve affirmative action pressure.

This dynamic is not likely to be operative at academically average and strong universities. These schools are likely to experience the full opportunity cost of athletic grants-in-aid and rely less or not at all on the advertising function of college sports. Indeed, the Ivy League, which was first formed as an eastern athletic conference rather than as a group of prestigious academic institutions, decided to leave the world of big-time sports behind in 1955, ending all athletic scholarships. Presumably, the stated rationale of maintaining the primacy of academics and avoiding the rampant corruption then prevalent in college sports was one motivation for this move. It is probable that another motivation was that the cost of big-time sports for the Ivy schools was higher and the advertising function was unnecessary.

GOING BIG TIME

Commercialization, media exposure, and the elusive potential for a financial payoff have led many schools to attempt to upgrade their athletic programs in recent years. This tendency has been fed by recent NCAA legislation that allows conferences to split into two divisions and run a lucrative postseason conference championship between the division leaders if the conference has at least twelve teams. Hence, several conferences have been looking to expand.

Between 1990 and 1997, 15 schools moved up to Division I, and another 5 schools are scheduled to make the jump by 1999.[38] L. Jay Oliva, president of New York University, which dropped from Division I to Division III in the 1980s, says that "every school wants to believe they will be the one to make it." But Division I is expensive. It requires that an institution sponsor at least 14 varsity sports, 10 more than Division II requires. Division I seasons are 50 percent longer than those in Division II.

The State University of New York at Albany decided in April 1997 to move up to Division I for the 1999–2000 season and increased student fees 54 percent to $128 to pay for it.[39] Since the University of North Carolina at Greensboro switched to Division I in 1991, student athletic fees have risen 80 percent to $422. Total student fees at Greensboro are now $1,003 a year—just $13 below in-state tuition.[40] And after six years in Division I, the Greensboro basketball team averages only 1,200 fans in attendance per game.

Within Division I, eight schools reclassified from IAA to IA between 1992 and 1997, and many more are contemplating the upgrade.[41] Dick Schultz, former NCAA Executive Director, says that the "real strong

IAA schools are making the move to Division IA now, or will very soon."[42] As the better IAA schools leave their conferences, those conferences weaken, thereby increasing the incentive for other schools to seek an upgrade.

Other schools already in Division IA have recommitted themselves to athletic success, allocating additional general funds to intercollegiate sports. The Tulane University Board of Administrators, for instance, decided to increase the athletics budget by $3.4 million for academic year 1996–97, at the same time that it was trimming $8.5 million from the university's overall budget, raising tuition 4 percent, and freezing faculty and staff salaries.[43]

Division IA takes its sports seriously, and upgrading is no easy matter. To seek membership in Division IA a school must: sponsor at least 14 varsity sports; play at least 60 percent of its games against other IA opponents; play football in a stadium with a capacity of at least 30,000; and experience an average football attendance of over 17,000 once in the previous four years.[44]

Thus, upgrading to IA is an expensive proposition. It usually entails the following: building a new or expanding an old stadium; increasing the number of football scholarships from 63 to 85; increasing the number of women's scholarships by approximately 22 to stay within Title IX guidelines; increasing team travel, recruitment, coaching staff and salaries; upgrading training and other facilities; enlarging academic support staff; increasing amenities; and making similar improvements for the women's program.

Without considering the costs of a new stadium, the University of Connecticut, which was seeking to join the Big East football conference, estimated that operating costs would increase by $2.1 million a year in 1994 by upgrading to IA.[45] The University of Massachusetts, still giddy from the meteoric rise of its basketball team under John Calipari, commissioned an upgrade study in 1996 and the results were sobering. Increased scholarship costs would approach $700,000, team travel would increase some $250,000, recruiting and equipment expenses would grow nearly $100,000 each, game operations would soar by over $200,000, and a stadium upgrade would cost over $52 million (not including needed improvements in the local transportation infrastructure).

The best scenario for UMass was that they would be allowed to join the Big East. Given that the average Big East football program was reported to be running a $600,000 yearly deficit, some may have found this opportunity something less than compelling. But the UMass task force put an interesting spin on the question: the school's football team was running a $1.7 million deficit in IAA, so the move to IA would save over $1 million a year (ignoring the debt service and maintenance cost on the new stadium and assuming that UMass was able to perform financially as well as the average established school in the conference). A different spin might have been that by eliminating football altogether the school could have saved $1.7 million directly and even more indirectly by lowering overhead and Title IX obligations.

The record of schools which have upgraded to IA is less than encouraging. When the University of Akron played in IAA in 1986, the football team sold 5,000 season tickets. The school upgraded to IA in 1987. Going from a leading team in IAA to a bottom dweller in IA, by 1994 the team sold only 2,500 season tickets.[46] Jacksonville State University upgraded in 1996, and their AD, Jerry Cole, reports on the transition to IA: "However expensive you think it may be, however much trouble you think it may be, double that." Richard Sheehan surveyed the universities that upgraded from IAA to IA and concluded that "no school has made that jump and also made significant profits."[47]

Since it is only the top IA schools that generate significant positive net income, it is not surprising that new arrivals to the big time do not flourish financially. Still, some maintain that big-time athletics provides an incalculable promotional value, boosting applications and donations—more pie in the sky as we shall see presently.

INDIRECT EFFECTS

Not infrequently one hears the claim that even though a college's intercollegiate athletic program necessitates a subsidy to carry out its yearly operations, there are indirect benefits from college sports that accrue to the university. These purported benefits are twofold. On the one hand, it is alleged that strong athletic teams increase donations to the school's endowment. On the other, it is averred that successful athletic performance provides positive advertising to the school, thereby raising its popularity, increasing its applications, and allowing the admissions process to be more selective—resulting in a more qualified student body and higher SAT scores. We shall examine the evidence on each of these contentions in turn.

Increased Donations

The logic is reasonable enough. A school goes to the Rose Bowl or to the Final Four. Alumni feel proud and open up their pocketbooks. The empirical evidence, however, does not support the logic. Apart from two very limited and statistically sloppy studies, all the published literature suggests that there is no reliably positive impact of athletic success on giving to the general endowment of a university.[48] This literature consists of at least twelve separate studies and, in some cases, a significantly negative effect is found.[49]

There are several possible reasons why there is no statistical relationship between athletic success and general endowment gifts. First, the main contributors who seem to respond to athletic prominence are boosters, not the typical alumnus or academic philanthropist. Boosters tend not to be graduates of the school, but rather local business people who also happen to be avid sports fans. The boosters at the University of Iowa, for instance, include over eight thousand individuals who were not students at the school.[50]

And boosters give to athletics, not the general fund. Richard Conklin, a top administrator at Notre Dame, comments: "We at Notre Dame have had extensive experience trying to turn athletic interests of 'subway alumni' [read: boosters] to academic development purposes—and we have had no success. There is no evidence that the typical, nonalumnus fan of Notre Dame has much interest in the educational mission."[51]

John DiBiaggio, former President of Michigan State University, reaffirms Conklin: "No data support the oft-heard claim that wins on the field or on the court bring in more private dollars or more state and federal funding. Losses do not result in decreased financial support either. To be sure, wins can and do often bring in more support for athletic programs. But the myth of institutional dependency on athletic revenues—therefore on athletic victories—needs to be aggressively refuted."[52]

Yet, if normal alumni are approached about giving specifically to athletics, some seem to respond positively. Unfortunately, this comes at the expense of giving to the general fund. Consider the following concern expressed in the minority report of the University of Massachusetts task force about upgrading to Division IA: "Major fundraising around support of a major upgrade for football and a capital campaign is likely to lure dollars away from general University giving and toward athletics. Related to this concern is athletic department information from UConn where athletic department giving rose from $0.9 million in 1988–89 to $4.29 million in 1992–93. At the same time a decrease from $7.5 million down to $4.5 million took place for total university giving."[53]

Even if it were true that upticks in donations occasionally followed stellar athletic years (particularly for teams that rise from oblivion to prominence over the course of one or two years), it is probable that downticks in donations would offset these gains when the teams dropped from prominence. It is also likely that a team penalized by the NCAA for rule infractions would face a degree of ignominy, resulting in diminutions of academic giving. Consider this assessment from the majority task force report at the University of Massachusetts: "A further risk, as we saw with the negative *Boston Globe* and *Sports Illustrated* articles about UMass basketball, is that sport success can have its dark side. If any prominent athletic program is seen as lowering academic standards or if improprieties become public, the University risks a backlash from alumni and others. Further, the danger of a 'sports only' or 'sports first' message to alumni, the community, and legislators risks diminishing the fragile reputation of UMass as a solid academic institution."[54]

Finally, it is no secret that most, if not all, Division I (and many Divisions II and III) schools follow an admissions policy of accepting "special admits." That is, gifted athletes who do not meet the school's academic criteria for admission are nonetheless admitted. Some schools are more shameless than others in this regard. The consequences of this practice are twofold: first, the educational/intellectual environment is vitiated; second, SAT scores drop which hurts the college's ranking and diminishes its reputation. Each of these outcomes might reduce academic giving.

Improved Student Body

Several years ago Xavier University in Cincinnati began to use athletics as one of nine keys in its strategic plan for university development. Michael Graham, Xavier's Vice President for University Relations, explains: "There are few things that are a better calling card. When a prospective student receives a letter from you, you have five seconds in which he or she decides to open that letter or pitch it. And whether that student opens the letter . . . depends upon what they know of you. So does the basketball program win students? Well, no. Does it help to get that letter opened? Oh yeah."[55]

The College of Charleston in South Carolina is the thirteenth-oldest college in the United States and one of its three original board members was a signer of the U.S. Constitution. Yet some administrators at the school believe that the school languished in obscurity until its basketball team made it to the NCAA basketball tournament in March 1997 and won its first game. The school believes that their two tournament games on national television provided $3.3 million worth of publicity. Applications to the school jumped 6 percent.[56]

Northwestern University, long a cellar dweller in the Big Ten, defied all odds and went to the Rose Bowl in 1995. Applications jumped 30 percent. George Washington University went to the Sweet 16 in March 1993 and its applications surged 23 percent.

Similar examples of athletic prominence producing leaps in applications are plentiful, though they are not universal. The University of Wisconsin, for instance, made a rare appearance in the Rose Bowl in 1993 and its applications were unaffected. And it appears clear that the effect is more pronounced for schools which experience sudden bursts of athletic success. That is, if the University of Kentucky goes to the Sweet 16, it is unlikely to have the same positive effect on applications, as it did for the University of Massachusetts which rose from obscurity to the Sweet 16 in 1992.

Further, there are two crucial questions. One, since schools can't stay on the top athletically forever, what happens to applications when the school's performance drops off? Two, what kind of students are motivated to apply to a school just because it has a good basketball or football team? Are these the kind of students who will have better than average SAT scores and allow the school's admissions policy to become more selective? Moreover, does the increase in applications also lead to a higher yield (the percent of admitted students who end up enrolling in the school)? That is, does the increase in applications sustain itself and does it lead to a better quality student body?

The following analysis from an internal study at the University of Massachusetts is not encouraging.

> The period fall 1988 to fall 1990 did not include outstanding basketball years. In 1991, UMass was a semi-finalist in the NIT and in the four years since has been featured consistently on national television, has been ranked consistently in the top twenty and has gone to the NCAA tournament. . . . It is clear that after double digit declines in out-of-state applications from fall 1988 to fall 1991, we experienced two years of double digit increases in fall 1993 and 1994. It has been suggested that this bump in applications might be related to, among other things, the greater awareness of the University beyond Massachusetts, at least partially as a result of the success in basketball.
>
> It has been reported that the University of Connecticut experienced a similar application increase after their very successful Elite Eight season in 1991, with a 26% increase in out-of-state and 6% increase of in-state applications. Despite the growth of applications correlated with UConn basketball success, the conclusion was that there was no impact on yield (enrollment divided by admittances). With the numbers of applications up, it would also be expected that the quality of students enrolled might increase

because of a larger pool on which to draw. The Connecticut experience indicates no change in the quality of students. In the UMass figures there was a decrease in the SAT scores of applicants and enrolled students for both in- and out-of-state students. In fact, this [1995–96] was the first year that the SAT scores of out-of-state students fell below in-state. None of this suggests that team success carries beyond the application stage. In fact, in the year following the "Dream Season," UConn applications dropped back to earlier numbers. Their conclusion was that there was no lasting impact on the admission numbers.[57]

Of course, anecdotal information from individual colleges does not tell us whether or not there is a systematic relationship between athletic success and quality of the student body. One study of 44 colleges from 1971 to 1984 tested whether, controlling for other relevant factors, increase in the win percentage of a school's football team led to higher SAT scores. The coefficient of football success was not statistically significant at the 10 percent level.[58] Another study of 119 schools using data from 1989 finds that neither membership in a big-time athletic conference nor success in football or men's basketball improves the average SAT scores of the student body.[59]

To update these studies and provide a more robust test of this relationship, I gathered data for 86 Division IA colleges from 1980 through 1995 and performed a variety of econometric tests. The tests revealed that, while there was some tendency for athletic success to increase applications, there was no significant relationship between various measures of athletic success (win percent in football and basketball, appearance in postseason tournaments or bowls, ranking in AP polls, number of All-American players at the school, among others) and average school SAT scores. The athletic success variable also did not improve the yield.[60]

The only possible institutional justification, then, for supporting athletic success is that it might enable a university to expand the size of its student body. Of course, the positive correlation between athletic success and applications also means that poor athletic performance will lead to fewer applications. Thus, this is a risky strategy for a school to follow.

CONCLUSION

The common arguments frequently made to justify committing large resources to college athletics—that they directly or indirectly support the school's educational mission or its finances—do not stand up to empirical scrutiny. Not only do the vast majority of schools in Divisions IAA,

IAAA, II, and III run a significant deficit from their athletic programs, but the majority of schools in Division IA do as well. It is true that a handful of schools consistently earn surpluses from the intercollegiate athletic programs and they seem to generate sufficient stimulus for scores of universities to try to emulate their success. As NCAA restrictions are increasingly challenged in court, as television dollars for sporting events become more competitive, and as the collegiate licensing market wanes, it is unlikely that the financial fortunes of big-time college sports will improve in the coming years.

CHAPTER EIGHT

The NCAA

MANAGING THE SYSTEM

I must say that I thought the NCAA was very fair.
—Peter McPherson, President of Michigan State University, commenting
on the light NCAA penalties imposed after the school was found guilty
of fraud in 1997 for helping three athletes become eligible to play

We were thankful with what they gave us.
—Gary Abernathy, Sports Information Director at Texas Southern
University, commenting on NCAA penalties imposed in 1997 following
numerous violations in several sports going back five years

*The NCAA is so mad at Kentucky they're gonna give Cleveland
State two more years' probation.*
—Jerry Tarkanian, head basketball coach at Fresno State University,
remarking on a common perception that the NCAA makes exemplary
penalties of athletically less important schools and treats the
big-time schools with kid gloves

JUST as the Bible distinguishes between venial and mortal sin, the
NCAA has two categories of infractions: secondary and major. And just
as God created night and day, the NCAA Manual in Article 17, Section 1, Subsection 5 provides humanity with a "Definition of Day": "A
day shall be defined as a calendar day (i.e., 12:01 A.M. to midnight).
Adopted 1/10/91," leaving one to wonder how "Genesis" could have
been written before the NCAA Manual.

One might think that with 964 schools, 3 volumes, and 1,268 pages
of rules and regulations, and an annual budget of $283 million, the
NCAA might have more than 15 investigators looking into infractions
by its member schools. The budget of its enforcement staff is not

reported in the NCAA's annual budget, but one NCAA financial officer cited the joint enforcement and initial eligibility budget in 1997–98
as $3.1 million. Since $1.6–2.0 million was budgeted for initial eligibility, this leaves between $1.1 and $1.5 million for enforcement.[1] To be
sure, the 15 enforcement gumshoes seem to be less than handsomely
remunerated since as much as one-third of the staff turns over in some
years.

The Association readily acknowledges that there is a labor shortage in
the enforcement area. David Berst, the NCAA's chief of enforcement
from 1988 to 1998, estimates that every day at least ten of the biggest
universities are involved in a serious violation of NCAA rules.[2] David
Swank, chair of the Infractions Committee that hears the cases and levies
the penalties, is unequivocal: "They don't have the manpower to look at
everything, even if they wanted to."[3]

Making matters even more impossible, the 1,268 pages of rules and
regulations mean that minor rules are being violated every hour of the
day and schools are not loathe to report secondary transgressions. Thus,
Berst says that his office receives 3,000 calls a year from colleges to report that one of their players has, say, illegally received a lift across campus or been the improper beneficiary of an ice-cream cone.[4] One former
enforcement staffer suggested a resemblance between NCAA investigators and Inspector Javert in *Les Misérables* who spent 20 years chasing
Jean Valjean for breaking parole after his incarceration for stealing a loaf
of bread.[5] When all is said and done, Berst's office conducts 20–25 in-
vestigations a year—not many if Berst is correct that there are 10 major
infractions per day, just among the big schools.

Since the NCAA does not have the resources to investigate even
1 percent of the major infractions, it now routinely follows the practice
of allowing the schools to investigate themselves. Sometimes, to lend an
air of independence and legitimacy to the self-investigation, the university hires an outside firm to do the sleuthing, such as it is. According to
Mike McGraw at the *Kansas City Star*, since 1986 one-third of the
schools with major cases before the NCAA hired the same sleuth, attorney Michael S. Glazier of the Kansas City firm Bond, Schoeneck & King.
Glazier had worked for seven years with Berst, as an NCAA top enforcement officer before entering this new lucrative venture. Glazier's cre-
dentials are further enhanced by the serendipity that his former law
partner, Michael Slive, is now chair of the NCAA Division I Infractions
Appeals Committee.

Just in case there is any doubt, Berst readily endorses Glazier's work
to prospective client schools. Berst, it happens, is not only Glazier's
former work colleague, but he is also his golfing buddy. In Glazier's own words: "Dave [Berst] and I worked together for seven years.

Our families know each other. He's somebody who taught me a lot of good things, skills I still try and use today. So when I play golf with Dave Berst, it's because we both enjoy golf."[6] Berst even has attempted to discourage other firms from competing with Glazier's investigating services.[7]

Glazier's services are well compensated. He charged the University of Maine $544,930 in 1996 for a report, Florida State $500,000 for an earlier engagement, and Michigan State nearly $1 million for three cases. Glazier also worked on a report for the University of Michigan in 1997 to research the allegations against a booster, Ed Martin, his connection to basketball coach Steve Fisher, and "huge" gifts given to star players Chris Webber, Maurice Taylor, and Jalen Rose.

Sixty-three-year-old Ed Martin has been a fixture in Detroit playgrounds since 1980. Known as the "godfather," he would arrive in his gold Mercedes with boxes of Nikes to dispense to select players. One source claimed that Martin gave $100,000 to both Webber and Taylor. Other sources and information indicated that Martin provided an apartment and living expenses for the players, threw them parties, and possibly made a $47,000 car available to Taylor.

The main issue of the investigation was the extent to which coach Fisher and his staff were involved with Martin. Was Martin encouraged and abetted by Fisher or was he acting on his own? If the former, then Michigan would be guilty of a major infraction; if the latter, then the infraction would be secondary. It was known that Martin received complimentary tickets to at least thirty Michigan games. Handwriting analysis was used to determine who wrote the notes arranging for Martin's complimentary seats and the results pointed to Fisher. At one 1994 game, there was a handwritten note from coach Fisher to his secretary requesting that a prize recruit be seated with Martin. Telephone records show that Fisher made at least three calls to Martin and that Fisher's staff made at least thirty-nine additional calls to him.

This and other evidence of institutional complicity notwithstanding, Glazier's report concluded that Ed Martin was acting on his own and that the University of Michigan was not guilty of a major violation. It recommended no penalties against the university. Glazier's report stated that it explored the allegations and was unable to uncover conclusive evidence against Fisher and the school. One of the reasons that sufficient corroborating information was not obtained is that neither Glazier's firm nor the NCAA has the power of subpoena. If an individual does not wish to cooperate with the investigation, he or she does not have to talk. Keeping mum is precisely what Martin, Webber, Rose, and many others did.[8] Michigan self-imposed a reduction of official recruiting visits on its basketball team and the NCAA levied no additional penalties.

The potential for extensive stonewalling by key witnesses is the Achilles' heel of the entire NCAA enforcement apparatus, as it would be for any system of justice. When it is combined with the old boys' network confounding independent investigation and a severe lack of resources, the NCAA enforcement mechanism has all the credibility of Gus Hall running for president.

Back in 1989, coach Jim Valvano's basketball program at North Carolina State was under investigation because it was discovered that his players sold their complimentary game tickets as well as their free sneakers over a five-year period. There were also allegations of changing grades of players to make them eligible and hiding positive drug tests. NC State did not lose its rights to appear on television, which in the 1980s was a common punishment for a major violation such as this. The report from the NCAA infractions committee stated that television rights were preserved because of NC State's cooperation with the investigation and their self-imposed penalties, including the elimination of off-campus recruiting for a year.[9]

In 1993 two sports agents treated football players at Florida State University (FSU) to a free shopping spree at a Foot Locker store in Tallahassee. Many now call FSU, Free Shoes University. The shopping spree was one of several incidents with agents and players at the school between 1992 and 1994. The NCAA conducted its own investigation which again was hampered by uncooperative suspects. One suspect was FSU wide receiver Lawrence Dawsey. The NCAA attempted to contact him several times for an interview. Dawsey finally replied with a fax, stating: "I have already said all I intend to say about the FSU investigation. I never broke any NCAA rules while I was their [*sic*] and know nothing about any violation. Please don't bother me at One Bucs [*sic*] Place about this matter anymore."[10]

Three years later the NCAA ruled that FSU did not commit a major violation. They were not even guilty of a lack of institutional control; rather, they committed only a secondary infraction in failing to take appropriate action in response to information indicating ties between agents and players. The NCAA Infractions Committee put the school on probation for one year, which amounts to no more than a public slap on the wrist. It just so happens that Bob Minnix, who previously worked on the NCAA enforcement staff, was hired by FSU as the Associate Athletic Director after the Foot Locker incident. The revolving door of regulators and regulatees never stops.

During the 1995–96 year, Jim Harrick, then head basketball coach at UCLA, engaged in a number of recruiting violations. Among them, he invited guests to a $1,000-plus recruitment dinner which is proscribed by Association rules. He provided free tickets to UCLA games and a

1995 championship ring to the coach of a club team in Los Angeles whose players included potential recruits. He also provided free transportation to ineligible persons, gave his players free tickets to L.A. Lakers games, and exceeded the permitted number of recruiting calls. Harrick filed a false expense account report regarding the recruiting dinner and then lied about it to his superiors in the athletics department. He was fired from UCLA in November 1996.

UCLA got three slaps on the wrist (three years' probation) and a reduction from twelve to six in the number of official visits to the campus by recruits over two years. Harrick received no penalty from the NCAA and was back coaching at the University of Rhode Island for the 1997–98 season.

Sometimes the NCAA imposes a real penalty, but even then it is generally too light to be an effective deterrent. Consider the strange case of University of Massachusetts star Marcus Camby. Subsequent to UMass earning its five units in the 1995–96 NCAA tournament, it was revealed that Camby had received tens of thousands of dollars in payments and gifts from an individual who was hoping to be Camby's agent when he turned professional. Camby was being paid when he was still an amateur and, thus, had broken NCAA rules. He was an illegal player and UMass's tournament performance was nullified.

A logical inference would be that, since UMass did not legally earn its way into the tournament and its tournament record was officially obliterated, the penalty would be the removal of all its revenue units. Far from it. The NCAA levied a 45 percent penalty only on UMass's first-year payout (not the remaining five years). Hence, only $151,617 had to be returned out of present-value earnings of $2.02 million. So, the NCAA penalty came to only 7.5 percent of the total earnings from the tournament.

In the spring of 1997 the University of Texas at El Paso (UTEP) was nailed for various eligibility violations and improper recruiting enticements. The school was on probation at the time of these new infractions and, thus, was subject to the repeat-violator rule which made it a candidate for the "death penalty" (team suspension of play for a year or more). Not only was there no death penalty applied, but UTEP did not get either a postseason or TV ban. Instead, its penalty was five more years on probation and some scholarship reductions.

At UC-Berkeley in 1995, the men's basketball coach was caught sending $30,000 to the family of a player. In July 1997, the NCAA verdict came down: three years' probation, a one-year postseason ban, and reduction of basketball scholarships for two years. No TV ban.

There is a pattern to each of these incidents that is repeated over and over in the NCAA. If a violation is detected (and only a small minority of them ever is), the penalty ultimately imposed is *de minimus* and getting smaller.

Back at the 1985 convention, the NCAA had approved a distinction between major and secondary infractions. A major infraction was defined as one where there is a pattern of willful disregard of regulations or a school is given a distinct competitive advantage. A major infraction brought a minimum penalty: two years' probation, one-year ban on TV appearances and postseason play, one-year prohibition on recruiting, and a one-year suspension without pay for involved coaches and staff. A second major violation within a five-year period also brought a death penalty for one or two years, no athletic scholarships for the entire school for two years, and the loss of voting privileges in the NCAA.

But these sanctions were never applied and were eventually taken off the books. The death penalty was last applied in 1987 when Southern Methodist University, after being caught cheating several times, was caught again paying $61,000 to its football players and was suspended from all play for one year. The death penalty has not been applied since.

And the frequency of applying suspensions from postseason play or appearances on television, the two most costly penalties, is dropping rapidly, as the data in Table 8.1 make clear.[11] Even though the average number of reported major infractions in football and basketball per year has steadily risen from 5.1 during the 1950s, to 10.9 in the 1970s, and to 14.0 during 1990–95, the number of schools facing postseason suspensions has fallen from 91 during the 1970s (9.1 per year) to 41 during the first six years of the 1990s (6.8 per year), and the number of schools facing television suspensions fell from 80 during the 1970s (8.0 per year) to 12 during the first six years of the 1990s (2.0 per year). It is natural that TV suspensions were infrequent during the 1950s and 1960s because the vast majority of teams then were not televised and the amount of money involved was relatively small. Further, not only has the frequency of suspensions diminished, but the average lengths of the postseason and television suspensions have fallen sharply: from .83 years in the 1970s to .49 years in the 1990s for postseason sanctions, and from .73 years to .14 years for television sanctions.

The NCAA argues that it has reduced television suspensions for a good reason. Here's what they said in response to a broadside attack from the *Kansas City Star* in 1997: "It is true that television bans have declined in recent years; the decline is intentional. The Committee on Infractions, a membership peer group responsible for the enforcement process, moved away from such bans because they impact other schools and student-athletes not in violation." That is, suppose Nebraska is hit with a TV ban. When it plays Oklahoma, the Oklahoma team loses a TV opportunity and the associated exposure and revenue. Further, suppose

TABLE 8.1
Major Infractions and Penalties, 1950–1995

Years	No. of Infractions		Years on Probation (no. of years)		Postseason Prohibition (no. of years)		TV Prohibition (no. of years)	
	Total	Avg./yr	Total	Average	Total	Average	Total	Average
1950–59	51	5.1	65.2	1.28	38	.75	23	.46
1960–69	68	6.8	77.7	1.14	58	.85	25	.37
1970–79	109	10.9	121.0	1.11	91	.83	80	.73
1980–89	141	14.1	191.2	1.36	78	.55	46	.33
1990–95	84	14.0	145.5	1.73	41	.49	12	.14

Source: Data compiled from official NCAA statistics. NCAA, *Enforcement Summary* and *Supplement to the Enforcement Summary.*

Notes: Applies only to football and basketball. Years counted within the period in which the penalty began. Data available through November 1, 1995.

Nebraska was sanctioned because one player took $10,000 from an agent. Is it fair for the rest of the team to be prohibited from appearing on television?

To be sure, the NCAA has a point. Yet, it would be possible to allow Nebraska to appear on television but prevented from receiving any revenue from the appearance. This would penalize neither Oklahoma nor the other Nebraska players. It would only hurt the program's finances. Moreover, this logic does not apply directly to a ban on postseason play. If the NCAA argues that it applies indirectly, because when the team is disallowed to appear in a bowl game or the NCAA tournament it injures the other players, then the Committee on Infractions might as well close its shutters and lock its doors. All penalties will have some indirect bearing on the innocent athletes. John Weistart, professor of law at Duke and an expert on sports law, has a different interpretation of the NCAA's vanishing will to levy postseason or TV bans: "They're essentially conceding that the money is just too important and that the financial structure is too important."[12] Bucks over books again.

Two researchers, using data from 35 Division IA schools, found that net income and total revenues of "athletic programs that [got caught] violat[ing] NCAA rules during the 1980s are consistently higher than the programs that have not violated the rules. On average, programs that were penalized by the NCAA at any point in the 1980s generated about $1 million in additional revenues or profits in 1989."[13] In short, during the eighties it paid to cheat. Since the frequency and severity of tangible penalties has diminished in the nineties while the revenue payoff to athletic success has increased appreciably, what was true for the 1980s must be even more valid for the 1990s.[14]

While the incentive structure encourages the average school to cheat, it provides a still stronger stimulus to the perennially successful schools to do whatever is necessary to stay on top. Since the NCAA recognizes that it can only catch a small fraction of actual violations, the enforcement apparatus must be selective in choosing which schools to investigate. The schools that come to the NCAA's attention as well as the attention of its competitor schools are not the ones that have strong winning records year after year; rather, it is schools that move from rags to riches—the ones that transform themselves from losing schools to top contenders overnight. They are the ones usually suspected of cheating and the ones most frequently investigated.

Arthur Fleisher, Brian Goff, and Robert Tollison did a statistical study of eighty-five big-time schools from 1953 to 1983 and found that the likelihood of being investigated is correlated positively with the variability of a school's performance.[15] That is, schools that do poorly one year and well the next are likely candidates to be investigated; schools that consistently do poorly or well are not likely candidates.

Compounding the problems from the old boys' network, the inadequately funded enforcement system, and the inverted incentive structure, the NCAA has some poorly formulated rules. Consider the issue of agent abuse of college athletes.[16] According to the NCAA's in-house newspaper, the *NCAA News*, somewhere between 50 and 90 percent of agents offer inducements to college athletes with remaining eligibility.[17] Further, as of October 1995, this source asserted that the problem with agents was getting worse.[18] The number of reported cases of improper agent involvement with athletes increased fifteenfold between 1989–92 and 1995.[19] An athlete who is caught accepting any inducement is disqualified, but few are ever caught. And agents are outside the NCAA's control. Some twenty-seven U.S. states have passed legislation attempting to aid the NCAA in punishing agent misbehavior. But too few agents are caught. So the problem grows.

One case where the players and agent were identified occurred in 1996. The University of Connecticut's senior center, Kirk King, was suspended for the balance of the season because he accepted a plane ticket home from would-be agent John Lounsbury. Lounsbury also supplied a ticket to King to pass on to team point guard Ricky Moore. Moore argued dubiously that he did not know the source of the ticket, so he was only given a five-game suspension. Later that year it came to light that two basketball players from St. John's University, Felipe Lopez and Zendon Hamilton, accepted plane tickets to Las Vegas for a basketball workout. Lopez and Hamilton got their tickets from Adidas ringmaster Sonny Vaccaro. Since Vaccaro is not formally an agent, the provision of free tickets to Lopez and Hamilton did not violate any

NCAA rules. So Lopez and Hamilton were not suspended, and King and Moore were, despite the fact that the latter were visiting home and the former were promoting their professional careers at a basketball workout.

In short, the NCAA enforcement apparatus is ineffectual. The NCAA used to have mandatory penalties for certain transgressions but ended up granting exceptions 80 percent of the time. In 1994 the NCAA finally scrapped mandatory sentences altogether. Businesses do not usually punish themselves for doing good business.

Nowadays schools are invited to investigate themselves and they can hire a tacitly designated "independent" investigator with a wink. Without subpoena power, hard evidence is difficult to come by. If schools are deemed to be cooperative during an investigation, the NCAA Infractions Committee invariably reduces their sentence (often to little or nothing more than a symbolic probation) for good behavior. The outcome protects the athletic powerhouses. The number of probationary wrist slaps grows as the number of tangible penalties shrinks.

THE ADMINISTRATORS

What the NCAA saves on its enforcement budget seems to find its way into financing a life of luxury for the Association's top executives. In the fiscal year ending August 31, 1997, Cedric Dempsey, the NCAA's Executive Director since 1994, had a total compensation of $647,332, according to "the 990" tax forms the Association is required to file with the IRS.[20] This represented an increase of over $150,000 from Dempsey's fiscal 1996 compensation, a gain of over 30 percent. The next five highest-paid administrators at the NCAA headquarters all averaged compensation above $200,000.

The NCAA refuses to divulge Dempsey's fiscal 1998 or 1999 compensation, but defends his salary as dictated by the market. What is the market for executive directors of monopoly college athletic associations? Gene Corrigan, then president of the NCAA, and Sam Smith, president at Washington State University, determined Dempsey's salary and claim to have studied the compensation levels paid to officials on the U.S. Olympic Committee, commissioners of professional sports leagues, football coaches and athletic directors at major universities, and executives at other associations.

In particular, the NCAA argues that Dempsey's salary is comparable to that of the executive directors of the largest nonprofit organizations in the country. This is questionable. In fiscal 1997, Elizabeth Dole earned $204,400 as chief of the American Red Cross and John Seffrin earned $293,700 as head of the American Cancer Society.[21] The highest paid university president in 1996–97 was Judith Rodin at the University of Pennsylvania. Her salary was $498,536. Only four other university presidents had salaries above $400,000 that year.[22] According to a 1997 survey whose results were published in the *Chronicle of Philanthropy*, the median compensation for the chief executives of the 207 largest non-profits was $193,206.[23] Even Thomas Lofton, who runs the $12.7 billion Lilly Endowment (the nation's largest foundation), has a compensation package of $613,648, approximately $33,000 below that of Dempsey.[24] The Lilly Foundation's budget is 45 times the size of the NCAA's.

Whatever the proper level of Dempsey's salary, it is peculiar that it is set by two individuals, one of whom has his salary set in part by Dempsey. Further, since the basis of comparison used for Dempsey's salary included athletic directors, conference commissioners, and football coaches, among others, it is clear that the entire hierarchy of intercollegiate athletics benefits from a ratchet effect on each others' salaries. Unfortunately, none of these salaries is set by profit-making entities operating in a competitive environment. There is, then, a closed circle of college athletic administrators who promote each other's value to the rest of the world with no effective litmus test.

Dempsey's real compensation, however, does not stop with his salary, deferred compensation, and payments to his benefits plan. He profits from a long tradition of perquisites established during Walter Byers's 36-year reign atop the Association. In 1978 and again in 1982, Byers purchased houses with no-interest loans from the NCAA. By 1988, the year after Byers retired, no-interest loans were approved by the Executive Committee for ten top NCAA officials.

Byers's successor, Dick Shultz, raised the perk bar. Schultz had been athletic director at the University of Virginia and served on a number of high-level NCAA committees prior to assuming the Association's top post in 1987. His first perk was persuading the NCAA to buy his house in Charlottesville, Virginia, for $600,000 to facilitate his move to Kansas City. The NCAA put the house up for sale immediately and found a buyer four months later for $550,000.[25]

Next, he convinced the executive committee to buy a $1.7 million Learjet in June 1988. Schultz, pilot license in hand, wasted little time in putting the jet to good use. An NCAA log reveals that in 1989 Schultz made more than three hundred flights, including his wife as passenger on more than half these trips. Four trips were made with his wife to Decorah, Iowa, and Elmira, New York. The couple had a son living in each town.

One of the trips in 1989 left Kansas City with Schultz and two businessmen aboard. The first stop was Fayetteville, Arkansas, where Schultz picked up University of Arkansas AD Frank Broyles. The next stop was the Augusta National Golf Club in Georgia, famed home of the Masters Tournament. Schultz said it was a business trip. One of the businessmen, Warren Weaver, has a different recollection: "No. No. It was not business at all. Not a bit. We were talking about golf scores."[26] During 1992–93 it cost the NCAA $388,251 to maintain and operate the jet.[27]

Schultz had another remunerative scam he ran at the NCAA's expense. While on several Association committees Schultz was hired as a consultant to American Sports Underwriters. According to the *Kansas City Star*, among his services to the company were efforts to persuade fellow committee members to have the NCAA buy its insurance from American Sports Underwriters. Schultz also provided the company with mailing lists of NCAA member schools and helped the company establish hospitality suites at NCAA conventions. Schultz's consulting income from the company amounted to over $120,000, and some of the payments to him were made after he became the NCAA executive director.

In 1993 a scandal broke out when it was revealed that there had been thousands of dollars in improper loans made to athletes at the University of Virginia during 1990–91, when Schultz was its athletic director. Worse, an investigation found that Schultz knew of at least some of these loans. Pressure eventually forced Schultz to resign, but not before the Association gave him a golden handshake of at least $700,000. Today, Schultz is the executive director of the U.S. Olympic Committee for which he receives a compensation package of around $506,000.

Dempsey took over on January 2, 1994, in style. He previously had served as AD at the University of Arizona. Unable to sell his home he arranged for the NCAA to buy it from him for $685,000 in 1994. The Association also had difficulty selling it. In December 1996 the NCAA finally struck a deal at $562,500, taking a $122,500 capital loss plus lost interest. Dempsey also received a $411,000 subsidized mortgage to buy his new house. Similar subsidies have been provided to 11 other top NCAA officials. In February 1994, Dempsey and his wife were invited by CBS on an all-expenses-paid trip to the winter Olympics in Lillehammer, Norway. Ten months later CBS negotiated an extension on its contract to televise the annual NCAA basketball tournament.

Other perks are disseminated among the top administrators—from golf club memberships, to the use of cars, to first-class travel for committee members and staffers when flying on trips over 1,200 miles.[28] During the month of June 1998 alone, various NCAA committee meetings took place at the LaCosta Resort and Spa in Carlsbad, California; the Tahoe Seasons Resort in South Lake Tahoe, California; the Wild Dunes Resort in Isle of Palms, South Carolina; and the Elkhorn Resort in Sun Valley, Idaho. Earlier in the year an NCAA committee met for three days at an oceanfront resort in Santa Barbara, California, to discuss the location for the winter 1999 meetings. Dempsey says that while greater cost-efficiency in the Association is needed, "I don't necessarily believe that means we stop all resort-type hotels."[29]

All this might not be so objectionable if compensation and employment were set at effective levels elsewhere in the Association. But when the enforcement staff has only fifteen investigators and as many as five per year leave for better jobs, then one wonders whether the NCAA has its labor market priorities set straight.

IS IT ALL LEGAL?

Dempsey's 30-plus-percent raise to the contrary, 1997–98 was a difficult year for the NCAA. The Association paid out $2.5 million to settle long-standing litigation with Jerry Tarkanian. In March 1998, the Third Circuit Court of Appeals in Philadelphia found against the Association in *Smith v. NCAA*, stating that since its member institutions received federal subsidies, the NCAA itself was subject to Title IX. This ruling, among other things, opens to legal scrutiny the NCAA's rules about grants-in-aid limits for various sports, since these rules (such as 85 scholarships for men's football) affect each school's ability to reach gender parity. In May 1998, the Association signed an agreement with the U.S. Justice Department to modify its eligibility rules that were found in conflict with the Americans with Disabilities Act. It still faces an unresolved lawsuit in Philadelphia that charges the Association's standardized test score requirements discriminate against minorities and another suit by Adidas which charges the Association's rules on logo size on uniforms violates antitrust law.

More significantly perhaps, the NCAA lost one case which may threaten the basic premise for much of the Association's rule making. Back in 1993 five assistant basketball coaches filed a class action suit against the NCAA's restricted earnings rule pertaining to third assistant coaches on basketball teams. At its 1991 Convention, on the recommendation of a committee on cost cutting, the NCAA voted to restrict the earnings of the third assistant basketball coach to $12,000 during the school year (plus $4,000 in the summer) as well as to restrict individuals to five years in this position and to prohibit them from doing off-campus recruiting. The rule went into effect in 1992. The irony that the cost-cutting committee chose to put a lid on the earnings of the lowest-paid of four basketball coaches to save a few thousand dollars and did nothing to thwart the upward march of the head coaches' half-million-plus compensation packages seemed to escape everyone.

Prior to this rule the coaching staff of men's basketball teams included a head coach and three assistants. Not persuaded that it was necessary to have four coaches for twelve players, the presidents of NCAA colleges urged the cost-cutting committee to recommend the elimination of the third assistant. Head coaches, on the other hand, pleaded with the committee to retain the third assistant. The committee came up with what it thought was a magnanimous compromise: allow the third coach, but restrict his earnings to $12,000 during the school year. The committee came up with an additional rationale for retaining the third coach—it would enable teams to hire graduate students or other young aspiring individuals in order to train them to be coaches. Gene Corrigan, NCAA president and chair of the cost-cutting committee, explained: "We gave them that position out of the goodness of our hearts." The Convention was persuaded that the committee's idea was a good one.

One immediate problem surfaced with the implementation of the restricted-earnings coach rule. Head coaches preferred to hire experienced individuals for the position rather than novices. In the presence of college basketball's growing commercialism and lucrative sneaker contracts, these experienced assistant coaches soon began to resent their restricted salaries.

The case, *Law v. NCAA*, was heard in Kansas City District Court in 1995. Judge Kathryn Vratil ruled that the restrictive-earnings legislation by controlling the price of labor was a violation of antitrust statutes. The NCAA argued that the legislation actually permitted more employment, because the alternative would have been one fewer coach. Back in 1977, the U.S. Court of Appeals for the Fifth Circuit upheld the legality of the NCAA's restriction on the number of coaches, so the NCAA assumed that the alternative of two assistant coaches would have been legal. From this perspective, the restrictive-earnings legislation allowed for an additional coach and, hence, by creating more commerce, was procompetitive.

Moreover, back in 1984 the Supreme Court (in *NCAA v. Board of Regents of the University of Oklahoma*, discussed in chapter 5) recognized that some of the NCAA's restrictions helped to preserve the amateur character of college sports and, therefore, were legitimate. In the majority opinion of the 1984 decision, Justice John Paul Stevens wrote: "The NCAA plays a critical role in the maintenance of a revered tradition of amateurism in college sports. There can be no question but that it needs ample latitude to play that role, or that the preservation of the student-athlete in higher education adds richness and diversity to intercollegiate athletics and is entirely consistent with the goals of the Sherman Act."

But first Judge Vratil, and then in January 1998 the Court of Appeals for the Tenth Circuit, held that the restrictive-earnings rule was purely commercial in scope and had nothing to do with preserving amateurism. Thus, whereas limiting the number of games to be played by college basketball and football teams or even proscribing payment for college athlete services may be legitimate functions of the NCAA to preserve amateurism, direct price controls which impact on the labor market of nonstudents are not an acceptable restraint of trade. In June 1998 the NCAA announced that it would appeal these rulings to the Supreme Court.

Once liability was determined in *Law v. NCAA*, a jury trial for damages was set for April 1998. The action by the basketball coaches was joined by coaches from baseball and lacrosse who were also affected by the restrictive-earnings legislation. In all, the class action claimed to be on behalf of at least 1,900 assistant coaches. The jury found damages of $22.3 million, which are automatically tripled in an antitrust case to $67 million. Further, the NCAA is responsible for legal costs of the plaintiffs, estimated at $10 million, and an additional $13 million has been tacked on to cover inflation and interest.[30] The NCAA, believing that Judge Vratil's handling of the case and her instructions to the jury were prejudicial, appealed the damage award to the Circuit Court of Appeals.

Judge Vratil's attitude toward the NCAA seemed to have been influenced by a letter sent from Executive Director Dempsey to the 300-plus presidents of Division I colleges suggesting that the schools did not have to provide athletic financial information to the plaintiffs. The plaintiffs sought the information in order to calculate damages in the case. Vratil termed the NCAA's behavior as "contemptuous, malicious and calculated to severely delay and frustrate the discovery process." Vratil then ordered the NCAA to pay the costs for the plaintiffs' lawyers to travel to all the schools to procure the necessary information, helping to raise legal fees above $10 million.

The case has potential importance beyond the damage award, in itself roughly one-fourth of the NCAA's annual budget and more than one-half of what the NCAA distributes back to its member schools. The courts have been less than rigorous in defining a consistent set of standards to identify when the NCAA is acting legitimately to preserve amateurism and when it is acting illegitimately to restrain trade. In October 1998, the Supreme Court upheld the *Law v. NCAA* decision by the

Tenth Circuit, calling into question a whole gamut of NCAA rules: the limitation on the number of scholarships per sport; the new $2,000 limit per year on the wages athletes can earn in jobs during the school year; limits on the number of games teams can play; limits on the size of coaching staffs; limits on the items covered in full grants-in-aid; and the general limitation on paying athletes for their services, among others.

Prudently, the NCAA has engaged a law firm specializing in antitrust to do a thorough review of its manual to advise it on the legality of its rules. The NCAA explicitly budgets over $3 million a year for legal services. Its actual legal bill probably at least doubles that figure.

The Association, then, is coming to a legal crossroads at the same time that it confronts new economic challenges. Similar to the Japanese economy, strong and steady growth has hidden many of intercollegiate athletics' infirmities. With more and more competition for the entertainment dollar and an economy poised for a pause, revenue growth for college sports is likely to slow. The professional sports are counting on opening new international markets to spur ongoing growth. While it makes sense that households in Japan would be interested in watching Hideki Irabu pitch in New York, it takes a vast leap of imagination to expect European or Asian households to express much excitement about sporting contests between U.S. colleges.

Many of the NCAA's contradictions and weaknesses are already coming to the fore. Growth has enabled the Association to thrive in spite of them. What will happen as the growth subsides and what can be done about it? These questions are addressed in the next chapter.

CHAPTER NINE

Whither Big-Time College Sports?

REFORM AND THE FUTURE

*We really don't know what's going to happen, but the pressures build-
ing in the system are so great it's hard to imagine college sports stay-
ing the same.*

> —Gary Roberts, professor of sports law at Tulane University
> and NCAA athletic representative

*We believe the culture and environment surrounding the develop-
ment and recruitment of the elite youth player is so contaminated
that failure to adopt a series of structural changes in the sport will
undoubtedly lead to further tragedy and scandal.*

> —Jim Delany, commissioner Big Ten Conference

*I would be very surprised if there aren't substantial and comprehen-
sive changes within the next year in men's basketball. College basketball is a wonderful sport, but it is time to expunge the worst elements
that are in the game today.*

> —Robert Bowlsby, athletic director of the University of Iowa
> and chairperson of the new Division I Management Council

*The type of reformers I refer to are those who play with questions for
public consumption. . . . I wonder if there are not grounds to suspect
that the reformers . . . protest too much, that their zeal may be an
excuse for their own negligence in reforming themselves . . . true reform in athletics will not be accomplished by the mere publishing of
noble, high-sounding codes which are often hypocritically evaded in
actual practice.*

> —Notre Dame President John Cavanaugh, January 1947

History shows that the NCAA is not going to do anything unless it's forced to.

—Tom McMillen, former NCAA and NBA basketball player,
former member of U.S. Congress, cochair of
President's Council on Physical Fitness

We are losing our way. We need to find a way back from this athletics excess. . . . It's unheard of in our society for someone to say, "Stop now, that's enough."

—Rick Burns, coach at Drury College

IN MANY real senses, the history of the NCAA is a history of reform—failed reform. The Association was born out of the need to diminish violence in football at a time when commercialism was already rampant. As documented in earlier chapters, these problems were readily perceived, and educational leaders energetically railed against the excesses of college sports.

Throughout the decades various reforms have been essayed, each with a certain sincerity and optimism. As the Association has tinkered with eligibility requirements, length of the playing season, revenue distribution formulae, rules of amateurism, etc., the problems of college sports have continued to mount.

Early on, it was assumed that the proper approach to reform was to subordinate athletics to academics and coaches to faculty. At the NCAA Convention in 1916 at New York City's Hotel Astor, then NCAA President Le Baron R. Briggs of Harvard University told the assembled delegates: "Despite the principle of supply and demand, there may be reasons why the athletic coach should not receive three times as much salary as the professor of Greek; but there is no inherent reason why he should not hold a position of equal dignity. . . . Faculty control, then, in the best sense, means taking coaches into the faculty team. It means choosing coaches who are not out of place therein."[1]

Somehow matters drifted farther and farther out of the hands of faculty and academic administrators. By the 1970s the American Council on Education (ACE), a policy forum and lobbying group for college presidents, began to express increasing alarm at what had become of college sports. Some of the presidents must have felt like Dr. Frankenstein when they unsuccessfully attempted to assert their rightful control over the NCAA.

The NCAA, after all, was a one-college, one-vote organization where legislation was set every year at the convention. Each school's voting delegate to the convention was appointed by the college president. It would seem, then, that presidential control over the NCAA would be a foregone conclusion. It didn't work out that way.

Following a 1982 study commissioned by Derek Bok, president of ACE and of Harvard University at the time, the ACE decided to lobby at the 1984 convention for the creation of a Board of Presidents which would have veto power over the legislation passed at the convention. The irony of this request escaped no one. The presidents wanted to be able to veto the decisions of the people they sent to the convention. The presidents, it appeared, already had the power if they cared to exercise it.

No matter. The convention turned the ACE down. The message was clear: the NCAA is independent of its source. Perhaps the presidents did not really want control in the first place, it being much easier to scapegoat the convention or the NCAA Executive Committee for the errant path of college sports.

Just to preserve the semblance of order, however, the 1984 convention concocted a face-saving compromise—the Presidents' Commission. The Presidents' Commission would have no legislative or veto powers, but it could place items on the convention's agenda and it could make recommendations; that is, it was an advisory body. The Commission did weigh in on getting coaches to report outside income to the university, on raising athlete initial eligibility standards, and on promoting various cost-cutting measures, such as the restricted-earnings coach and reduced numbers of grants-in-aid. But none of these tinkerings altered the basic problematic of intercollegiate athletics.

Indeed, after living with the Presidents' Commission for a little more than a decade, the NCAA decided that it might as well make the nominal power of presidents official. The 1997 "restructuring" placed college presidents in charge of the most important decision-making bodies.

Why did athletic directors, coaches, and conference commissioners find nominal control by college presidents so compatible with their interests? One reason is public relations. The Knight Commission on intercollegiate athletics had been pestering the NCAA since the 1980s to put college presidents and academic priorities in control. The 1997 restructuring enabled the Knight Commission to proclaim victory. A second reason is that the presidents, through their activity on the Presidents' Commission, showed themselves to be a largely uninterested and ineffectual force.

Most college presidents fell into one of two categories: those with little interest in sports and those with intense interest. The presidents with little interest delegate worrying about the NCAA to the school's AD or its faculty representative. The presidents with intense interest are sports fans, enjoy associating themselves with big-time college sports and its attendant perks, and have no desire to upset the apple cart. Walter Byers, former NCAA Executive Director, puts it poignantly: "The so-called presidential reform movement, which is about 10 years old, has been all form and no substance. Presidential control has merely led to increased commercialization and a clear commitment by the presidents to achieve as much money in the marketplace as they possibly can."[2]

Further, college presidents turn over with rapidity. Between 1990 and 1995, 58 percent of the presidents of Division IA colleges changed jobs, and between 1985 and 1995, the figure was 81 percent. They are simply not going to be around long enough to warrant the investment of their time and energy in athletics, given the enormity of their other responsibilities.

The few presidents who did decide to make a commitment to reforming college sports found other impediments, such as a school's alumni, boosters, trustees, or state legislators. In 1990 the president of Michigan State University, John DiBiaggio, went to the mat trying to prevent the school's football coach from also being named its athletic director. DiBiaggio had the strange thoughts that values might be compromised and that a nationwide equal opportunity search was desirable. MSU's Board of Trustees, reportedly afraid that the football coach would leave to go to the New York Jets, reversed DiBiaggio and gave the coach a ten-year appointment as athletic director. DiBiaggio has since fled to Tufts University, a Division III school where the athletic stakes are lower.

At Clemson University, during the 1989–90 academic year, President A. Max Lennon and AD Bobby Robinson negotiated the resignation of the school's football coach. The coach, Danny Ford, had been implicated in fourteen NCAA rules violations. In the week following Ford's resignation (which cost Clemson over $1 million in settlement payments!), Tiger fans called for the resignation of both the president and the AD. The AD was given round-the-clock security protection by the state police after several death threats were received. President Lennon's predecessor had quit in 1985 in a dispute with the trustees over the athletics' program.[3]

Still another line of defense was built into the Presidents' Commission, as explained by Sam Magill, one of the Commission's members and president of Monmouth College. "I found that the real decisions were not made by the whole commission, but only by the IA folks and those who toadied up to them."[4] So, by 1997, the NCAA no longer had much to fear from the presidents, and they had much legitimacy to gain from putting them in nominal control.

Thus, the January 1996 convention voted in restructuring to take effect on August 1, 1997. Stripped of its rhetoric, restructuring has two principal prongs: "presidential" control and divisional autonomy. The presidential control is enforced because atop each division is a council composed of college presidents. Atop the entire association is the Executive Committee, consisting of 16 presidents. Of these, 12 are from Division I and, of these 12, 8 are from Division IA. That is, Division I with one-third of the membership has three-fourths of the representation on the Association's highest body, and Division IA with 15 percent of the membership has 50 percent of the representation on this body.

The major consolation for Divisions II and III is that the Executive Committee will have little power. It is supposed to assure that the three divisions continue to operate according to the general principles of the Association. The actual policy making will take place within each division.

Divisions II and III will continue to pass legislation at annual conventions where each school has one vote. Division I, however, has abandoned the democratic, one-school, one-vote model and abandoned policy making at its annual convention. Rather, Division I is now governed by a Board of Directors and Management Council. The Board consists of presidents from 15 schools, 9 of which are from Division IA so that IA with roughly one-third of the membership in Division I has 60 percent control over the Board. Of the 9 from IA, 8 are from the so-called equity or big-time conferences,[5] and the 9th position is split between the Big West and MAC conferences.

The Management Council consists of 34 athletic administrators and faculty representatives. Of these, 18 are from Division IA. The Council is charged with adopting the operating bylaws and rules to govern Division I, subject to the approval of the Board of Directors, and with interpreting these bylaws. As with the Board, Division IA has disproportionate and effective operating control on the Council. The Council clearly is the active policy maker with what amounts to veto power vested in the hands of the Board. The expectation is that the Board will primarily serve as a rubber stamp for the Council's decisions.

Any pretense of one-school, one-vote has been jettisoned in favor of clear control to the most commercialized elements within Division I. And Division I will now be able to pass legislation appropriate for its further commercialization without any constraints imposed from the less commercially oriented Divisions II and III. Whether this will mean longer seasons, lower eligibility standards, more on-field advertising, greater revenue inequality, or lower graduation rates has yet to be seen. The deck has been cleared for untrammeled commercialization. Further, while decision making in Divisions II and III continues to take place at the annual meetings and to be open to the public, decision making in Division I takes place within private committee meetings and is now obscured from open public discussion and scrutiny.

Larry Gerlach, longtime member of the former NCAA Council, the second highest body prior to restructuring, opines: "My sense is that the restructuring would never have passed if institutions voted their sense of things. The hidden agenda carried the day—if the Big Boys didn't get their way, they would bolt the NCAA. That was made very clear. Lots of people are unhappy and concerned, but there is no organized opposition because of the fear of secession by the folks who bring in the dollars." Dick Schultz, former NCAA Executive Director, conveyed a similar message to a closed meeting with the Knight Commission in 1995, stating that the top half-dozen conferences and their presidents were ready to tell the NCAA that "it is our way or the highway." Then Schultz characterized their motivations: "While greed and mistrust is a factor, it is not the only factor."[6]

As television, marketing, advertising, and facility revenues have grown, the several dozen financially successful schools have found they have less and less in common with the 900-plus remaining members of the Association. Why should they be bound by the revenue-sharing requirements and rule-making procedures of the NCAA? It was precisely this tension that produced the separation into three divisions in 1973, the bifurcation of Division I into IA and IAA in 1978, the formation of the CFA in 1977, and now the restructuring of 1997.

The schools from Divisions II and III were given no choice. Either go along with restructuring and Division I independence and new, undemocratic structures or the big-time schools would take their money and leave. The payoff to Divisions II and III for acceding to restructuring is that they are guaranteed 4.37 percent and 3.18 percent, respectively, of NCCA net revenues from traditional sources. Their shares do not apply to revenue from new sources, such as a possible postseason football playoff. In 1997–98 these shares amounted to $11.1 million for Division II and $8.1 million for Division III.[7] These funds are used to finance championships in these divisions. While making a significant contribution, these monies pale in comparison to the $146.4 million allocated to Division I.

What's in it for the big-time schools? In exchange for approximately 7.5 percent of their net revenues, the big-time schools buy hoped-for legitimacy by holding the NCAA together. They also buy continued recognition as amateur, non-profit entities along with accompanying special tax exemptions and the privilege of not having to pay their athletes.

But, as I write in the fall of 1998, the restructured NCAA has been functioning for scarcely a year and turmoil in the system is already brewing. Sneaker companies are reeling from lower sales and are beginning to question their financial commitment to college sports and hero promotion. TV ratings for the NCAA basketball men's finals have fallen 22 percent since 1992. Regular season football ratings are falling as more and more games find their way onto network and cable channels. And as televised sporting events of all kinds proliferate, many insiders wonder whether the next round of television contracts will be as rich as the last. Some wonder whether the big-time conferences may have been offered sweetened deals from the networks to get them to bolt from the CFA. Now that the CFA is defunct, there may be no sweetener next time around. Attendance at football games by students is also dropping as is youth participation in football, and the NCAA has undertaken a major public relations campaign to increase interest in college football.

Another chink in the armor of amateurism has appeared in the form of allowing athletes to work and earn up to $2,000 during the school year. ADs and compliance officers are biting their nails in anticipation of the enforcement nightmare this policy will engender. How, for instance, will they be able to prevent boosters from offering athletes phantom jobs, where they receive pay for no work? And now that $2,000 earnings are allowed, what is the next step? Will such a restriction stand up to antitrust scrutiny?

Boston University lost $2.91 million on its football team in 1997–98. Despite its reputation as a big sports and party school with a football team since 1884, BU has decided it can no longer afford this luxury. BU Provost Dennis Berkey took advantage of the opportunity to proclaim victory: "We have to stop increasing the amount of money we are spending in areas that are not at the heart of what the university is here to do, and that is to educate young people and to conduct research and advance knowledge."[8]

The separation of rich and poor athletics programs continues to grow, as do the financial pressures from Title IX. Twenty-two schools have dropped their football program in this decade (five of these from Division I), and there will be more.

The athletic conferences continue to go through their mergers and acquisition stage, attempting to position themselves into the most lucrative television and postseason markets. The most recent spin-off occurred in the spring of 1998 when the Western Athletic Conference split in half, the self-perceived strong football schools feeling dragged down by the rest. Rumors have Notre Dame joining the Big Ten, along with its eleven existing members (but who's counting) and a reconfiguration in the Big East, among others. According to new NCAA rules, any conference with twelve or more schools can create two divisions and then run a postseason conference championship. The dollars are sufficiently alluring to keep the mergers and acquisitions phase alive and well for the foreseeable future.

Meanwhile, the restricted-earnings case has the NCAA in a true identity crisis, wondering what it can and cannot do. In October 1998 the Supreme Court refused to hear the NCAA's appeal to the liability ruling, allowing to stand the lower court ruling that the NCAA's limit of $16,000 per year on earning for certain assistant coaches violated the antitrust laws. Whatever is decided in the appeals to the damages portion of this case, the ambiguity in interpreting the rule of reason in antitrust cases is sure to keep the Association's lawyers guessing.

If, as college sports continues to commercialize, the NCAA loses some of its cartel powers and tax benefits, then many predict the 1997 restructuring will be followed by a formal exodus of big-time schools. Thus, while many thought that restructuring would sap the centrifugal energy in intercollegiate athletics and give way to an era of stability, as we prepare for the new century significant change seems more inevitable than ever before. What kind of change is possible and what kind is desirable?

REFORM AND THE FUTURE

Any dispassionate observer would concur that the piecemeal reforms in the NCAA over the past several decades have accomplished little. At best, the NCAA is on a treadmill, working hard to go nowhere. Former Executive Director Walter Byers has harsh words about the reform process: "The rewards have become so huge that the beneficiaries simply will not deny themselves even part of current or future spoils. I believe the record clearly shows the major hope for reform lies outside the collegiate structure."[9]

That is, there is a commercial juggernaut that Byers believes is impossible to stop from within. The problem, however, is that the outside options are not very encouraging either. Congress has intermittently shown an interest in reforming college sports. The last spate of Congressional reform bills occurred during 1988–90 and was largely inspired by then Maryland Representative Tom McMillen. None of McMillen's efforts made it out of committee.[10] These days folks in Washington seem to get most worked up about the reduction of male sports in the face of Title IX requirements. Representatives in state legislatures have focused mainly on curbing the encroachments of agents into high schools.

To further minimize the risk that Congress act against the NCAA, the Association opened an office in Washington, D.C., in April 1995. An article in the *NCAA News* provided a rather cynical account of this opening: "An early and intuitive decision by Doris Dixon, director of federal relations, and other NCAA administrators was to locate the office at One Dupont Circle alongside other higher education associations— including the American Council on Education. 'Because of our office location, we are perceived as and treated as one of the higher education associations,' Dixon said. 'It has improved and developed our position with the higher education community.'"[11] Appearances, it seems, are everything.

Writing for the *Chronicle of Higher Education*, Debra Blum describes Dixon: "She knows how to make contacts and keep them. She knows when to talk, listen, and ask. She knows how to cut a deal. Most of all, she knows how to handle the tricky business of handing out tickets to one of the most popular sporting events in the country—the finals of the NCAA Division I men's basketball tournament."[12] As long as the mass of the constituents of members of Congress remain apathetic about reforming college sports[13] and the NCAA follows a proactive policy of providing perks to members and lobbying staffers, there is small chance for Congress to play a progressive role.

The other alternative is a genuine reform movement among college presidents and trustees who have not bought into the assumptions and privileges of the NCAA. This too is a long shot, but given the substantial financial losses incurred by more than 95 percent of college athletic programs, the pressures from Title IX, the antitrust legal challenges, and the abiding contradictions of college sports, perhaps it is not too late for sensible ideas to mobilize for serious structural reform.

Any serious structural reform must begin with a repudiation of tinkering. The underlying incentive system must be attacked and the pressures to raise revenue must be relieved. Reform must be far-reaching and its components must be articulated and self-reinforcing. While it is tempting to begin with a clean slate, it is also unrealistic. College sports are too popular and too ingrained in our culture to re-engineer them from the ground up. Even though the vast majority of athletic programs run a deficit, college athletics create significant positive externalities and have powerful support constituencies. The ten-point program I propose below is composed of measures which can all be feasibly implemented from the current structure. Further, each step should be able to develop a substantial constituency within academia, giving the program a *prima facie* viability.

Step 1: Change the Relationship between Professional and College Sports

Major League Baseball (MLB) provides a modest subsidy to college baseball every year to help support the summer leagues. There are sixteen such leagues around the country where the top college players go to hone their skills and be observed and appraised by baseball scouts. This subsidy, on the order of $350,000 per year, is the only one provided by professional team sports to intercollegiate athletics.[14]

There is a sharp irony here. MLB has its own player development system—an extensive network of over 160 minor league clubs and winter leagues that cost each major league team an average of over $9 million annually. That is, MLB already carries a stiff charge for player development. Beyond this, they support, albeit modestly, college baseball.

The reverse is true for the National Basketball Association (NBA) and the National Football League (NFL). Neither the NBA nor the NFL has player development systems, and their teams do not have substantial player development expenses. Practically all their player development occurs at the college level. (In basketball, some player development also occurs at the high school level as well as at the Nike and Adidas summer camps.) Yet neither the NBA nor the NFL contributes a penny to college basketball or football.[15]

While the National Hockey League (NHL) does not contribute to college hockey, it does run its own player development program, though it is less extensive than that of MLB. As of 1997, even the United States Olympic Committee (USOC) recognizes the player development role of intercollegiate athletics. The USOC voted to provide $2 million a year for four years to college conferences in support of Olympic sports.

The NFL and NBA are wealthy leagues. The average NBA team earns over $65 million a year in revenue. The average NFL team earns over $80 million. And these numbers apply to the 1997–98 season, prior to their new television contracts. Each league more than doubled its average yearly guaranteed revenues from national television rights, raising the per team annual revenues by $36.7 million in football and by $13.3 million in basketball.

Why does the NCAA pay for the player development of these teams? Why does the NCAA do their bidding when it comes to the amateur drafts? Prior to 1997, the NCAA had a rule that a player lost his eligibility if he signed with an agent, whether or not he was paid by a professional league. The leagues didn't like this rule because it meant that the top players could enter their amateur drafts without signing with an agent. If players didn't like the team which picked them or the salary offered them, they could turn the team down and return to play college ball if they had eligibility remaining. Such a system gave players some bargaining leverage with the teams.

The NBA found a partial way around this by requiring players to go to team-sponsored workouts prior to the amateur draft and making it clear that agents were to arrange for the players' appearance at such workouts. Nominally, these workouts gave the teams a chance to evaluate the players' talent. In reality, no such thing happened. The workouts occurred several months after the end of the college season, when the players were out of game shape. And the workouts lasted for only a few hours. Any team that thought it was going to learn more about a player at such a workout than from several years of college basketball was badly deluded. Rather, the workouts appear to have been ruses to prompt players to sign with agents and lose their eligibility under NCAA rules.

Still, the NBA wanted a tighter system. So when the league met with the NCAA's Professional Sports Liaison Committee in 1996, it requested that the NCAA change its eligibility rule. The NCAA obliged at its 1997 Convention. The new rule stated that any player entering the NBA draft lost his eligibility. Meanwhile, the NBA stiffened its own rules to give the drafting team rights to bargain with a player for two years, rather than one.

In the 1997 NBA draft, forty college players with remaining eligibility made themselves available for the draft. Nine were picked in the first round; 21 were not picked at all.[16] Under the new rules, these 21 would not be allowed to return to play in college. And most of those picked in round two never receive an NBA contract.

If the NCAA were really trying to support student athletes as Cedric Dempsey continually claims, then it would not make it harder for the player to return to college. There is no good reason why a player can't be considered an amateur, so long as he has not been paid to play his sport. The proper policy is to allow college athletes to test the market. If they like what they get, they can decide to turn pro. At such a point they should lose their eligibility, not before. Such a system would give college students direct market information about their professional prospects.[17] If a student entered the draft and was not selected, he might be induced to take his studies more seriously. Next, if the NCAA wants to support its athletes, it could challenge the new NBA draft rule as an unfair restraint of trade.

Further, rather than assuming a supine posture vis-à-vis the NBA and NFL, the NCAA should seek its rightful compensation for providing a crucial player development function. Start with the $9 million per team spent by MLB clubs on their player development systems. Be conservative and cut the number in half, and charge the NBA and NFL $4.5 million per team. This modest sum is only 33.8 percent of the increase in TV revenues for the NBA teams from its new national contract and only 12.3 percent of the increase for the NFL teams. Such a charge would produce a yearly subsidy of $130.5 million from the NBA and $135 million from the NFL. The NCAA could even use the potential challenge of the NBA's and NFL's draft practices as leverage in seeking this financial support.

The NCAA should then take the resulting $265.5 million and divide it equally among all its 964 members. Each school would receive $275,000-plus to relieve some of the financial pressure from Title IX. It could be used to add scholarships for women, add teams for women, or retain "non-revenue" sports such as swimming or gymnastics for men.

Of course, restructuring legislation stipulates that any new sources of revenue to Division I (and the NBA and NFL money presumably would go overwhelmingly to Division I) are not subject to distribution without a two-thirds vote of membership. Division I has enough votes to veto such a change, so an arrangement would have to be made with the NFL and NBA to distribute its payments to all three divisions. Alternatively, the $265.5 million might be distributed disproportionately to Division I schools and used to support some of the programs described in step 2.

Step 2: Professionalize the Team or Allow a Quota of Nonmatriculated Athletes

One of the saddest charades in college sports occurs because many young athletes see college as the only route to the pros. Kids who have no academic talent and/or interest in attending college are compelled to be there. Schools prostitute themselves by accepting "special admits" and offering them phony curricula. There is no integrity in this process.

There are several ways to avert this cynicism and hypocrisy. One way would be to professionalize the big-time college sports. The University of Michigan Wolverines could still be the Michigan Wolverines and play their games in Ann Arbor, but the football players would have no necessary connection to the university. Rather, the team, with subsidies from the pros, would be a separate business entity. It would rent the stadium or arena from the university and some of its players might be part-time students. But all its players would be paid as minor league football or basketball players. The Michigan students could still root for their local team, the way they might root for the Detroit Lions or Pistons. Only now the team would be playing on their campus and the connection would be closer. Michigan boosters should be just as happy either way. If the schools that run perennially profitable football or basketball teams resist such a change, then they might be offered the option of owning the team as a separate entity. In any event, the school can earn money by renting and operating the stadium, retaining student athletic fees, or providing room and board for the players.

While such a change would be radical, there certainly is ample precedent for this type of professional and independent presence on a university campus. One prominent example is the Loeb Theater at Harvard University. The theater itself is owned by the Harvard Faculty of Arts and Sciences. Harvard students perform their own plays in the main theater twelve weeks a year, while a professional company, the American Repertory Theater, performs there thirty weeks a year. When the professional company performs, graduate students in a Harvard certificate program may also act or otherwise assist in productions. Sometimes undergraduates participate as well. The professional company also runs theater workshops and does advising for the certificate and undergraduate students.[18]

Still, if the independent entity model is too radical a departure from the status quo, a hybrid model is available. The NCAA could allow each Division IA football team to have, say, 15 of its 85 players be nonmatriculated athletes and 5 of its 13 basketball players. These 15 students would receive a modest salary, similar perhaps to the $2,500 per month earned by Triple A minor league baseball players. They could also hold a part-time job or attend classes, but they would not be degree students. There might also be a promise that if any of the nonmatriculated athletes later desired to return for a degree and had the appropriate qualifications, then a four-year full scholarship would be made available to them. Financial support for this hybrid model might be sought from the NBA and NFL.

Another variant would be to promote the introduction of new player development leagues unaffiliated with college sports. The National Rookie League for basketball is scheduled to begin play during the summer of 1999. The league is intended for high school students who do not want or are not qualified to go to college. This league does not have the financial backing of the NBA, but the league hopes to support itself partially by selling its top players to NBA teams. The International Basketball League and the Collegiate Professional Basketball League also hope to commence play in the fall of 1999 and to recruit talent from high schools and colleges.[19] The financial basis for all three leagues appears tenuous. The good news for colleges is that any such league would reduce the problem of special admits and phony curricula; the bad news is that, if successful, such leagues would drain college sports of some of its top athletes and lessen the interest in college sports. For this reason, either of the first two models might be preferable from the NCAA's perspective. (If aspects of this second step are adopted, several other steps would need to be modified or may be obviated altogether.)

Step 3: Take Enforcement Seriously

NCAA enforcement has many problems, from insufficient due process to occasional dubious behavior of staff, but its fatal failure is that it does not enforce a system of sanctions that effectively deters flouting of rules. The NCAA needs to triple or quadruple its enforcement staff, improve their training, and offer them salaries sufficiently attractive to keep them in the job. Spending under $2 million a year to enforce over a thousand pages of rules and regulations at 964 colleges is a joke. The Association generates practically $300 million annually. If it is serious about amateurism and level playing fields, then it needs to allocate $10–15 million or whatever it takes to get the job done.

Once sufficient resources are in place, minimum penalties should be restored. Back in the mid-eighties there were mandatory penalties for all major infractions and mandatory "death penalties" for all repeat major infractions within a five-year period. Unless real, painful penalties are reinstated, including prohibitions on postseason play and earning money from TV appearances, the incentive structure will continue to promote violations and cheating.

Step 4: Establish Clear Criteria for Students in Good Standing

The NCAA has raised the initial eligibility bar on several occasions since 1984. This bar has incurred the wrath of the Black Coaches' Association, necessitated the creation of the $2 million-a-year National Clearinghouse, provoked litigation from high school students, and caused endless hours of debate among member schools. Although it has retracted its heavy hand a bit, the NCAA also went as far as deciding which high school classes were valid to establish one's grade point average. All this for initial eligibility.

But when it comes to certifying how a student is performing once in college, the NCAA basically leaves it up to each individual college. Student-athletes have to take a certain number of courses per semester, but the NCAA does not care whether the classes are in basket weaving or principles of basketball. The NCAA needs to worry less about high school classes and more about what happens in college. If there are going to be clearinghouses to oversee the content of courses, let them inspect what happens in the hallowed halls of academia.

Step 5: Eliminate Freshman Eligibility

Back when people still had their wits about them, it was taken for granted that first-year students should not be involved in intercollegiate athletics. It was not until 1972, for financial reasons, that the NCAA capitulated and passed an Association-wide rule to allow freshmen to play.[20]

First-year students have just left home and usually are on their own for the first time. They need to adjust socially and emotionally to their new environment. They also need to establish a firm foundation for their studies. If they lose their way in their first year, they may lose their confidence and ability to stay on top of their work. If the model is student-athlete and not athlete-student, then this step is a no-brainer.

Step 6: Substantially Cut the Number of Grants-in-Aid for Division I Football

Between December 2, 1945, and October 7, 1950, the Notre Dame football team did not lose a single game. During this period, the team traveled to its away games with a squad of 38 players.[21]

NFL teams today have maximum active rosters of 45 players.[22] When you have to pay them, you find ways to trim the fat. The last time I counted there were only 11 football players on the field per team. Allowing for 11 players on defense, 11 on offense, 11 others on special teams, one punter, one placekicker, and 10 substitutes is enough. (If freshman eligibility is eliminated, then 60 grants-in-aid would be necessary for this player endowment. Of course, walk-ons could still fill out the roster and Division IA could reconsider the possibility of allowing partial scholarships for football players.)[23]

As might be expected, coaches will kick and scream, and concoct rationales as to why this is impossible, just as they did when the number of grants-in-aid was reduced from 105 to 95 and, then, to the present 85. If 40 grants are cut from football, that will save over $500,000 per school. The money can be used to foster gender equity in participation rates, scholarships or facilities, or it can be used to keep that men's water polo team. Not to worry—football will survive and thrive.

Step 7: Take Control over the Summer Camps

The Nike/Adidas recruiting networks are pernicious. They teach kids to be on the take at an early age. They encourage false dreams and deflect responsible behavior. Summer camps, organized and run by Nike and Adidas, are the culmination of this process.

Jim Delany, Big Ten Commissioner, proposed the elimination of summer camps to the NCAA later in 1998. Not a bad idea, but it would be difficult for small college programs to continue their recruiting without the camps. Camps centralize the talent and save recruiters the time and money of traveling to dozens of schools. Big Ten schools perhaps could absorb this extra cost. The majority of Division I schools running deficits would be put at a further competitive disadvantage.

Instead of eliminating the camps, the NCAA should take them over. The number of camps could be substantially reduced. Payoffs and agents could be kept at a distance. It's worth a serious try.

Step 8: Shorten Seasons and Hours

The number of football and basketball games per year has found a way to keep growing. Special preseason charity games (which raise as much money for the participating schools as for the charities) or tournaments always find a way of creeping onto the schedule. The NCAA is now contemplating adding a twelfth football game to the season in lieu of preseason charity contests when the season permits.

The number of hours per week of obligatory practice is set at 20, but everyone knows this is a farce. Including non-obligatory activities in the absence of a coach, such as informal practice, weight training, tape viewing, attendance at special functions, and travel, athletes can spend 50 or 60 hours a week on their sport in season. Out of season in Division I they still practice and train.

Again, if the model is student-athlete, then the schedule should be set so that more hours are spent studying and in the classroom than preparing for intercollegiate competition.

Step 9: Give Coaches Long-Term Contracts and No Sneaker Money

Big-time basketball and football coaches are paid well, too well. For their pay, they are expected to produce winners. If they don't, they are shown the door. If they are caught cheating, they are given a golden handshake, take a year off, and go coach at another school. The incentive is clear: do all you can to win. Whatever it takes.

This is backwards. College coaches don't need to make $500,000 to $1,000,000 a year and up. Their remuneration is artificially bloated by boosters who make inflated deals advertising on coaches' shows on TV, radio, and the internet. It is also bloated by payoffs from sneaker companies. Georgetown's John Thompson gets $400,000 a year from Nike for having his players wear Nike shoes and garments, not to mention millions of dollars in stock options. Why should Thompson get the money and not the players? He shouldn't. The players can't get it because they are amateurs says the NCAA. But maybe that rule could be relaxed. For instance, some licensing money could go to pay for parents and siblings to travel to postseason competition. Anything left over can support the general athletic program.

Instead of paying the coaches for what they don't do, pay them for what they produce through their base salary. The vast majority will earn between $100,000 and $300,000. They'll still be better remunerated than 99 percent of the faculty and many college presidents.

But like the faculty, also give them the opportunity to have secure jobs. Nearly one-quarter of Division IA football teams began the 1997–98 season with new football coaches, including 4 new coaches in the Big Ten and 4 more in the WAC.[24] Only 3 of the 24 coaching changes in Division IA football were made at schools that had winning records in 1996–97, and, of those 3, 2 were retirements. If coaches don't win but run a solid program with proper priorities, they should be given long-term contracts.

Step 10: Don't Compromise on Free Speech

The value of free speech is the sine qua non of academic life. It should never be compromised.[25] The NCAA needs an Association-wide, clear policy that prohibits commercial contracts with sneaker or other companies that include any form of no-taping or no-criticism clauses.[26] Further, if athletes wish to protest labor or other policies of the sneaker companies in Asia, they should not be required to wear their products. Coaches who penalize such players should be sanctioned. University contracts with sneaker or other companies should only stipulate that athletes will be encouraged to use certain products.

The foregoing ten steps include no explicit measures either about pay for student-athletes or about gender equity. This is because I believe the present policies basically are appropriate. As long as we have student-athletes, they should not receive monetary remuneration directly for their play. Full scholarship rides, special eating and housing privileges (which persist notwithstanding legislation passed at the 1991 Convention), the right to carry Pell Grants on top of their scholarship, to earn up to $2,000 additional income during the school year, to receive several hundred dollars a year in special needs support, and preferential access to summer jobs are all adequate remuneration. Yes, there are star football and basketball players who may generate a half-million dollars of revenue or more for their teams, but many of these stars will soon earn millions in the pros and they can leave college anytime they like. With their scholarships and other benefits college athletes on average are treated at least as well as minor league players in baseball.

The NCAA should follow more pro-student-athlete policies, as noted throughout this book, but paying each athlete according to his marginal revenue product (MRP) is neither economically feasible nor desirable. Many Division I football and basketball players would be found to have MRPs below the value of their grant-in-aid. To begin to create a real labor market for student-athletes would create too many invidious distinctions, administrative headaches, and tax burdens. The only sensible modifications to the present policy are described in steps 2 and 9 above.

Title IX is also moving in the right direction. Strides in women's sports have been enormous and gender equity continues to advance. This is as it should be. Wherever possible, more resources should be assigned to promote the goals of Title IX. The naysayers, who complain that women's sports don't generate revenue as men's football and basketball do and, hence, should receive fewer resources, cannot have their cake and eat it too. If college sports continue to adhere to the amateur model (and benefit from not paying athletes, the panoply of tax exemptions described in chapter 6, and the antitrust privileges described in chapters 5 and 8), then it should not matter if one sport produces net revenue and another does not. All that should matter is that the sport is contributing to the well-rounded development of the student body.

The naysayers should also pay closer attention to the experience of women's sports. Some teams are beginning to generate net revenue and the quality of play is improving rapidly as the Title IX generation reaches college age. The commercial viability of women's sports is adumbrated by the early success of professional women's basketball.

It is abundantly apparent that intercollegiate athletics cannot stand still. Even NCAA Executive Director Cedric Dempsey acknowledges that the Association is in flux and must accept dynamic change if it is to survive. College presidents, faculty, students, and politicians need to repudiate piecemeal and superficial reform and embrace a commitment to thoughtful and profound structural transformation.

A reform movement is necessarily more than a series of steps that gets rationally implemented by well-meaning individuals. Rather, reform entails political analysis and coalition building. Some schools and educational leaders will be more receptive than others, depending on the structural and economic circumstances of their schools' athletic program as well as on the preferences of the individuals involved. My intention here has not been to plot out the political strategy for a reform movement, but rather to point out the reasons reform is needed, what type of reform makes sense, and to which constituencies reform might be appealing.

The NCAA and college sports are now in a period of legal turmoil and rapid economic change. This is the right time to implement far-reaching change. Change can happen at the hands of public officials or the often capricious decisions of the court system, or it can happen under the auspices of university academic officers engaging in considered, long-range planning. One way or another, change will happen.

The foregoing reform plan will no doubt appear too radical to some and too mild to others. To be sure, the obstacles to serious reform are formidable. Like any package of serious reforms that strike at the basic incentives of the system, it will be resisted by a large number of Division I schools. This resistance might crystallize into a secessionist movement, much like the CFA of the early 1980s. Seceding from the NCAA, however, is risky for university athletic programs for the following reasons: *(a)* they may lose the legitimacy gained by being perceived as amateur and congruent with the academic program; *(b)* they may lose legal challenges about whether their athletes are employees entitled to workmen's compensation coverage; *(c)* they may be more vulnerable to antitrust complaints; and *(d)* they may lose their tax-exempt privileges. These risks should give reformers ample latitude, particularly if the changes are prepared properly and cohesively. If a few dozen big-time schools still choose to secede, then so be it. The remaining nine hundred colleges can carry on, perhaps more modestly, but they will also be more faithful to the amateur vision and the educational mission.

Preface

1. These numbers refer to the share of the 1990–91 entering class which graduated within six years and are taken from the NCAA's *1997 NCAA Division I Graduation-Rates Report*, Overland Park, Kansas, June 1997.

2. These GPA scores are averages for the players from the entering classes of 1993/94 through 1996/97; data, ibid.

3. These data refer to averages for entering classes for the years 1993/94 through 1996/97. A complementary explanation for the lower SAT scores for basketball and football players at Stanford is that there is probably a much higher proportion of ethnic minorities among them. As a private California school, Stanford is still able to practice affirmative action. Some schools are known to de-emphasize standardized test scores and rely more heavily on high school grades and letters of recommendation for minority students as part of their affirmative action effort. Robert Kinnally, the Dean of Admission and Financial Aid at Stanford, would not confirm or deny the existence of such a policy. He did, however, point out that the Stanford statement of admission criteria explicitly states that "the Department of Athletics may designate outstanding athletes for special attention."

Chapter One

Epigraph: Hutchins is quoted in Richard Sheehan, *Keeping Score: The Economics of Big Time Sports*, South Bend, Indiana: Diamond Communications, 1996.

1. *Chronicle of Higher Education*, December 20, 1996, p. A35.

2. Jim Naughton, "Debate Over Championship Game in Football Reflects Larger Tensions in College Sports," *Chronicle of Higher Education*, September 19, 1997.

3. Welch Suggs, "A Different Final Four to Win," *Kansas City Star*, March 11, 1997, p. D1.

4. Mike McGraw et al., *Money Games: Inside the NCAA*, reprint from the *Kansas City Star*, 1997, p. 6.

5. Ibid., p. 2. In the summer of 1998 the NCAA issued new rules that limit the amount Final Four host cities can spend to $500,000. In March 1998 San Antonio had a budget of $1.2 million for hosting the Final Four. The apparent reason behind this limit is to help protect the investment of the NCAA's national corporate sponsor. The more local money spent, the more local sponsorship is needed and the more the national sponsor's presence is diluted.

6. Presumably, college sports also produce consumer surplus. Even though college sporting events employ price discrimination through ticket pricing and premiums (e.g., booster contributions), there are likely tens of thousands, if not millions, of fans who derive more utility from attending these events than it

costs them to attend the events. This consumer surplus, of course, also enhances welfare.

7. Steve Rushin, "Inside the Moat," *Sports Illustrated*, March 3, 1997, p. 82.

8. Hal Sears, "The Moral Threat of Intercollegiate Sports," *Journal of Sport History*, vol. 19, no. 3 (winter 1992).

9. Eric Leifer, *Making the Majors: The Transformation of Team Sports in America*, Cambridge: Harvard University Press, 1995, p. 39.

10. Robert Brown, "Revenue Sharing and Economic Incentives...," Ph.D. Dissertation. Walter Byers, *Unsportsmanlike Conduct: Exploiting College Athletes*, Ann Arbor: University of Michigan Press, 1995, p. 38.

11. Athur Fleisher, Brian Goff, and Robert Tollison, *The NCAA: A Study in Cartel Behavior*, Chicago: University of Chicago Press, 1992, p. 45.

12. *Intercollegiate Sports*. Hearings Before the Subcommittee on Commerce, Consumer Protection, and Competitiveness of the Committee on Energy and Commerce. House of Representatives. 102d Congress, 1st Session. Washington, D.C.: USGPO, 1992, p. 105.

13. Francis Dealy, *Win at Any Cost*, p. 68.

14. Brian Porto, "Completing the Revolution: Title IX as Catalyst for an Alternative Model of College Sports," *Seton Hall Journal of Sport Law*, vol. 8, no. 2, 1998, p. 398n.

15. Frank Deford, "A Critical Look at Sports in America," *Academe*, January–February 1991.

16. Cited in Sears, "Moral Threat of Intercollegiate Sports," p. 218.

17. The fatality figures were originally reported in the *Boston Globe* and cited in Dealy, *Win at Any Cost*, pp. 67–68.

18. Lawrence Debrock and Wallace Hendricks, "Setting Rules in the NCAA Cartel," in Wallace Hendricks, ed., *Advances in the Economics of Sport*, Greenwich, Connecticut: JAI Press, 1997, p. 182.

19. More precisely, it was the Intercollegiate Athletic Association of the United States that was formed in 1905. This association changed its name to the National Collegiate Athletic Association in 1910.

20. John Thelin, *Games Colleges Play: Scandal and Reform in Intercollegiate Athletics*, Baltimore: Johns Hopkins University Press, 1994, p. 26.

21. An interesting review of this period can be found in Paul R. Lawrence, *Unsportsmanlike Conduct: The National Collegiate Athletic Association and the Business of College Football*, New York: Praeger, 1987.

22. There is a fascinating discussion of the depiction of college sports in celluloid and in the media in Murray Sperber's *Onward to Victory*, New York: Henry Holt, 1998.

23. Ibid., p. 42.

24. With many of the stronger players drafted for the war effort, coaches complained that those remaining to play football were not talented enough to play both defense and offense. This problem together with free substitution rules led to the gradual introduction of two-platoon (different players for offense and defense) football beginning in 1942. See Sperber, 1998, p. 112 and chap. 26.

25. Quoted in ibid., p. 168.

26. Ibid, p. 169.

27. For an excellent discussion of the atmosphere of college sports and their changing perception in society, see Sperber, 1998.

28. Parts of the Code were eliminated in 1951, but were reinstated along with other modifications over time. See Lawrence, 1987.

29. Cited in Byers, pp. 56–67.

30. Sperber, 1998, p. 340. Judge Streit's views are reinforced by the conclusion of a report to the Governor of Kentucky in 1947 by a prestigious Chicago consulting firm, Griffenhagan Associates: "[At the University of Kentucky] it is impossible to put football and basketball in its proper place in university education because some of the alumni, fans, and sports writers demand winning teams with such force that their demands cannot be resisted. . . . Athletics in the University of Kentucky, as in many other universities, has become professionalized, though it is still considered to be amateur. As such, athletics has no worthy place in a university. The University of Kentucky and many other state universities, as soon as possible, should return intercollegiate athletics to its amateur standing." Quoted in Sperber, 1998, p. 330.

31. Daniel Fulks, *Revenues and Expenses of Intercollegiate Athletics Programs*, Overland Park, Kansas: NCAA, August 1994, pp. 13–18.

32. Robert Brown, "An Estimate of the Rent Generated by a Premium College Football Player," *Economic Inquiry*, vol. 31, October 1993, pp. 671–84.

33. The average Division IA men's football had reported revenues of $4.34 million in 1989 and $6.44 million in 1995 (an increase of 48.4%) while the average men's basketball team had reported revenues of $1.64 million in 1989 and $2.5 million in 1995 (an increase of 52.4%). Unreported revenues, such as off-budget contributions to the coaches' incomes from sneaker companies and booster groups, have skyrocketed since the 1980s. Daniel Fulks, *Revenues and Expenses of Intercollegiate Athletics Programs: Financial Trends and Relationships, 1995*, Overland Park, Kansas: NCAA, 1996.

34. Robert Brown, "Measuring Cartel Rents in the College Basketball Player Recruitment Market," *Applied Economics*, January 1994, pp. 27–34.

35. There is a large literature on the transgressions and excesses in college sports. Some of the more interesting treatments are: Murray Sperber, *College Sports, Inc.*, New York: Henry Holt, 1991; James Michener, *Sports in America*, New York: Random House, 1976, esp. chap. 7; John Thelin, *Games Colleges Play*, Baltimore: Johns Hopkins University Press, 1994; Tom McMillen with Paul Coggins, *Out of Bounds*, New York: Simon & Schuster, 1992; Don Yaeger, *Undue Process: The NCAA's Unjustice for All*, Champaign, Illinois: Sagamore, 1991; Francis Dealy, *Win at Any Cost: The Sell Out of College Athletics*, New York: Birch Lane, 1990; Gary Shaw, *Meat on the Hoof: The Hidden World of Texas Football*, New York: St. Martin's Press, 1972; David Whitford, *A Payroll to Meet: A Story of Greed, Corruption, and Football at SMU*, New York: Macmillan, 1989; Rick Telander, *The Hundred Yard Lie: The Corruption of College Football and What We Can Do to Stop It*, New York: Simon & Schuster, 1989; and Peter Golenbock, *Personal Fouls*, New York: Penguin Books, 1989.

36. *Intercollegiate Sports.* Hearings Before the Subcommittee on Commerce, Consumer Protection, and Competitiveness of the Committee on

Energy and Commerce. House of Representatives. 102d Congress, 1st Session. Washington, D.C.: USGPO, 1992, p. 83.

37. NCAA, *1997 NCAA Division I Graduation-Rates Report*, Overland Park, Kansas: NCAA, June 1997, p. 626. These percentages refer to the four-class average for the entering classes between 1987–88 and 1990–91.

38. Robert Simon, "Intercollegiate Athletics: Do They Belong on Campus?" in Judith Andre and David James, *Rethinking College Athletics*, Philadelphia: Temple University Press, 1991, p. 44.

39. Some schools are beginning to offer full scholarship rides to high school valedictorians and other top students, but this practice is still not nearly as prevalent or extensive as athletic grants-in-aid. See Michael McPherson and Morton Schapiro, *The Student Aid Game*, Princeton: Princeton University Press, 1998.

40. Cited in Sperber, 1998, p. 506.

41. Thelin, p. 115. Statement was made in February 1951.

42. A 1997 CBS News poll of 1,037 adults found that 47 percent believed sports in college were overemphasized and among college graduates 62 percent thought so. Porto, "Completing the Revolution," p. 394.

43. *Intercollegiate Sports*. Hearings, House of Representatives, p. 9.

44. Women's Sports Foundation, *Women's Sports Facts*, East Meadow, N.Y., 1995, p. 1.

45. This result is from a 1998 study of a nationally representative sample of 11,000 students in grades 9 through 12. It found that female athletes of this age cohort were less likely to have sex and more likely to use contraceptives. Women's Sports Foundation, "Sport and Teen Pregnancy" East Meadow, N.Y.

46. Norma Cantu, Assistant Secretary of Civil Rights, U.S. Department of Education, Statement before the Subcommittee on Consumer Affairs, Foreign Commerce and Tourism, Committee on Commerce, Science and Transportation, U.S. Senate, October 18, 1995, p. 4.

47. Ibid., p. 2.

Chapter Two

Epigraphs: Tom McMillen quote is from his *Out of Bounds*; Popular Amusements Committee Report, in *Kansas Annual Conference of the Methodist Episcopal Church, Official Minutes of the Thirty-ninth Session*, Abilene, Kansas, March 7–12, 1894; Edwin Locke, n.d. Cited in Hal Sears, "The Moral Threat of Intercollegiate Sports, *Journal of Sport History*, vol. 19, no. 3 (winter 1992).

1. The graduation rates refer to the entering class of 1990–91. The data are from *1997 NCAA Division I Graduation-Rates Report*, Overland Park, Kansas: NCAA, 1997.

2. The NCAA measures graduation rates over six-year periods from the time of each entering class. As we shall see, graduation rates is a rather deficient measure of academic achievement. *1997 NCAA Division I Graduation-Rates Report*, Overland Park, Kansas: NCAA, 1997.

3. The story of Kenny Blakeney is taken from Gene Wojciechowski, "College Basketball: How Two Athletes Survive," *Los Angeles Times*, March 31, 1995, p. C1.

4. Walter Byers, *Unsportsmanlike Conduct: Exploiting College Athletes*, Ann Arbor: University of Michigan Press, 1995, p. 367. This refers to Krzyzewski's salary in the mid-1990s.

5. Information on Chad Wright comes from "Athletic Notes," in *Chronicle of Higher Education*, November 8, 1996, p. A40.

6. The pre-1973 era which allowed four-year guaranteed scholarships often did not function any better. In *Meat on the Hoof: The Hidden World of Texas Football*, New York: St. Martin's Press, 1972, former University of Texas football player Gary Shaw tells some chilling stories about how UT coaches ran the weaker players off the team. In the late 1960s, the Southwest Conference allowed two hundred football scholarships per team. Large numbers of players were given scholarships but did not make the first or second teams. UT coaches put these players through a draconian boot camp experience in practice (called "shit drills" by Shaw), often resulting in serious injuries, and the coaches did not allow these players to travel with the team. At the same time, these weaker players were denied access to the athletic department's special tutoring services. Actually, in 1967, the NCAA passed legislation that allowed schools to revoke grants of players who broke team discipline.

7. Steve Rushin, "Inside the Moat," *Sports Illustrated*, March 3, 1997, p. 73.

8. Ibid.

9. *Intercollegiate Sports.* Hearings Before the Subcommittee on Commerce, Consumer Protection, and Competitiveness of the Committee on Energy and Commerce. House of Representatives. 102d Congress, 1st Session, Washington, D.C.: USGPO, 1992, p. 193.

10. Alexander Wolff and Armen Keteyian, *Raw Recruits*, New York: Pocket Books, 1990, p. 268.

11. Byers, *Unsportsmanlike Conduct*, p. 346.

12. Goldie Blumenstyk, "NCAA Director Says Colleges Should Rethink Rules on Amateurism," *Chronicle of Higher Education*, June 21, 1996, p. A31.

13. Gary Becker, "College Athletes Should Get Paid What They're Worth," *Business Week*, September 30, 1995, p. 18.

14. The Atlantic Coast and Big Ten Conferences had adopted similar athletic aid standards a few years earlier.

15. Dealy, *Win at Any Cost*, p. 118.

16. Thelin, *Games Colleges Play*, pp. 53–54.

17. Thelin, p. 132. Apparently, McElhenny used these words in self-description. He also said about his final year in college: "As things now stand, I've got three cars, $30,000 (worth around $270,000 in 1998 dollars) in the bank, the promise of a lifetime job from four companies, and two professional teams are paying my way through school. Also a wealthy guy puts big bucks under my pillow every time I score a touchdown. Hell, I can't afford to graduate." Quoted in Sperber, 1998, p. 467.

18. Byers, pp. 56–57.

19. See Sperber, 1998, chaps. 30–34.

20. General violations of the Code were rampant during this time. In the words of legendary baseball executive Branch Rickey speaking at the January 1948 NCAA Convention: "There is not a professional [sports] club which does

not have written evidence and, in quantity, that the colleges have 'professionally' induced boys to enter [to play sports for them]—boys, too, who are kept in college on such terms that we . . . define as professionalism. Such men are just as much professional . . . as if they were on our [pro team] payrolls, but frequently with the added feature that neither the boys nor the college admit it. Surely, it is not part of the educational process to create or permit hypocrisy." Cited in Sperber, 1998, p. 231.

21. For a lucid exposition of this discussion within the NCAA, see Sperber, 1998, chaps. 23–24.

22. Byers, *Unsportsmanlike Conduct*, p. 28.

23. Dealy, *Win at Any Cost*, pp. 170–73.

24. Byers, chap. 2. See also Dealy, p. 174.

25. Sperber, 1998, p. 203.

26. *Chronicle of Higher Education*, March 7, 1990, p. A37.

27. Dealy, *Win at Any Cost*, p. 175.

28. Kenneth Shropshire, *Agents of Opportunity*, Philadelphia: University of Pennsylvania Press, 1992, p. 1.

29. The survey was sent out to 3,500 active and retired NFL players. Only 1,182 responded, suggesting that these percentages may be understated. See discussion in ibid., pp. 62–65. Another view is provided in Don Heinrich's 1988 publication *College Football*, called by Murray Sperber "the most authoritative annual guide." Heinrich divides cheating into three categories: (1) those programs that make outright illegal payments to players (estimated to be 15–25% of Division IA schools); (2) those programs that will assure a students physical and social comfort (about 65%); and (3) those programs that will occasionally bend a rule (15–20%). Cited in Sperber, 1998, p. 245. Sperber also states that Bobby Knight estimates that 50 percent of Division I schools cheat in basketball.

30. *Chronicle of Higher Education*, August 1, 1997, p. A34.

31. Ibid.

32. CBS Sportsline USA, internet service at www.sportsline.com, May 31, 1997.

33. *Chronicle of Higher Education*, July 18, 1997, p. A35.

34. T. McMillen, *Out of Bounds*, p. 108.

35. Ibid., p. 63.

36. Quoted in Shropshire, *Agents of Opportunity*, p. 38.

37. Ibid. See also Tom McMillen, *Out of Bounds*.

38. David Armstrong and Daniel Golden, "Many Saw Dollar Signs in Camby's Rising Star," *Boston Globe*, June 30, 1996, p. 10.

39. "Agent: Camby Got More Money," Associated Press, July 11, 1996 (no byline).

40. The number of high schoolers who declared themselves eligible for the NBA draft jumped from one in 1995 to three (including Kobe Bryant) in 1996.

41. Alan Gutmann, in A. James, p. 26.

42. Michael Lufrano, "The NCAA's Involvement in Setting Academic Standards: Legality and Desirability," *Seton Hall Journal of Sport Law*, vol. 4, no. 1 (1994), p. 98.

43. The 700 SAT score corresponds to a 68 ACT score. Further, with SAT

recentering, the 700 score became 820 in April 1995. Unless otherwise indicated, score references in the text are to the pre-1995 standard.

44. The NCAA approved somewhat substantial criteria for satisfactory progress in 1992: 25 percent of degree requirements had to be completed by the beginning of a student's third year, 50 percent by the beginning of the fourth year, and 75 percent by the beginning of the fifth year. These criteria, however, are sufficiently lax that they seldom come into play.

45. A. Fleisher et al., *The NCAA: A Study in Cartel Behavior*, Chicago: University of Chicago Press, 1992, p. 132.

46. In 1994, a 270 on math denoted a raw score of 0 out of a possible 60, and a 200 on English denoted a raw score of 0 out of a possible 78. The College Board, *Handbook for the SAT Program*, 1995, p. 26.

47. Byers, p. 305.

48. Frederick Klein, "Student Athlete Raises Questions About Education," *Wall Street Journal*, October 10, 1997, p. B11.

49. McGraw et al., *Money Games: Inside the NCAA*, p. 21.

50. This is what Tyrone Foster, basketball star at U. of Oklahoma during 1995–96, did at the Coffeyville Community College in Kansas. Ibid.

51. Thompson applied for this concession in 1996, but sensible interventions from Georgetown president Father Leo O'Donovan dissuaded him. Nor did the NCAA look favorably upon the prospect of Thompson becoming partners with Michael Gaughan, a casino owner and bookmaker. Gaughan was also the father of Bendan Gaughan, a walk-on on Georgetown's basketball team. Partnership with Gaughan, who booked bets on college basketball games, was too much for the NCAA to abide. According to an article in *Washington Magazine*, "NCAA investigators say they were prepared to jump in with both feet. . . . The fact that one of Thompson's players is the son of a man who books bets on Georgetown was not something Thompson wanted to let simmer." Chuck Conconi, "Thompson Quits Gambling Deal," *Washington Magazine*, May 1996.

52. The number of scholarships in football fell to 85 and in men's basketball to 13 in 1994–95.

53. Cited in Byers, p. 314.

54. Alexander Wolff and Don Yaeger, "Credit Risk," *Sports Illustrated*, August 7, 1995, p. 55.

55. Quoted in Lufrano, "NCAA's Involvement," p. 103.

56. These averages are from 1989, but the numbers are very steady year to year. The average for Hispanics was 801.

57. *NCAA News*, December 6, 1996, p. 1.

58. Cited in Byers, p. 303.

59. *NCAA Research Report*. Report 91–07, Overland Park, Kansas, 1994. See also Reports 91–01 to 91–06.

60. The main reason that this percentage has fallen is that blacks were hard hit by the new core course requirements put in place for the 1995–96 academic years. This is discussed in the next section.

61. Richard Lapchick and Kevin Matthews, *1997 Racial Report Card*, Boston: Northeastern University's Center for the Study of Sport in Society, 1998.

62. Again, I refer here to the pre-1995 scale. On the new scale the standard is 2.0 GPA and 1010 combined SAT or 2.5 GPA and 820 SAT.

63. *NCAA News*, August 4, 1997, p. 5.

64. Eligibility data come from *NCAA News*, December 23, 1996, p. 16, and June 30, 1997, p. 2.

65. *NCAA News*, February 2, 1998, p. 1.

66. Jim Naughton, "Athletes Lack Grades and Test Scores of Other Students," *Chronicle of Higher Education*, July 25, 1997, p. A43. At Vanderbilt University it is estimated that up to 80 percent of the men's basketball and football players are special admits, yet the average SAT scores of Vanderbilt basketball players are 200 points above those at Duke. David Climer, "Vandy Athletics Searching Its Soul," *The Tennessean*, October 22, 1995, p. 1A.

67. Porto, "Completing the Revolution," p. 390.

68. Ibid.

69. See the fascinating exposé on Southeastern Bible College: Wolff and Yaeger, "Credit Risk."

70. Cf. *Chronicle of Higher Education*, June 19, 1998, p. A42.

71. See, for instance, Sperber, Dealy, and McMillen.

72. Rick Reilly, "Class Struggle at Ohio State," *Sports Illustrated*, August 31, 1998, p. 156. Austin Murphy, "Kataclysm," *Sports Illustrated*, August 31, 1998. For an interesting anecdote about another Ohio State football player who received special treatment, see John Thelin and Lawrence Wiseman, "The Numbers Game: The Statistical Heritage in Intercollegiate Athletics," in B. Mallette and R. Howard, eds., *Monitoring and Assessing Intercollegiate Athletics*, San Francisco: Jossey-Bass, 1992.

73. *Economist*, March 30, 1996, p. 22.

74. This list of distinction includes: Georgetown, Iowa, Marquette, Louisville, UConn, Kansas, Iowa State, Syracuse, and Cincinnati. The graduation rate is for members of the basketball team entering college in 1989–90. Since the number of players on a basketball team from any given year might vary from, say, one to five, these percentages are not statistically robust. The NCAA uses a six-year graduation rate, and students who transfer and later graduate from another school are not counted in their original school's tally.

75. McGraw et al., *Money Games*, p. 22.

76. *USA Today*, January 8, 1998, p. 2B.

77. See Jim Naughton, "At Oregon State U., Athletes Graduate but Don't Win Many Games," *Chronicle of Higher Education*, February 7, 1997, p. A43.

78. McGraw et al., *Money Games*, p. 22. See also "Former Athletics Director at OSU Turns Cowboy," *Chronicle of Higher Education*, September 19, 1997.

79. These percentages refer both to the class entering in academic year 1991–92 as well as to the average of that class and the three preceding classes. See *1998 NCAA Division I Graduation-Rates Report*, Overland Park, Kansas: NCAA, November 1998.

80. In the entering class of 1990, for instance, the average GPA for men's basketball was 2.79 and for football it was 2.77, while the unweighted average for the other sports was 3.12. The average combined SAT for men's basketball

was 922 and for football it was 933, while the average for the other sports was 999.

81. Quoted in Frederick Klein, "Stay in School? Why? NBA Money Looks Too Good," *Wall Street Journal*, May 10, 1996, p. B7.

82. Cited in Sperber, p. 203.

83. Bailey and Littleton, 1991, p. 55.

84. See Frederick Klein, "Looking Back, Ex-Lineman Takes College Sports to Task," *Wall Street Journal*, September 25, 1995, p. W5.

85. *Chronicle of Higher Education*, July 12, 1996, p. A38. In another interesting case, Peggy Wroten, a psychology instructor at Northeast Mississippi Community College, sued her school for pressuring her to give basketball star Dontae Jones (drafted by the New York Knicks in 1996) a higher grade and then trying to fire her for making the matter public. Jones was taking summer school classes at this community college in order to transfer credits to become eligible for an athletic scholarship at Mississippi State. Mike Waller, "Professor Sues 2-Year College Over Changes to Athlete's Grade," *Chronicle of Higher Education*, May 2, 1997, p. A46.

86. Mike Waller, "Texas Tech Tightens Academic Rules for Athletes," *Chronicle of Higher Education*, March 7, 1997, p. A42.

87. Simon, in A. James, p. 53.

88. James Thelin, *Games Colleges Play: Scandal and Reform in Intercollegiate Athletics*, Baltimore: Johns Hopkins University Press, 1994, p. 180.

89. Opinion piece from the *Orlando Sentinel* reprinted in the *NCAA News*, June 23, 1997. The U.S. Department of Education reports that 25 to 30 percent of high school senior football and basketball players leave high school functionally illiterate. See McMillen, *Out of Bounds*, p. 79.

90. See, for instance, Roger Noll, "Economic Perspectives on the Athlete's Body," *Stanford Humanities Review*, fall 1998.

91. Two Division I conferences, the Ivy League and the Patriot League, have eschewed overt athletic scholarships. These conferences, at least nominally, claim to make only small concessions in admissions criteria for athletes. In practice, the schools in these conferences suffer from many of the same athletic maladies as those in the big-time conferences—the main difference being in degree, not kind. Further, in December 1996, the Patriot League, under pressure from Holy Cross, decided to reintroduce athletic scholarships. The competitive pressure from other conferences and the perceived need to retain a lucrative television contract stimulated this decision. As we shall see in later chapters, the economics of this move will not necessarily pay off for the conference.

92. D. Fulks, op. cit., 1998, p. 10.

93. This is equal to $25,000 divided by $(1 - .4605)$, where .4605 is the marginal tax rate. A family in this top bracket would not pay social security taxes on their marginal income, although they would pay 1.45 percent for FICA/medicare. So the marginal tax rate is 39.6 percent plus 5 percent plus 1.45 percent, or 46.05 percent. In 1998–99, however, the IRS began taxing part of the grant.

94. The degree completion fund is for former college athletes whose initial grant-in-aid has expired and want to return to college to obtain their degree. The fund has averaged annual expenditures of approximately $400,000.

95. Byers, p. 236.

96. The NCAA also found the University of Miami guilty of paying athletes $412,000 above the permitted allowance to live off campus during 1990–94. *Chronicle of Higher Education*, December 15, 1995.

97. *NCAA Register*, October 6, 1997, p. 11.

98. Welch Suggs, "Few Use Revised NCAA Rule," *Sports Business Journal*, September 28–October 4, 1998, pp. 1, 47.

99. In *Meat on the Hoof*, former University of Texas football player Gary Shaw relates that the head of academic support in the late 1960s himself had flunked out of UT his first time around and would explain to players that he figured out all the shortcuts in order to finally get his degree. The same academic support officer refused to give help to the less talented football players (p. 59).

100. Communication from Fred Stroock, director of academic support for athletes at USC, July 11, 1997.

101. Email communication from Bob Bradley, September 16, 1997, head of the academic tutoring for athletes program at the University of Kentucky.

102. Sperber (1998, p. 363) refers to Southern Methodist University as having a plush athletic dorm in 1951.

103. Alexander Wolff, "Upstairs, Downstairs," *Sports Illustrated*, October 14, 1991, p. 54.

104. Cited in Sears, "Moral Threat of Intercollegiate Sports," p. 218.

105. Quoted in Sperber, 1998, p. 18.

106. The evidence for such gains is reviewed in Ernest Pascarella and Patrick Terenzini, *How College Affects Students*, San Francisco: Jossey-Bass, 1991. The authors cite studies that support differential improvements in leadership and interpersonal skills among college athletes, but they also cite studies that reach the opposite conclusion. Further, they conclude that most of these studies do not sufficiently control for related factors (see especially pp. 151–52 and 477–78). See also discussion in text below under Psychosocial Detriments.

107. Danny Robbins, "It's Tapes 22, Auburn 0," *Los Angeles Times*, October 26, 1991, p. C1.

108. For a nice discussion of other examples of agent tampering and its legal interpretation, see Ricardo Bascuas, "Cheaters, Not Criminals: Antitrust Invalidation of Statutes Outlawing Sports Agent Recruitment of Student Athletes," *Yale Law Journal*, vol. 105, April 1996.

109. Joe Drape, "ND Halo Loses Some Glow After Recent Revelations," *New York Times*, August 14, 1998. For other Notre Dame transgressions, see Don Yaeger and Douglas Looney, *Under the Tarnished Dome: How Notre Dame Betrayed Its Ideals for Football Glory*, New York: Simon & Schuster, 1993.

110. See the excellent and thorough treatment of how Nike and other athletic shoe companies establish recruiting networks that affect junior and senior high school prospects in Wolff and Keteyian's *Raw Recruits*.

111. See the interesting discussion of his personal experience being recruited as a high school student by over 300 schools, in McMillen, *Out of Bounds*, chap. 2. McMillen's mother's recollection of that experience was quite vivid (p. 43): "It was a miserable, miserable time in my life. We were a peaceful, close family till your recruiting. It caused members of our family to take sides, and we had never done that before."

112. Quoted in Sperber, p. 309. Typical disregard for student-athletes' academic commitments was shown by the University of Wisconsin in rescheduling their last game of the 1993 season against Michigan State. Instead of playing in Madison, Wisconsin, on December 3, the university accepted an offer from Japanese sponsors to play the game in Tokyo. Not only was this a bad choice for students needing to complete the last weeks of the semester, but it backfired financially. See Rick Telander, *From Red Ink to Red Roses*, New York: Simon & Schuster, 1994, p. 295.

113. The 1993 study is A. Astin, *What Matters in College*, San Francisco: Jossey-Bass, 1993. The 1995 study is E. Pascarella et al., "Intercollegiate Athletic Participation and Freshman-Year Cognitive Outcomes," *Journal of Higher Education*, vol. 66, no. 4 (July/August 1995). Pascarella et al. suggest that the differences they observed for first-year students would actually grow larger over the four years of college.

114. Cited in Sperber, 1998, p. 506. Sperber, who is conducting his own research on the impact of college sports on college life, writes that the situation has only gotten worse in the 1990s. Sperber (p. 507) goes on to suggest another reason for this cynicism when he quotes an administrator from a Sun Belt university, who explained: "We certainly can't give our students a quality degree—not with class size growing geometrically and our 30-to-1 faculty/student ratio—but at least we can encourage students to have fun, and identify with our teams while they're here. . . . Football Saturdays are great here, and so are winter basketball nights. In our Admissions Office literature, we've stopped saying that we provide a good education—our lawyers warned us that we could get sued for misrepresentation—but we sure promote our college sports teams." See also Ted Gup, "Losses Surpass Victories, by Far, in Big-Time College Sports," *Chronicle of Higher Education*, December 18, 1998.

115. These cases are taken from Jeffrey Benedict, "Colleges Must Act Firmly When Scholarship Athletes Break Laws," *Chronicle of Higher Education*, May 9, 1977, p. B6.

116. *Chronicle of Higher Education*, July 25, 1997, p. A43.

117. Jack Cavenaugh, "Two Football Players Dismissed After Assault on Frat," *New York Times*, October 18, 1996.

118. *Chronicle of Higher Education*, November 29, 1996, p. A44.

119. Drape, "ND Halo Loses Some Glow."

120. Charlie Taylor, former standout end for the Washington Redskins, recounts his days at Arizona State: "In Spring training my sophomore year, I broke my neck—four vertebrae. 'Hey, coach,' I said, 'my neck don't feel good.' 'There's nothing wrong with your neck, you jackass,' he said. So the numb went away a little, and I made a tackle. When I went to get up, my body got up but my head just stayed there, right on the ground. The coach says, 'Hey, get this jackass off the field.' So the trainer put some ice on my neck and after practice they took me up to the infirmary for an X-ray. The doctor said, 'Son, your neck is broken. You got here ten minutes later, you'd be dead.' Dead! Man, that scared me. I mean those colleges let you lie right out there on the field and die. That's something to think about." Quoted in Shaw, op. cit., p. 130.

121. Joe Drape, "NCAA Ignores the Negatives, But Gambling Problem Begs for a Solution," *Sports Business Journal*, December 14–20, 1998, p. 11.

122. *Chronicle of Higher Education*, July 25, 1997, p. A45.

123. Kim Strosnider, "Boston College Football Team Is Embroiled in Scandal Over Gambling," *Chronicle of Higher Education*, November 16, 1996.

124. Mike Waller, "2 Probes of Alleged Point Shaving Roil College Basketball," *Chronicle of Higher Education*, March 21, 1997, p. A54. Jim Naughton, "Why Athletes Are Vulnerable to Gambling," *Chronicle of Higher Education*, April 17, 1998.

125. Pam Bulluck, "Two Former Northwestern Basketball Players Indicted for Fixing Games," *New York Times*, March 27, 1998; Jim Naughton and Jeffrey Selingo, "A Point-Shaving Scandal Rattles Northwestern U.," *Chronicle of Higher Education*, April 10, 1998; Ira Berkow, "A Player Caught in Gambling's Grip," *New York Times*, April 20, 1998.

126. The FBI was also looking into charges of player gambling at the University of Colorado. ESPN SportsZone, August 28, 1998.

127. Michael Cross and Ann Vollano, "The Extent and Nature of Gambling among College Student Athletes," unpublished ms., University of Michigan, October 1998.

128. *Chronicle of Higher Education*, November 22, 1996, p. A37.

129. Cross and Vollano, "The Extent and Nature of Gambling among College Student Athletes." To be sure, the gambling phenomenon extends throughout our whole society: gross wagering in the legal Nevada sports books grew from $0.4 billion in 1982 to $2.6 billion in 1995. *NCAA News*, February 3, 1997, p. 2.

130. Todd Crosset et al., "Male Student-Athletes and Violence Against Women," *Violence Against Women*, vol. 2, no. 2 (June 1996). See also Kim Strosnider, "Virginia Tech Player Convicted of Assault in Brawl," *Chronicle of Higher Education*, July 25, 1997, p. A45.

131. Jim Naughton, "Alcohol Abuse by Athletes Poses a Big Problem in Colleges," *Chronicle of Higher Education*, September 9, 1996, p. A47.

132. *Chronicle of Higher Education*, November 22, 1996, p. A37.

133. McMillen, *Out of Bounds*, p. 170. The interviewer asked each player what percentage of his opponents in his opinion used steroids. Dealy (p. 45) claims that while NCAA does drug testing, it is announced ahead of time, and cocaine and amphetamine users could abstain for a day and test negative.

134. The percent increased from approximately 0.25 percent in 1991–92 to approximately 1.7 percent in 1995–96, as reported in a chart in the *NCAA News*, June 23, 1997.

135. American Institutes for Research, *Report No. 1: Summary Results from the 1987–88 National Study of Intercollegiate Athletics*. Palo Alto, California, November 1988.

136. Joe Roberson, "Is It Student-Athlete or Athlete-Student?" *NCAA News*, September 16, 1996, p. 4.

137. He uses out-of-state tuition and fee charges for public schools. This is a compromise between using the economic return to a college degree and in-state tuition.

138. The recent experience at Southern Illinois University is not uncommon. Students at this school in 1996–97 paid $116 a year in athletic fees. In

May 1997 the administration decided to raise the fee gradually up to $276 per year. Both the undergraduate and graduate student body governments voted overwhelmingly against it. Following several angry meetings between students and administrators, the matter was referred to a study committee. *Chronicle of Higher Education*, June 13, 1997, p. A40. More striking still, in 1997–98 University of Illinois students were asked to vote whether they should be charged $34 every semester to cover debt service on Memorial Stadium. They voted 8 to 1 against the fee. The fee was imposed anyway. Fred Girard, "Big Ten Athletics Gobble up Profits," *The Detroit News*, November 11, 1998.

139. *Chronicle of Higher Education*, August 2, 1996.

140. See Pascarella and Terenzini, *How College Affects Students*, p. 478.

141. Not only do the Division I football and basketball players earn a decent implicit wage, according to a study by the U.S. Department of Education, as a group they appear to do relatively well economically in the first decade of their working lives, whether or not they have obtained a college degree. "[Basketball and football players] experienced less unemployment between ages 25 and 32, earned incomes above the mean for all students who attended four-year colleges, and owned homes at a higher rate (77%) than any other group of students." Clifford Adelman, *Light and Shadows for College Education*, Washington, D.C.: USGPO, 1990, pp. 301–2.

142. James Long and Steven Caudill, "The Impact of Participation in Intercollegiate Athletics on Income and Graduation," *Review of Economics and Statistics*, vol. 73, no. 3 (1991), pp. 525–31.

Chapter Three

Epigraphs: de Coubertin is quoted in Mahoney, "Taking a Shot at the Title," *Connecticut Law Review*, vol. 27, no. 3 (spring 1995); Byers is quoted in his *Unsportsmanlike Conduct: Exploiting College Athletes*, Ann Arbor: University of Michigan Press, 1995.

1. The stories of Jennifer Baldwin Cook and Amy Cohen are culled from a variety of journalistic sources and interviews. A major source is *Intercollegiate Sports (Part 2)*. Hearings Before the Subcommittee on Commerce, Consumer Protection, and Competitiveness of the Committee on Energy and Commerce, U.S. House of Representatives, 103d Congress, 1st Session, Washington, D.C.: USGPO, June 23 and August 4, 1993, written statements of Jennifer Baldwin Cook and Amy Cohen.

2. Ibid., p. 14.

3. The academic year 1970–71 is cited as 1971, that of 1972–73 as 1973, and so on, throughout the text.

4. NCAA, *Gender Equity Study: Summary of Results*, Overland Park, Kansas: NCAA, 1997.

5. McGraw et al., *Money Games: Inside the NCAA*, p. 17.

6. The history of the AIAW is discussed in Linda Jean Carpenter and R. Vivian Acosta, "Back to the Future," *Academe*, January–February 1991.

7. The actual number of head coaching jobs for women's teams increased by 209 between 1993–94 and 1995–96, but the number of these jobs held by

women decreased by 9 to 3,138. In 1995–96 there were 1,003 more head coaching jobs of women's teams than in 1985–86; of these, 333 jobs went to women and 670 went to men. R. Vivian Acosta and Linda Jean Carpenter, "Women in Intercollegiate Sport: A Longitudinal Study—Nineteen Year Update," Department of Physical Education, Brooklyn College, Brooklyn, N.Y., 1996, p. 7.

8. Ibid., p. 11. In 1996–97, of the 305 Division I schools, 17 had female athletic directors, and of the 111 Division I-A schools, 6 had female athletic directors, the latter being up from 1 in 1991–92. See "Female College Ads Slowly Making Their Marks," *USA Today*, October 2, 1996.

9. 802 F. Supp. 737 (N.D.N.Y. 1992).

10. Janet Judge et al., "Gender Equity in the 1990s: An Athletic Administrator's Survival Guide to Title IX and Gender Equity Compliance," *Seton Hall Journal of Sport Law*, vol. 5, no. 1, 1995, pp. 333–34.

11. Favia v. Indiana Univ. of Pa., 812 Supp. 578 (W.D. Pa. 1993).

12. See, for instance, Steven Rattner, "Ivy and Red Tape," *New York Times*, January 28, 1995, p. 19.

13. See, for one, J. Weistart, "Equal Opportunity: Title IX and Intercollegiate Sports," *Brookings Review*, vol. 16, no. 4, 1998.

14. NCAA, *Participation Statistics Report, 1982–95*, p. 124.

15. *NCAA News*, September 30, 1996, p. 2.

16. Ibid., February 19, 1996, p. 7.

17. The April 1997 NCAA *Gender Equity Study* reported that in 1995–96 women were 53 percent of the student body and 36.5 percent of the athletes, suggesting an increase of 1.2 percentage points between the academic years 1994–95 and 1995–96. It should be cautioned, however, that the survey instrument was different in the two cases and that the response rate for the gender equity study was only 82.3 percent.

18. *USA Today*, November 7, 1995, p. 4C.

19. The scholarship limit for Division IA football since 1994–95 is 85. The average squad size in 1994–95 for all Division IA football was 112 (NCAA, *Participation Statistics Report, 1982–95*, p. 116).

20. Ibid., p. 117. The University of Massachusetts reports that 235 students showed up for the organizational meeting of women's crew in 1995–96: a further affirmation of strong interest among female athletes. David Scott, "Women's Crew Rules," *Massachusetts*, vol. 7, no. 4 (summer 1996), p. 26.

21. In large part because of the tendency to redshirt most freshman in football but not in basketball, football players in Division I have had a higher graduation rate (by 3 to 5 percentage points) than basketball players.

22. McGraw et al., *Money Games*, p. 17.

23. For 1995–96, the total number of grants-in-aid to men and women averaged 276 per school in Division IA, 185 in Division IAA, and 148 in Division IAAA. Assuming the proportion of full grants was the same among men and women and that the number of grants was the same as the previous year, during 1994–95, in Division IA schools there were an average of 91 women receiving an average grant of $9,340, in Division IAA schools there were an average of 64.4 women receiving an average grant of $6,724, and in Division IAAA there were an average of 71.8 women receiving an average grant of $6,560.

24. The Office of Civil Rights refers to July 1998 interpretation of substantial proportionality as a "clarification" consistent with previous policy, but many ADs argue that it is a new standard. Stanford AD Ted Leland estimates that it will cost his school an additional $2 million yearly to comply with this standard. See Welch Suggs, "Title IX: Total Compliance Still Elusive," *Sports Business Journal*, September 7–13, 1998, p. 26.

25. NCAA, *Gender Equity Report*, April 1997, p. 14.

26. Ibid. The comparative spending data for 1996–97 are given in the table below.

	IA Men	IA Women	IAA Men	IAA Women	IAAA Men	IAAA Women
Per-athlete						
Spending	$27,000	$17,000	$10,000	$9,000	$11,000	$11,000
Scholarships	$1.83 m	$1.056 m	$0.945 m	$0.586 m	$0.624 m	$0.64 m
Coaching						
Salaries	$1.66 m	$0.74 m	$0.586 m	$0.291 m	$0.355 m	$0.269 m
Recruiting	$0.29 m	$0.10 m	$0.080 m	$0.035 m	$0.050 m	$0.032 m

Source: Welch Suggs, "Only NCAA's Star Schools Turn Profits," *Sports Business Journal*, October 19–25, 1998, p. 5.

Note: m = million.

27. Of course, some student-athletes may find employment off campus, especially through boosters. In the latter case, there will be a major enforcement problem, trying to ensure that the $2,000 does not become a stipend for fictitious work.

28. A small part of this gain is attributable to the fact that for the first time in 1996–97 NCAA schools were permitted to count the women's attendance as part of a doubleheader with men, as long as the fan count was taken by halftime of the women's game.

29. See, for instance, *NCAA News*, April 20, 1998, p. 7.

30. The league had projected an average attendance of 4,000 fans a game before its inaugural season began and then modified the projection upward to 6,500 midway through the season. In an assessment of the WNBA just after the midpoint of the first year, a *New York Times* piece reported: "The new women's league . . . has taken off like a rocket, exceeding twofold even the most optimistic predictions. Attendance across the eight-team league is averaging nearly 9,000." Jane Gross, "Girls Gleefully Claim a League of Their Own," *New York Times*, August 4, 1997. The league finished its first year with an average attendance of 9,669 during the regular season, attracting more than a million fans overall. Tarik El-Bashir, "WNBA Surpasses Its Goals," *New York Times*, September 1, 1997. Cited in D. Mahoney, "Taking a Shot at the Title," *Connecticut Law Review*, vol. 27, no. 3 (spring 1995).

31. Already, there is a sharp increase in corporate sponsorships of women's sports which rose from $285 million in 1992 to $600 million in 1997. See Ellen Zavian, "Sports Marketing Is Becoming Less and Less Gender Specific," *Sports Business Journal*, April 27–May 3, 1998.

32. A study of 15,000 predominantly female athletes completed in 1998 finds that women's sports are beginning to promote the same unhealthy values

and undesirable behavior as men's sports. Cited in espnet.sportszone.com, March 10, 1998. NCAA infractions by women's programs are also appearing with increasing frequency. In one recent incident the star pitcher of the 1995 national champion UCLA softball team returned home to Australia without taking her final exams and without earning any academic credit.

33. In December 1997 the National Coalition for Athletics Equity was formed as a lobbying group to fight the proportionality standard of Title IX.

34. *Chronicle of Higher Education*, October 17, 1997.

Chapter Four

Epigraphs: Marcum is quoted in M. Sperber, *College Sports, Inc.*; Olson is quoted in McGraw et al., *Money Games: Inside the NCAA*; Dodds is quoted in R. Bryce, "UT Big Wheels' Perks Outweigh Staff's Paychecks," *Austin Chronicle*, April 24, 1998; Jones is quoted in S. Fatsis and J. Weinbach, "College Football: Sis, Boom, Blah," *Wall Street Journal*, Nov. 20, 1998, as is Sanders.

1. This section on Marianne Crawford (Stanley) relies on discussions with Marianne Stanley, on Ann Killion, "For What She's Worth," *San Jose Mercury West*, November 24, 1996, and on Jane Gottesman, "An Odyssey of Championships and Hardships," *New York Times*, November 19, 1995.

2. Raveling, like other big-time college basketball coaches, earns several times more in auxiliary income than he does in base salary. Contracts with sneaker companies often bring in several hundred thousand dollars annually. Local television and radio shows, which are heavily subsidized by local boosters who pay advertising spot rates disproportionate to the low ratings, can generate tens of thousands of additional dollars. Summer camps, with free use of college facilities, can bring upwards of $30,000. Motivational speaking engagements can produce several hundred thousand dollars. College-financed mortgages, free use of cars, country club membership, extravagant severance pay, team performance bonuses, and other perks can be worth in excess of $100,000. Most, if not all, of this income is arranged through the university and is part of the compensation package bestowed upon a coach.

3. Richard Sandomir, "Raveling Happy to Leave Coaching," *New York Times*, March 7, 1995, p. B13.

4. The starting center had a dislocated shoulder and basically was playing with one arm. Other starters were also injured or altogether unavailable.

5. Frank Litsky, "Former Brooklyn Coach Wins Damages in Sex Bias Suit," *New York Times*, July 10, 1998.

6. This information on Conradt and UT is from Robert Bryce, "Is Rick Barnes Worth Three Jody Conradts?" *Austin Chronicle*, September 18, 1998.

7. Ibid.

8. Cited in Byers, *Unsportsmanlike Conduct: Exploiting College Athletes*, Ann Arbor: University of Michigan Press, 1995, p. 9.

9. This percentage is up from 51.5 percent recorded in the 1992 survey. The 1997 survey was conducted for the 1995–96 season. The 1992 survey was conducted for the 1990–91 season. At the Division IA level, 98 of 106 schools responded. The combined average salaries for the assistant coaches on the men's

team was $95,855 and $46,060 for the women's team during 1990–91 and $95,040 and $62,530, respectively, during 1995–96.

10. See, for instance, Dave Anderson's column in the paper on May 31, 1996, p. B9. See also Byers, *Unsportsmanlike Conduct*, for information on compensation of other coaches. Steve Spurrier was reportedly offered a multiyear contract in football worth $2 million annually at the University of Florida to commence with the 1997–98 academic year.

11. Sperber, *College Sports, Inc.*, p. 174, cites the following cases of extravagant severance packages to coaches who left their posts after being implicated in NCAA violations: Mike White of the University of Illinois, $300,000; Barry Switzer of the University of Oklahoma, $225,000; Jackie Sherrill of Texas A&M, $684,000 and a house; and, Danny Ford of Clemson, $1.1 million-plus. Separately, Robert Frank and Philip Cook in *The Winner Take-All Society* (New York: The Free Press, 1995, p. 80) report a $500,000 severance payment for Paul Hackett, football coach at the University of Pittsburgh, and a $600,000 payment for Jack Crowe, football coach at the University of Arkansas.

12. Unless otherwise indicated, the sources for these data on coach compensation are *USA Today*, November 21, 1997, p. 4C, and McGraw et al., *Money Games*, p. 7.

13. Bryce, "UT Big Wheels' Perks."

14. Ibid.

15. Anecdotes to support this doubt are plentiful. For instance, John Weistart, professor of law at Duke University, writes in the fall 1998 issue of the *Brookings Review* ("Equal Opportunity: Title IX and Intercollegiate Sports," vol. 16, no. 4, p. 39): "Bear Bryant, the legendary coach of the powerful University of Alabama football teams of the 1960s, 1970s, and 1980s, is remembered in faculty circles for his quick assessment of how athletics and academics should be ordered in higher education. In response to questions about how the athletic department could justify its independence from the usual regime of academic deliberations, Mr. Bryant offered that it was unlikely that 50,000 people would show up to watch an English professor give a final exam."

16. John Feinstein, *A March to Madness: The View from the Floor in the Atlantic Coast Conference*, New York: Little, Brown, 1998, p. 36.

17. McGraw et al., *Money Games*, p. 7.

18. Ibid.

19. *Chronicle of Higher Education*, June 5, 1998.

20. Sperber, *College Sports, Inc.*, p. 174.

21. *Ann Arbor News*, October 13, 1997.

22. The story of the UMass basketball team's meteoric rise is told engagingly and insightfully by Marty Dobrow in *Going Bigtime: The Spectacular Rise of UMASS Basketball*, Northampton, Massachusetts: Somerset Press, 1996. Among other things, Dobrow suggests that both Calipari and Pitino, as ambitious assistant coaches at the Universities of Pittsburgh, Kansas, and Hawaii, were not loathe to bend recruiting rules.

23. These figures do not include student fees of $526,019 and do not deduct the penalty levied by the NCAA due to Marcus Camby's ineligibility. They do however include gifts.

24. Pat Riley's 1995 multimillion deal in Miami and John Calipari's 1996 deal in New Jersey are part of a recent upward trend in coaches' salaries in the NBA. Both Riley and Calipari serve as de facto general managers as well as head coaches. Phil Jackson's one-year, multimillion-dollar deal with the Chicago Bulls for 1996 is a third case of this magnitude, but Jackson's circumstance also is unique because he appears to be a complementary factor of production to superstar Michael Jordan. To be sure, the NBA salary cap seems to permit coaches to capture some of the revenue generated by players. For the 1998-99 NBA season, twelve coaches had contracts of more than $2.8 million.

25. D. Fulks, *Revenues and Expenses of Division I and II Intercollegiate Athletics Programs, 1995, 1997*, Overland Park, Kansas: NCAA, 1996, 1998, pp. 15–16.

26. The literature on the relationship between product market competition or lack thereof and wages concludes that concentration and regulation establish permissive conditions for higher wages, which are then realized when other factors, such as strong unions, are present. (See, for instance, Wallace Hendricks, "Regulation and Labor Earnings," *Bell Journal of Economics* [autumn 1977]; D. Card, "Deregulation and Labor Earnings in the Airline Industry," unpublished manuscript, Department of Economics, Princeton University, 1996.) Similarly, where employers are not attempting to maximize profits, the compulsion to pay workers according to the value of their output is diminished. In each of the latter two cases, it is easier for noneconomic factors to enter into the determination of a worker's wage or salary.

27. Hallock, based on data from 700 major U.S. corporations and nearly 10,000 directors, identified cronyism between CEOs and directors as a significant factor in raising executive pay. After controlling for other determinants of compensation, Hallock finds that interlocks between executives and directors of two companies increased executive remuneration by 17 percent. Although such corporations face competition in their product markets, agency problems allow for buffering and cronyism to ratchet up pay. Kevin Hallock, "Reciprocally Interlocking Boards of Directors and Executive Compensation," unpublished manuscript, Department of Economics and Institute of Labor and Industrial Relations, University of Illinois-Champaign, May 1996.

28. See, for instance, John Rofe, "Commissioners' Top Priority: Marketing," *Sports Business Journal*, October 5–11, 1998, p. 25. See also Byers, *Unsportsmanlike Conduct*, pp. 365–73.

29. Fleisher et al., *The NCAA: A Study in Cartel Behavior*, Chicago: University of Chicago Press, 1992, p. 91, write, "Should coaches be paid only a competitive wage, they would become less likely to advocate cartel stability and more likely to oppose the redistribution of rents from players."

30. There are certain conditions under which this would not be so, such as persistent racist behavior by the fans.

31. This argument, of course, was originally formalized by Gary Becker in his book, *The Economics of Discrimination*, Chicago: University of Chicago Press, 1956.

32. One might sensibly ask whether professors of philosophy, chemistry, and other fields are not subject to the same favorable conditions. In fact, the circum-

stances are quite different. Professors operate within controls placed by and watched over by specific administrative business officers who do not benefit when professors' pay rises. Further, the absence of competitive market pressures in a profit-maximizing environment does not necessarily mean that salaries are bid up: it could just as well mean the opposite, depending on the culture and bargaining power of the two sides.

33. Daniel Fulks, *Revenues and Expenses of Intercollegiate Athletics Programs: Financial Trends and Relationships—1993*, Overland Park, Kansas: NCAA, August 1994, p. 15.

34. Some might argue that NBA and Division I coaches are in the same market because there are no barriers or other market restraints to separate them. By this reckoning, high school coaches are also in the same market. In fact, the markets are quite different. College coaches do recruiting, deal with academic issues, NCAA rules, a distinct culture, and the teams generate 1/20 the revenue of NBA teams. The fact that the markets are different, of course, does not mean that they are impermeable.

35. See Welch Suggs, "Athletic Directors Finally Being Treated Like the Campus CEOs They Are," *Sports Business Journal*, October 5–11, 1998, p. 24.

36. Bryce, "UT Big Wheels' Perks." Documents obtained by the *Austin Chronicle* indicated that between September 1990 and November 1991 athletic department personnel spent more than $21,000 on golf outings, food, and drink at the Barton Creek Country Club.

37. One sports economist who has used this approach is Gerald Scully in his book, *The Business of Major League Baseball*, University of Chicago Press, 1989, chap. 10. Scully purports to measure the baseball manager's ability to convert team player talent into team victories. The manager's efficiency in doing this determines the number of wins the manager contributes to team performance which, in turn, determines his value to the team. Through regression analysis, Scully estimates that in 1987 each additional win was worth about $244,000 to a franchise, and on this basis he estimates that Earl Weaver was worth $2.6 million to the Orioles in that year.

38. Arguably, of course, if the coach had the right ties in the business community, he could obtain a more remunerative job. Further, since most college coaches presumably have college degrees, the more appropriate comparison might be to males with bachelor's degrees. In 1993, the median earnings for such males aged 35–44 was $43,199 (Daniel Hecker, "Earnings of College Graduates, 1993," *Monthly Labor Review*, December 1995, pp. 3–17). In any event, even at $40–50,000 the reservation wage is well below the compensation levels being received by Division I head coaches of men's basketball.

39. I arrived at this estimate as follows. An NCAA men's basketball team that went from mediocrity to the Final Four might experience a revenue increase as high as $2 to $4 million, depending on the arena it played in, the concessions arrangement, the revenue-sharing practices of its conference, and licensing and sponsorship deals. The odds that an average coach could accomplish this might be roughly 1 in 75 (4 chances out of 305 Division I schools), while those for an excellent coach might be 1 in 30, yielding expected revenue growth of between $13,333 and $26,666 for an average coach and between $33,333 and $66,666

for an excellent coach. Add to this the average revenue gain from making it to the NCAA tournament multiplied by the odds of making it, and subtract the expected revenue loss from a possible downward drift in team performance. I estimate that the combined expected effect on total team revenues from these two latter eventualities is $19,124 for an average and $47,810 for an excellent coach. The total mathematical expectation of team revenue gains, then, varies from $32,457 to $45,790 for an average coach and from $81,143 to $114,476 for an excellent coach. Now, assume that half of this gain is attributable to the coach, the rest owing to the school's reputation, recruitment and promotional efforts, assistant coaches, training and playing facilities, etc. This produces an expected marginal revenue product range for an average Division I men's basketball coach of $16,229 to $22,895, and for an excellent Division I men's basketball coach of $40,572 to $57,238. Even assigning success odds that were twice as high and assuming that three-fourths of the team revenue growth was attributable solely to the head coach, the estimated marginal revenue product range for excellent Division I men's basketball coaches would be $121,716 to $171,714. This estimate is elaborated upon in greater detail in Andrew Zimbalist, "Gender Equity and the Economics of College Sports," in Wallace Hendricks, ed., *Advances in the Economics of Sports*, vol. 2, Greenwich, Connecticut: JAI Press, 1997.

40. Robert Brown, "Measuring Cartel Rents in the College Basketball Player Recruitment Market," *Applied Economics*, January 1994, pp. 27–34. Brown also employs a two-stage, least squares procedure to estimate the marginal revenue product of a premium Division IA college player. Also see his "An Estimate of the Rent Generated by a Premium College Football Player," *Economic Inquiry*, vol. 31, October 1993, pp. 671–84.

41. Here there is an interesting analogy to the historical regulation of the U.S. airline industry where, prior to 1978, the Civil Aeronautics Board set passenger fares and cargo rates and restricted entry. Unable to compete over prices, airlines competed instead over flight frequency, amenities, and advertising. See, for instance, Card, "Deregulation and Labor Earnings in the Airline Industry."

42. To the extent that Division I athletic departments resemble labor-managed firms, one would expect to see abnormally high compensation for the top executives.

43. See Jeffrey Selingo and Jim Naughton, "New Federal Guidelines Seek to Define Pay Equity for Men's and Women's Coaches," *Chronicle of Higher Education*, November 14, 1997.

44. The total compensation package for the male basketball coach at Tennessee, Kevin O'Neill, in 1996–97 was an estimated $475,000. Tom Kensler, "Coach at Summit in Money," *Denver Post*, March 21, 1997, p. C1.

Chapter Five

Epigraphs: Statement of Gary Roberts, before the Antitrust, Business Rights and Competition Committee of the Senate Judiciary Committee, May 22, 1997; Cavanaugh is quoted in Murray Sperber, *Onward to Victory*, 1998.

1. Ronald A. Smith, "Television, Antitrust Law, and the Conflict Between

Home Rule and a National NCAA Policy, 1939–1994," unpublished ms., Penn State University, 1994. Much of the discussion in this section relies on Smith's treatment. Other important sources are: Walter Byers, *Unsportsmanlike Conduct: Exploiting College Athletes*; Paul Lawrence, *Unsportsmanlike Conduct: The National Collegiate Athletic Association and the Business of College Football*, New York: Praeger, 1987; Jack Falla, *NCAA: The Voice of College Sports*, Mission, Kansas: NCAA, 1981; David Klatell and Marcus Norman, *Sports for Sale: Television, Money and the Fans*, New York: Oxford University Press, 1988; John Thelin, *Games Colleges Play: Scandal and Reform in Intercollegiate Athletics*, Baltimore: Johns Hopkins University Press, 1994; and Ronald Smith, *Sports and Freedom: The Rise of Big-Time College Athletics*, New York: Oxford University Press, 1988.

2. Smith, 1994, p. 14.

3. Sperber, 1998, pp. 82–86. Consistent with its amateur policy, Notre Dame also abjured participation in postseason bowl games and stood firmly against special scholarships or other payments to athletes.

4. The September 30, 1939, game between Waynesburg State and Fordham ended in a lopsided 34–7 victory for Fordham. See Keith Dunnavant, *The Forty-Year Seduction*, Newnan, Georgia: Solovox Publishing, 1997, chap. 1.

5. In its June 1984 decision in NCAA v. Board of Regents of the University of Oklahoma et al., the U.S. Supreme Court reports that the University of Pennsylvania actually televised its first game in 1938, and that at the time there were six television sets in all of Philadelphia.

6. The National Football League was already persuaded that TV had a deleterious impact on gate revenues and announced a ban on televising of its games for the 1949 season.

7. Ibid., pp. 23–24.

8. Sperber, 1998, chaps. 39–40.

9. Smith, 1994, p. 40.

10. Sperber, 1998, p. 402.

11. For an interesting discussion of Walter Byers's key and idiosyncratic role in developing the NCAA television policy, see Dunnavant, 1997, especially chaps. 5 and 6.

12. Smith, 1994, pp. 41–43.

13. Byers, p. 90; Lawrence, p. 99; Smith, 1994, p. 59.

14. Smith, 1994, p. 78.

15. Byers (p. 277) maintains that Switzer meant to say "$50 a month."

16. Ibid.

17. The portion of the rights fee retained by the participating school varied, depending on conference revenue sharing rules.

18. The NCAA TV contract was signed with CBS and ABC in July 1981 and covered the next four years. It provided for teams playing in a nationally televised game to receive $500,000 each in 1982, rising to $750,000 in 1983, and for teams playing in a regionally televised game to receive $350,000, rising to $400,000 in 1985. The contract with Turner provided for an additional $17.5 million in revenues over the four-year period. Lawrence, *Unsportsmanlike Conduct*, p. 103.

19. Before the Supreme Court the NCAA lawyers chose to emphasize another line of defense; namely, NCAA football was not a separate market from NFL football or, for that matter, other TV programming. Hence, there was ample competition, and the NCAA TV package did not represent an unreasonable restraint of trade. See, for one, Dunnavant, 1997, chaps. 12 and 13.

20. Supreme Court of the United States, NCAA v. Board of Regents of the University of Oklahoma et al., June 27, 1984.

21. This result is consistent with economic theory. The monopolist produces to the left of the point of unitary elasticity on the demand curve. The competitive industry may produce to the right of the point of unitary elasticity, especially if marginal costs rise slowly. The only significant marginal cost to the colleges from broadcasting an extra game is the possibility that gate attendance will be hurt. These costs are presumably sufficiently low that the competitive industry may produce further to the right of unitary elasticity than the monopoly was to the left of this point (assuming the total revenue curve has a zero second derivative with respect to output, i.e., a linear marginal revenue curve). If this is the case, then total revenues may be lower for the competitive industry.

In addition to the revenues from post-1984 network contracts cited in the text, many schools and conferences entered into local and regional television deals. The number of televised contests, therefore, expanded appreciably. Rights fees from these local deals, however, were small and did not compensate for the network shortfall. Among others, see Dunnavant, 1997, chaps. 13 and 16.

22. Jim Hodges, "College Football Bowl Games," *Los Angeles Times*, December 31, 1995, p. C1, cites the $17.2 million figure, while the *Fresno Bee*, September 2, 1996, cites the $23 million sum. The *Chronicle of Higher Education*, December 15, 1995, reported that each Fiesta Bowl participant on January 2, 1996, should receive a payment of $13 million.

23. Interestingly, early on the bowl organizing committees claimed their purpose was to raise money for charity. Sperber (1998, p. 179) describes the situation in the late 1940s: "In reality, the bowls ran a huge financial shell game. The top tier—Rose, Sugar, Orange and Cotton—paid well, but almost all of the others kept most of the revenue or never made any. Furthermore, according to a *Colliers'* investigation, even though all of the bowls claimed that they 'are conducted for the benefit of local charities' . . . the [bowl] contributions to charities are inconsequential. Figures revealed that only $5,000, or .003 per cent of the gross receipts, had been donated to charity by 16 bowls in 1947."

24. Cited in Jim Naughton, "Debate over the Championship Game in Football Reflects Larger Tensions in College Sports," *Chronicle of Higher Education*, September 19, 1997.

25. Ibid.

26. These three conferences are: Big West, Western Athletic (WAC), and Mid-American.

27. Another WAC team, Wyoming, finished with an impressive 10–2 record and No. 22 ranking, and was also not afforded an opportunity to play in an Alliance bowl. One of Wyoming's two losses was to BYU in overtime.

28. The guaranteed minimum payout per team in each game of the Bowl Championship Series will be $12.5 million. "Equity" conferences (ACC, Big

East, SEC, Big Ten, Pac-10, and Big 12) that have teams in two Bowl Championship games will be guaranteed a minimum of $25 million, plus many will receive revenue from lesser bowl games. The guaranteed minimum total from all bowls for the SEC in 1998–99 is $26.65 million (the highest among Division IA conferences) and the guaranteed minimum for the Big West is only $750,000 (the lowest among Division IA conferences). See Welch Suggs, "Football Playoff: Don't Hold Your Breath," *Sports Business Journal*, September 7–13, 1998, pp. 24–25.

29. For 1997–98 the Big 12 Conference was offering a special two-game ticket package, including one seat each to its Dr. Pepper Big 12 Football Championship Game and the Builders Square Alamo Bowl, with a range of $55.50–$145.50, or $27.75–$72.75 per game.

30. Frederick Klein, "Gridiron Gridlock," *Wall Street Journal*, December 18, 1998, p. W10.

31. See, for instance, Tim Layden, "Going to a Football Bowl Game—Unless It's One of the Biggies—Makes Little Financial Sense for Most Schools," *Sports Illustrated*, December 26, 1994. See also Klein, "Gridiron Gridlock," p. W10.

32. The total number of postseason bowl games has grown over time from 12 in 1977–78, to 16 in 1986–87, to 18 in 1989–90, to 23 in 1998–99.

33. For example, it would be possible to have a team ranked number one in either the coaches' or the AP poll, or ranked number one in both polls, not to appear in the championship game. If such a team went on to win its bowl game, then there certainly would be widespread skepticism, if not disillusionment, about the crowning of a national champion. This reaction would only be compounded if this team won a lopsided victory while the "national champion" won in a close contest.

34. Others have offered similar estimates. See, for instance, Dunnavant, 1997, p. 187, who cites estimates of television revenues from a 16-team playoff at $200 million a year or more. This would provide $100 million more than is currently provided in rights fees from the Bowl Championship Series.

35. Unless otherwise noted, these and following numbers come from *Revenues and Expenses of Intercollegiate Athletic Programs*, a volume published periodically by the NCAA. The last volume was published in 1998 and the previous ones were published in 1996, 1993, 1990, 1986, 1982, 1978, and 1970. The latest two volumes were written by Daniel Fulks and all previous volumes were written by Mitchell Raiborn.

36. Data through 1985 were based on a slightly different classification of the top basketball schools, but the 1985 proportion under the old classification scheme (Class A) and under the new scheme (Division IA) was 15 percent in each case.

37. For a fuller discussion, see A. Fleischer et al., 1992, pp. 55–56.

38. John Helyar, "NCAA Basketball, Minus Stars, Proves It Still Has the Game," *Wall Street Journal*, March 14, 1997, p. B5.

39. Mike McGraw, Steven Rock, and Karen Dillon, "Revenues Dominate College Sports," *Kansas City Star*, October 5, 1997, p. 3. It is part of a special series entitled *Money Games: Inside the NCAA*, appearing October 5–11, 1997.

40. *Chronicle of Higher Education*, June 20, 1990.

41. The payoff from a single tournament game grew at roughly 6.2 percent annually from 1989 through 1997. Assuming that the payoff per game played continued to grow at 6.2 percent per year, that game would be worth $78,588 in 1997–98, $83,460 in 1998–99, $88,635 in 1999–2000, $94,130 in 2000–2001, and $99,967 in 2001–2002. If we take 6.2 percent to be a reasonable discount rate for a riskless asset, the present value of this income stream is equal to $444,000.

42. The coefficient of variation (a measure of the overall equality of distribution) remained virtually unchanged over this period (1.16 in 1991 and 1.15 in 1997). It did, however, drop slightly after the new distribution plan was introduced in 1991 (it was 1.23 in 1989). The spread, which was $4.67 million in 1989, also dropped.

43. In some cases, the conference sells a sports package to a network, including rights to televise football, men's and women's basketball, and other sports. For example, in July 1997, the Big Ten signed a ten-year deal with ABC and ESPN for over $500 million to begin in 1998. The payout per school will average approximately $4.6 million annually.

44. Camby was traded to the New York Knicks prior to the 1998–99 season.

45. Actually, UMass does better still due to the revenue sharing system within the Atlantic 10. In 1995–96, the Atlantic 10 rewarded $40,000 per institution in the first round of the tournament, $30,000 per institution in the second round, $20,000 in the third round, $20,000 in the regional final, and $50,000 in the final four. Thus, the total payment to UMass (since it made it to the final four) would have been $160,000, while the penalty forfeited to the NCAA was $8,383 less than this sum.

46. Quoted in the *New York Times*, April 1, 1990, p. S10.

47. Ibid., June 14, 1990, p. D27.

48. Through 1985, the NCAA published data according to a different classification of schools that included Class A through Class F institutions. Class A roughly corresponds to what today would be Divisions IA and IAA. The actual number of schools reporting over the 1962–1995 period in this group varies between 73 and 143. Through 1984 the NCAA reported only the mean and median school revenues for the various groups, for 1985 it reported the mean, median, and top school revenues, and after 1985 it reported only the mean and top school revenues. I linked the two series using the ratios of top/mean and median/mean for 1985. The series was also adjusted for the fact that prior to 1985 the universe of Class A institutions included 143 schools, while the universe of Division IA schools in 1995 included 110 schools. This adjustment was made by applying the ratio in 1985 of the top to average revenue for the Class A schools to the top to average revenue for the Division IA schools to the post-1985 figures. Further, since top revenue schools are more likely to receive revenue from unreported sources, the actual growth of revenue inequality over time is probably understated in the table. Finally, it should be pointed out that prior to 1985 the NCAA studies refer only to revenue from men's sports. This practice is unlikely to bias the distribution figures.

49. There are a number of ways to measure competitive balance. I refer here

to the ratio of the standard deviation of the win percentage to idealized standard deviation (if teams were of exactly even playing strength and the number of games played in each league were adjusted for). Results would be similar if a measure of championship concentration, excess tail frequency, or gini coefficients were used. See, for one, James Quirk and Rodney Fort, *Pay Dirt: The Business of Professional Team Sports*, Princeton: Princeton University Press, 1992, chap. 7.

50. For instance, a conference with 10 members might divide the conference tournament revenue into 13 shares with one share going to each school, one share going to the conference for administrative expenses, and two extra shares going to the school that participated in the tournament. See also Welch Suggs, "There Are a Lot of Fingers in the Bowl," *Sports Business Journal*, September 9–13, 1998, p. 21.

51. Article VI of the 1995–96 Atlantic 10 Conference Constitution and By-laws, p. 14.

52. Jim Hodges, "College Football Bowl Games," *Los Angeles Times*, December 31, 1995, p. C1.

53. Richard Sandomir, "Big Bowl Payouts Don't Always Offset Teams' Expenses," *New York Times*, December 30, 1997.

54. The equalization is measured by either a fall in the gini coefficient or in the standard deviation of win percentages. Fort and Quirk provide an empirical analysis of this phenomenon for the Big Ten and Pac-10 conferences. See R. Fort and J. Quirk, "Introducing a Competitive Environment into Professional Sports," in Wallace Hendricks, ed., *Advances in the Economics of Sport*, vol. 2, Greenwich, Connecticut: JAI Press, 1997.

Chapter Six

Epigraphs: Roberson is quoted in Jim Naughton, "The Travails of an Athletics Director Show the Many Tensions of the Job," *Chronicle of Higher Education*, October 17, 1997; Vaccaro is quoted in Sharon Fink et al., "A Battle for Heart and Sole," *St. Petersburg Times*, March 22, 1998.

1. Information on USC is from Peter Monaghan, "Fighting Over Seats," *Chronicle of Higher Education*, September 22, 1995, pp. A55–56. For a survey of ticket prices for Division IA football in 1998, see *Sports Business Journal*, September 28–October 4, 1998. The highest ticket price for an individual game seat is $50 for the Cal-Berkeley/Stanford game. The highest season ticket price is $250 at Nebraska, but to buy it one has to make a $1,000 donation.

2. Ibid.

3. Smith reportedly split the lion's share of his yearly stipend with his assistant coaches and staff and also allotted part of it to fund a scholarship. Jacalyn Carfagno, "Nike's Contract with Heels' Coach, School Is Public," *Lexington Herald Leader*, March 10, 1996, p. A15.

4. Communications with Marion Traub-Werner and Harvey Araton, "Students Protest Share Nike Athletes," *New York Times*, November 22, 1997.

5. The highest employee count I found was at the University of Texas where there are 130 athletic department staffers connected to men's sports and 76 staffers connected to women's sports, for a total of 206. (See Robert Bryce, "Is Rick

Barnes Worth Three Jody Conradts?" *Austin Chronicle*, September 18, 1998.)
The next highest employee count I found was 169 at the University of Virginia
athletic department, with the University of North Carolina close behind at 167.
Of course, these numbers include only those personnel on the employment roll
of athletics. There are others, such as building and grounds employees who
work on the athletic facilities or athletic dormitory personnel, who are hired
principally to service the athletic program but are not counted here.

6. The various provisions discussed here are found in the IRS Code in Sections 501, 511, and 512.

7. Quoted in Dennis Zimmerman, "Corporate Title Sponsorship Payments
to Nonprofit College Football Bowl Games: Should They Be Taxed?" Congressional Research Report for Congress, February 11, 1992, p. 6.

8. Cited in Zimmerman, ibid., p. 8.

9. It is nevertheless true that some individuals and most corporations claim
expenditures on arena and stadium tickets or luxury boxes as a business expense.
Since the 1986 Tax Reform Act, only 50 percent of such expenses has been
deemed tax-deductible.

10. NACUBO Report, 1993, and Survey of Division IA Athletic Directors.

11. Vice Chancellor for Legal and Executive Affairs, University of Wisconsin,
Potential NCAA Infractions: Self Report, March 19, 1998.

12. Administrators in the athletics department of Nebraska state that no such
practice exists.

13. Some booster activities are just plain goofy. Salyersville National Bank in
Lexington, Kentucky, offers a 12-month CD with a minimum $1,000 deposit
and a starting interest rate of 4.4 percent. For every touchdown the University
of Kentucky football team scores, the rate goes up 0.01 percentage point.

14. Thomas York, "Buck of the Month Adds to Millions," *Sports Business
Journal*, September 7–13, 1998, p. 20.

15. Roger Noll and Andrew Zimbalist, eds., *Sports, Jobs and Taxes: The Economic Impact of Sports Teams and Stadiums*, Washington, D.C.: Brookings Institution, 1997, p. 294.

16. Kenneth Lelen, "Kicking Off Luxury Boxes for Colleges," *Philadelphia
Inquirer*, July 12, 1993, p. E5. According to this source, at these 106 venues
there were 458 suites.

17. Bill Brubaker and Mark Asher, "A Building Boom in College Sports,"
Washington Post, November 3, 1998, p. A1.

18. Steve Traiman, "$2 Billion in New Construction in Midwest Sports Facilities," *Amusement Business*, June 1, 1998. According to Welch Suggs ("Facilities," *Sports Business Journal*, August 31–September 6, 1998, p. 15), Ohio
State signed up 16 corporate sponsors for the 1998–99 season at $75,000 to
$250,000 each.

19. Welch Suggs, "Ohio State Investing in Major Upgrades," *Sports Business
Journal*, September 7–13, 1998, p. 13.

20. Welch Suggs, "Colleges, Minor Leagues Won't Let Stadium Boom Lose
Momentum," *Sports Business Journal*, June 1–7, 1998, p. 17.

21. John Feinstein, *A March to Madness: The View from the Floor in the Atlantic Coast Conference*, Boston: Little, Brown, 1998, p. 261.

22. *Sports Business Journal*, June 15–21, 1998, p. 36.

23. Jerry Wizig, "Drexler's Hiring Paying Dividends at Ticket Window," *Houston Chronicle*, March 25, 1998, p. 4.

24. Alan Friedman, "Inside the Deal," *Sports Business Journal*, August 3–9, 1998, p. 9.

25. *Sports Business Journal*, August 10–16, 1998, p. 43.

26. "Schools Considering Corporate Name," Associated Press release, June 19, 1998.

27. Phil Axelrod, "Build a Gazillion-Dollar Gym," *Pittsburgh Post-Gazette*, February 15, 1998, p. D3.

28. Michigan was also number one in licensing revenues in 1997–98 at $5.8 million. *Sports Business Daily*, July 31, 1998.

29. For the 1997–98 academic year the top ten universities in logo sales in order were: Michigan, Kentucky, North Carolina, Penn State, Nebraska, Florida, Tennessee, Florida State, Alabama, and Wisconsin. The top ten apparel manufacturers of university logo products in order were: Nike, Starter, Nutmeg Mills, Champion Products, Gear for Sports, LogoAthletic, Pro Player, Jansport, Inc., T-Shirt International, and the Russell Corporation. The top ten non-apparel manufacturers of university logo products in order were: EA Sports, Mattel, Commem Brands, Sony, Jostens, Huffy Sports, Hunter Manufacturing Group, Deluxe Corporation, Licensed Lifestyles, Inc., and Wilson Sporting Goods. Data on licensing income come from: the Collegiate Licensing Company; Roger Thurow, "Go Team, Go: Win One for the Logo!" *Wall Street Journal*, November 22, 1996, p. B13; Goldie Blumenstyk, "Money-Making Champs," *Chronicle of Higher Education*, April 19, 1996; short pieces in the *Chronicle of Higher Education* on November 30, 1994, and March 22, 1996; Don Muret, "Has Collegiate Licensing Peaked?" *Amusement Business*, March 25, 1996; Jacalyn Carfagno, "Dressed to Sell," *Lexington Herald-Leader*, March 10, 1996; George Cantor, "Revenue Bonanza Will Hail the Victors of NCAA Tourney," *Detroit News*, March 30, 1997; John Bobel, "The Color of Money Is Blue," *Lane Report*, May 1996; Lee Barfknecht, "NU Athletics Removes Red from Budget," *Omaha World Herald*, October 8, 1995; Jon Marcus, "University Gains from Trademark, Technology," *Daily Hampshire Gazette*, September 9, 1996; and from individual school sources.

30. Data provided to the author by the Collegiate Licensing Company.

31. Some estimates go as high as $2.5 billion for gross retail sales, but the NCAA reports the figure at $2 billion (see, for instance, *NCAA News*, April 1, 1996, p. 2, and April 13, 1998, p. 2). Approximately 15 percent of this total is sold at local campus stores. Around 80 percent of all logo sales are for apparel.

32. Carfagno, "Dressed to Sell," p. A1.

33. The jersey was produced by the Authentic American Athletic Apparel Company.

34. Although the payment is described as a licensing fee, presumably part of the payment is also for marketing assistance from Converse for the production company.

35. In August 1998, Adidas outcompeted Reebok and signed a six-year, $18 million deal with UCLA which included cash, products, in-kind contributions,

and internships for students. Liz Mullen, "Adidas Ties Up UCLA Deal," *Sports Business Journal*, August 31–September 6, 1998, p. 10.

36. In one standout deal, University of Florida's Stever Spurrier will receive $900,000 a year from Nike as part of the company's five-year, $9 million contract with the school. *Sports Business Daily*, September 3, 1998.

37. Donald Katz, *Just Do It: The Nike Spirit in the Corporate World*, Holbrook, Massachusetts: Adams Pub. Co., 1994, p. 242.

38. The advertising figure comes from Bill Meyers, "Nike vs. Oakley: Swooshed," *USA Today*, December 12, 1997, p. 17C.

39. Sharon Fink et al., "A Battle for Heart and Sole," *St. Petersburg Times*, March 22, 1998.

40. The first "cattle-call" camps tied to shoe companies were set up by Chicago high school teacher Chick Shearer. He called them "AFBE" camps for Athletes for Better Education. Today's descendents are called "ABCD" camps, for Academic Betterment and Career Development. Communication from Alex Wolff, July 7, 1998.

41. Quoted in Alexander Wolff and Armen Keteyian, *Raw Recruits*, New York: Pocket Books, 1990, p. 2.

42. Quoted in Robert Lipsyte, "Basketball: If It's Gotta Be the Shoes, He's Gotta Be the Guy," *New York Times*, July 6, 1997. Vaccaro conveyed similar sentiments to me during an interview on June 24, 1998.

43. The recruitment network is also described and analyzed cogently by Wolff and Keteyian in *Raw Recruits*, op. cit.

44. At the 1998 Nike summer camp there were 209 boys. Rick Majerus, head coach of the University of Utah, who was at the camp looking for prospects, estimates that only 4 or 5 of them will ever go on to play one game in the NBA. The top 200 high school prospects generally spend an entire summer playing at camps and in leagues to display their talent to college coaches. See Karla Haworth, "The Pressure and Profits of Top Basketball Camps," *Chronicle of Higher Education*, August 7, 1998.

45. Quoted in Sharon Fink et al., "A Battle for Heart and Sole."

46. Ibid.

47. *Sports Business Journal*, June 15–21, 1998, p. 12.

48. These figures apply for the 1998–99 season. The salary continues to fall down to $535,600 for the 29th pick in the first round. *NBA Collective Bargaining Agreement*, September 1995, p. B-4.

49. Chris Carroll, "German Shoe Maker Is Helping Push Teenagers from Preps to Pros," *Sports Business Journal*, May 4–10, 1998. Interview with Sonny Vaccaro June 24, 1998.

50. The Garuda factory story is taken from Richard Read, "Nike's Code of Conduct Hasn't Eased Everyone's Lot," *The Oregonian*, June 14, 1998.

51. Richard Read, "Nike Trips: Asian Workers Take the Fall," *The Oregonian*, June 14, 1998.

52. Child labor in a Nike soccer ball factory in Pakistan was reported in *Life* magazine in May 1996. As of November 1997, Nike was still unable to give assurances that this factory does not employ child labor. Jeff Manning, "Nike Battles Back, But Activists Hold the High Ground," *The Oregonian*, November 10, 1997.

53. Jeff Manning, "Poverty's Legions Flock to Nike," *The Oregonian*, November 10, 1997. Manning describes a scene at the Dongguan factory in China which employs 65,000 workers: "The workers, mostly young women, stride in place in a vacant third-story room of a sun-bleached shoe factory. As instructed by their Chinese and Taiwanese supervisors, they chant: 'Loyalty to your boss, loyalty to your boss.' " The factory manager is a former Taiwanese infantry officer. See also Anita Chan, "Boot Camp at the Shoe Factory," *Washington Post*, November 3, 1996.

54. Richard Read, "Nike Trips."

55. Craig Smith and Craig Copetas, "For Adidas, China Could Prove Trouble," *Wall Street Journal*, June 26, 1998, p. A13.

56. Email communication to the author, June 24, 1998.

57. This is from page 7 of the draft.

58. Quoted in Jim Naughton, "Exclusive Deal with Reebok Brings U. of Wisconsin Millions of Dollars and Unexpected Criticism," *Chronicle of Higher Education*, September 6, 1996, p. A65.

59. Quoted in the *Sports Business Daily*, September 2, 1998.

60. Jim Naughton, "Colleges Eye Restrictions on Promotions by Brewing Companies," *Chronicle of Higher Education*, January 9, 1998.

61. Quoted in ibid.

62. Kay Hawes, "A Brewing Dilemma on Campus," *NCAA News*, April 6, 1998.

63. Bill Meyers, "Nike vs. Oakley: Swooshed," p. 17C.

64. Quoted in Jeff Manning, "Slump Speeds Slowdown of Spending on Athletes," *The Oregonian*, May 25, 1998.

65. *Chronicle of Higher Education*, March 22, 1996, p. A37.

66. Quoted in *Sports Business Daily*, August 19, 1998. In Reebok's second quarter, 1998 sales fell 11 percent and profits fell 70 percent.

67. Ellen Zavian, "Still a Few Steps Behind on Shoe Deals," *Sports Business Journal*, June 8–14, 1998, p. 16.

68. Manning, "Slump Speeds Slowdown," and Stefan Fatsis, "NBA's Problems Mount," *Wall Street Journal*, April 28, 1998, p. W9.

69. Sonny Vaccaro predicted to me that the average contract would fall by at least 50 percent for the June 1998 draftees. See also Josh Gotthelf, "Bargaining Table," *Sports Business Journal*, June 22–28, 1998. On Nike's problems in 1998, see Timothy Egan, "The Swoon of the Swoosh," *New York Times Magazine*, September 13, 1998.

70. David Pickle, "Corporate-Partner Program Enters New Era," *NCAA News*, February 23, 1998.

71. Steve Rushin, "Inside the Moat," *Sports Illustrated*, March 3, 1997, p. 74. See also Byers, *Unsportsmanlike Conduct*, p. 93.

Chapter Seven

Epigraphs: Byers is quoted in his *Unsportsmanlike Conduct*, as is Alexander's report.

1. Naturally, to assert that there are no entire programs that run surpluses is not to deny that individual sports may do so. In particular, there are a dozen or

so schools that have maintained top-level basketball programs (such as the University of Massachusetts, Temple, or the University of Connecticut), but have football teams playing in IAA or IAAA. When these basketball programs are having successful years, it is quite possible for them to generate surpluses up to one or two million dollars.

2. D. Fulk, *Revenues and Expenses, 1997*, p. 11.

3. Ibid., p. 20.

4. The most prominent adherents to this school are Fleisher, Goff, and Tollison (1992), and Lawrence (1987). See also Melvin Borland et al., "College Athletics: Financial Burden or Boon?" in *Advances in the Economics of Sports*, vol. 1, Greenwich, Connecticut: JAI Press, 1992, pp. 215–35.

5. The foremost exponent of this line of argument is Sperber (1991).

6. A similar public relations purpose is evident in *Sidelines*, the publication of the former College Football Association.

7. Quoted and discussed in Andrew Zimbalist, *Baseball and Billions*, New York: Basic Books, 1992, p. 62.

8. A clear sense of the extensive use and misuse of booster monies is provided in the University of Wisconsin's audit, *Potential NCAA Infractions: Self Report*, March 19, 1998.

9. Communication from Fred Stroock, director of athletic tutoring services at USC, July 11, 1997.

10. These irregularities and inconsistencies have been noted in various reports. See, for instance, NACUBO's 1993 publication *Managing an Intercollegiate Athletics Program* and the U.S. Department of Education Secretary's 1992 Report to Congress, *Revenues and Expenditures in Intercollegiate Athletics: The Feasibility of Collecting National Data by Sport.*

11. Douglas Lederman, "Arkansas Seeks to Learn How Much Colleges Really Spend on Sports," *Chronicle of Higher Education*, September 4, 1991.

12. These numbers are based on an AP story from May 19, 1997, and an interview with Ruth Yanka of the University of Massachusetts on May 21, 1997. In fact, of the $50 million cost to build the facility, $25 million was raised from a bond issue by the University of Massachusetts Building Authority and the other $25 million was a state appropriation. See also David Strupeck et al., "Financial Management at Georgia Tech," *Management Accounting*, February 1993, vol. 74, no. 8.

13. Debra Blum, "Trying to Reconcile Academics and Athletics," *Chronicle of Higher Education*, April 26, 1996, pp. A51–52. There is another possible angle to this calculus. If Vanderbilt dropped its Division I sports, its black student population would fall from around 4 percent to 2 percent. If the latter proportion was deemed to be unacceptably low, then a sizable share of the $3 million would have to be spent on financial aid for minority students. Of course, in this case those receiving financial aid would be receiving it based on academic, not athletic, merit.

14. To be sure, the university took more substantial measures at the same time which also helped to rescue the athletics program. Douglas Lederman, "University of Wisconsin Plots Strategy to End Overdependence on Football Revenues," *Chronicle of Higher Education*, March 14, 1990, pp. A41–42. See

also Rick Telander, *From Red Ink to Roses: The Turbulent Transformation of a Big Ten Program*, New York: Simon & Schuster, 1994. For other examples of similar practices, see Byers, op. cit., pp. 221–24.

15. Naturally, neither did the revenue appear in the budget, so there is only a net loss to the school if this money would otherwise have gone to the general fund.

16. Data are from the Big Ten Conference Athletic Operations Survey for 1994–95.

17. Cited in University of Massachusetts, *Final Report of the IA Task Force*, September 5, 1996, p. 45.

18. NACUBO, 1993, p. 18.

19. In his 1996 book, *Keeping Score: The Economics of Big-Time Sports*, Richard Sheehan estimates that only 41 Division IA schools make money in football, and, of these, 31 make more than $1 million.

20. See Peter Hughes, "Time to Tell the Whole Story," *NACUBO Business Officer*, May 1992. Hughes argues that overhead expenses should be allocated in proportion to the revenue generated by each sport and that such a procedure would generate a conservative estimate of the expense share incurred by the big-time sports.

21. Actually, in two of the three years the recorded medical expense for men's basketball was zero and in one year it was the paltry sum of $1,947.

22. The discrepancies for the other Big Ten schools were as follows:

	Big Ten Survey ($million)	EADA Survey ($million)
Purdue	5.14	5.01
Ohio State	7.27	2.97
Northwestern	5.98	3.95
Minnesota	4.65	2.77
Michigan State	6.46	3.16
Michigan	8.22	4.77
Iowa	5.54	2.67
Indiana	4.72	2.15
Illinois	5.90	3.65

In *Keeping Score*, Richard Sheehan reports that Notre Dame's athletic budget excludes "most of its television revenue from its football contract with NBC" (p. 263).

23. Gannett News Service, February 19, 1991.

24. Within Division IA overall, the standard deviation of athletic revenues increased from 5,534 in 1989, to 6,889 in 1993, and to 7,203 in 1995. By this measure, revenue inequality increased by 30.2 percent between 1989 and 1995. However, since the mean revenue grew more rapidly than the standard deviation, the coefficient of variation decreased from .57 to .47 over this period. (The NCAA provided the standard deviation measure for 1989, but the estimates for 1993 and 1995 were done by the author using the grouped data in the NCAA reports on revenues and expenses.)

25. *Los Angeles Times*, July 15, 1990. Also cited in Thelin, op. cit., p. 186. It is interesting to note in light of our discussion of the fungibility of financial performance that Byers reports Michigan ran a $0.7 million surplus in 1988–89 (op. cit. p. 224).

26. William Honan, "Costly Football Stadiums Bring Booms or Busts to Campuses," *New York Times*, December 26, 1997, p. A32. According to Michigan's 1997–98 EADA report, football revenue rose to $23.4 million in that year and football net income to $14.5 million.

27. Attendance for that game was a woeful 93,857. The Wolverines have led the nation in average attendance every year since 1974.

28. Valerie Reitman, "To My Beloved Football Tickets, I Sadly Bid a Fond Farewell," *Wall Street Journal*, September 17, 1997.

29. The Pac-10 and Big Ten schools never joined the CFA.

30. In addition to irregular accounting practices, the profit margins for many of the schools in 1995 must have been exiguous. According to the 1998 NCAA financial survey, only 60 percent of Division IA programs were profitable in 1997, including institutional subsidies. Without such subsidies, the share falls to 43 percent.

31. These data are from the *Division IA Athletic Directors' Association Financial Survey, 1995–96*, published in June 1997 by Pacey Economics in Boulder, Colorado.

32. That is, if investment income were reduced by the share of subsidies in total revenues, investment income would fall by 0.34 percentage points. This amount is added to the subsidy calculation.

33. Although the Coaches' survey does not explicitly state this, the 1996 figure for debt service in the Coaches' survey is just slightly above the 1995 figure for debt service in the NCAA study, and the NCAA figure only includes interest payments.

34. Arguably, some of the student fees (approximately one-half) go toward the purchase of free or reduced-price student tickets and should not be counted as subsidy. If half of the student fee was excluded, then the subsidy would become 13.84 percent of revenues and the average deficit without subsidy would be $1.65 million, instead of $2.08 million.

35. *Division IA Athletic Directors' Association Financial Survey, 1995–96*.

36. The top schools, as noted in the last chapter, may also earn one or two million dollars in licensing income each year, and this money is still often shared with the central university budget. The average Division IA school earns less than $200,000 from this source. To the extent that some of this money goes directly to the central university budget, rather than to athletics, the average deficit estimated in the text would be smaller.

37. *Sports Business Journal*, June 8–14, 1998, p. 41.

38. Mike Dodd, "Winning One for the Admissions Office," *USA Today*, July 11, 1997, p. 1A.

39. Jeffrey Selingo, "Institutions Gain Visibility, But Many Question the Expense and Fear the Impact on Academics," *Chronicle of Higher Education*, October 31, 1997.

40. Ibid.

41. Sally Huggins, "Why Division I?" *NCAA News*, September 22, 1997.

42. Cited in ibid., p. 27.

43. Debra Blum, "Faculty is Furious Over Six-fold Budget Increase for Athletics," *Chronicle of Higher Education*, February 16, 1996, p. A40.

44. There are a few exceptions to these rules, but they apply mostly to schools already in Division IA which are seeking to retain their status.

45. Greg Garber, "UCONN Upgrade Passes for Now," *Hartford Courant*, November 12, 1994.

46. University of Massachusetts, *Final Report of IA Task Forc*, p. 64.

47. Sheehan, op. cit., p. 269.

48. The two studies are Brooker and Klastorin, "To the Victors Belong the Spoils? College Athletics and Alumni Giving," *Social Science Quarterly*, vol. 62 (1981), pp. 744–50, and Paul Grimes and George Chressanthis, "Alumni Contributions to Academics: The Role of Intercollegiate Sports and NCAA Sanctions," *American Journal of Economics and Sociology*, vol. 53, no. 1 (January 1994). The first ran tests on 1,740 coefficients and found 1.7 percent of them to be significant at the 10 percent level. This is fewer than the number that would be expected by chance. Also, the authors do not report the magnitude of the impact. The second is based on data for only one school, Mississippi State University (MSU), over a 30-year period. As such, it is difficult to generalize about their results. They test whether winning percentages in football, basketball, and baseball had a significant impact on alumni contributions at MSU. Football and baseball each have t-statistics of 0.17, and the coefficient on football is negative. The coefficient on basketball has a t-statistic of 1.93, which with 21 degrees of freedom (eight independent variables in their model) is not significant at the .05 level with a two-tailed test. The authors inappropriately use a one-tail test, which in effect discards the possibility that athletic success can negatively impact on contributions. As explained in the text, there is as much reason to expect a positive as a negative effect.

49. For summaries of these studies, see James Frey, "The Winning-Team Myth," *Currents*, January 1985, and Judy Grace, "Good Sports? Three Studies Examine Athletic Fund-Raising Programs," *Currents*, July/August 1988.

50. Murray Sperber, 1991, p. 71.

51. Cited in ibid., p. 72.

52. Quoted in Porto, op. cit., p. 387. Tom McMillen echoes this in his book *Out of Bounds* (p. 125): "As the national chairman of the President's Club, a fundraising arm of the University of Maryland, which recently embarked on a $200 million campaign over five years, I have seen no link between our fundraising success for the school's educational programs and the fortunes of our sports teams."

53. University of Massachusetts Football Task Force, *Minority Report for IA Football Task Force*, p. 72.

54. University of Massachusetts Football Task Force, *Final Report of the IA Football Task Force*, September 5, 1996, p. 18.

55. Mike Dodd, "Winning One for the Admissions Office," *USA Today*, July 11, 1997, p. 1A.

56. Ibid.

57. University of Massachusetts Football Task Force, *Final Report of the IA Football Task Force*, pp. 16–17.

58. Robert McCormick and Maurice Tinsley, "Athletics Versus Academics: Evidence from SAT Scores," in Goff and Tollison, eds., *Sportometrics*, College Station: Texas A&M Press, 1990. The authors state that the coefficient is "marginally significant," which does not have any statistical meaning. In a two-tailed test, the coefficient is not significant at the 10 percent level. A 10 percent cutoff is a very lenient significance level. Normally, a 1 or 5 percent cutoff is used to reject the null hypothesis of a coefficient equal to zero. The authors tested several specifications and in no instance was the coefficient on football success significant at the 10 percent level.

59. Dale Bremmer and Randall Kesselring, "The Advertising Effect of University Athletic Success: A Reappraisal of the Evidence," *Quarterly Review of Economics and Finance*, vol. 33, no. 4 (winter 1993), pp. 409–21. See also Mike Simpson, "The Impact of the *U.S. News and World Report* Rankings on the Demand for Individual Colleges and Universities," Senior Honors Thesis, Department of Economics, Vanderbilt University, April 1996. Another study found a positive correlation between success in the NCAA basketball tournament over the years and out-of-state tuition, but the equation was underspecified; see F. Mixon and R. Ressler, "An Empirical Note on the Impact of College Athletics on Tuition Revenues," *Applied Economic Letters*, vol. 2, 1995, pp. 383–87. Further, the results of the foregoing paper are not sustained in F. Mixon and Y. Hsing, "The Determinants of Out-of-State Enrollments in Higher Education: A Tobit Analysis," *Economics of Education Review*, vol. 13, no. 4, 1994, pp. 329–35. This paper considers data from 220 institutions for 1990. It tests three specifications of the effect of NCAA division in a model attempting to predict the share of enrollments from out-of-state students. The models again are underspecified, and in two of the three specifications NCAA division did not have a statistically significant effect; in the other one it was significant at the 10 percent level.

60. Some schools use ACT rather than SAT scores. The College Board provides a formula for converting one to the other which I used. Recentered SAT scores were converted to the pre-1995 system. SAT and ACT data are from the annual yearbook of the College Board (*The College Handbook*), 1980–1996. Data on college characteristics are from *Barron's Guide to Colleges*, various years. Again, with these tests I employed a number of different specifications. The basic model was fixed effects (using year and university dummies) with panel data. Linear and loglinear relationships were tested. Also, rates of change among the variables were tested in a formulation that explicitly included educational characteristics of the schools. None of the many athletic performance variables had a significant impact on entering-class SAT scores under any specification. Some had a significant impact on the number of applications, but these never translated into a significant effect on yield or on SAT scores. Another study of 55 Division IA schools from the six major football conferences during 1978–87, also using a fixed effects model with panel data and appropriate control variables, obtained very similar results to my tests. Namely, a school's football suc-

cess had a statistically significant, albeit weak, effect of increasing the number of a school's applicants. In particular, an increase in a team's win percentage from .500 to .750 (a 50 percent increase) increases the number of applications by 1.3 percent the next year. See Robert Murphy and Gregory Trandel, "The Relation Between a University's Football Record and the Size of Its Applicant Pool," *Economics of Education Review*, vol. 13, no. 3, 1994, pp. 265–70. A 1993 study by Tuck and Amato, using data from 1989 for 63 leading Division IA schools, finds that neither football nor basketball ranking over the previous 10 years has a statistically significant effect on SAT scores of the entering class. However, when the dependent variable is the change in SAT scores between 1980 and 1989, football ranking is found to have a significant and modest, positive effect. Irwin Tucker and Louis Amato, "Does Big-time Success in Football or Basketball Affect SAT Scores?" *Economics of Education Review*, vol. 12, no. 2, 1993, pp. 177–81. In my econometric work, which involved more schools and more years, various measurements of athletic success did not have a significant effect on the change in SAT scores.

Chapter Eight

Epigraphs: Mcpherson is quoted in M. McGraw et al., *Money Games: Inside the NCAA*, as are Abernathy and Tarkanian.

1. Email communication from Keith Martin, July 10, 1998.
2. Ibid., p. 9.
3. Ibid.
4. Steve Rushin, "Inside the Moat," *Sports Illustrated*, March 3, 1997, p. 76.
5. Ibid., p. 71.
6. Mike McGraw et al., op. cit., p. 12.
7. Ibid.
8. Stories on the Michigan imbroglio appeared in the *Ann Arbor News*, October 9, 1997, and the *Detroit News*, October 10, 1997.
9. Charles Chandler, "General News," Knight-Ridder Newspapers, December 12, 1989. Barry Jacobs, "Valvano Tones It Down," *New York Times*, December 27, 1989.
10. Ron Kaspriske, "NCAA Clears FSU of Major Violations," *Tampa Tribune*, January 24, 1996.
11. Although the data in this table suggest a leveling of the number of major infractions, a year-by-year breakdown suggests an upward pattern has persisted since 1988. The average number of infractions per year during the following three-year periods were: 1988–1990, 11.7; 1991–93, 13.3; and, 1994–96, 14.
12. Quoted in McGraw et al., op. cit., p. 10.
13. Arthur Padilla and David Baumer, "Big-Time College Sports: Management and Economic Issues," *Journal of Sport and Social Issues*, May 1994, p. 133.
14. Indeed, Richard Sheehan, using data from 1991 to 1996 for Division IA football programs and multiple regression analysis, finds the same pattern. Football programs with more infractions have higher rankings. Richard Sheehan, "Athletics, Academics and Finances," draft manuscript, June 1998.

15. A. Fleisher et al., *The National Collegiate Athletic Association: A Study in Cartel Behavior*, chap. 5. The authors, however, fail to recognize that their quadratic modeling of the relationship shows that when the coefficient of variation of the school's win percentage surpasses .434, the probability of enforcement begins to decline, and when the coefficient of variation exceeds .868 the net effect of enforcement becomes negative. Although no schools in the authors' sample have coefficients of variation above .868, a significant portion have ones between .434 and .868. That is, the positive relationship between the likelihood of being investigated and the variability of a school's performance holds until a coefficient of variation of .868, but the degree of this positive relationship declines after the coefficient reaches .434.

16. An excellent overview of this problem is provided in Ricardo Bascuas, "Cheaters, Not Criminals: Antitrust Invalidation of Statutes Outlawing Sports Agent Recruitment of Student Athletes," *Yale Law Review*, vol. 105, no. 6 (1996).

17. Stephen Hagwell and Ronald Mott, "Agents Confirm Problems Run Deep," *NCAA News*, September 25, 1995.

18. Stephen Hagwell and Ronald Mott, "Schools Struggle to Combat Agent Issue," *NCAA News*, October 16, 1995.

19. *NCAA News*, January 15, 1996, p. 6.

20. Steve Rock, "NCAA's Dempsey Got Big Salary Boost," *Kansas City Star*, June 22, 1998.

21. McGraw et al., op. cit., p. 6.

22. *Chronicle of Higher Education*, October 20, 1998.

23. Rock, op. cit.

24. Judith Havemann, "Executive Pay Soars at Major Charities," *Hartford Courant*, July 5, 1998, p. 1.

25. This and other information on executive perquisites comes from Mc-Graw et al., op. cit., pp. 6–8.

26. Quoted in ibid., p. 8.

27. Steve Rock, "Lush Life Endangered: NCAA Looks at Cost-Cutting Measures," *Kansas City Star*, August 11, 1998.

28. The 1,200-mile limit was installed in 1998. The previous limit was 600 miles.

29. Steve Rock, "Lush Life Endangered," and interview with Dempsey in *Kansas City Star*, August 19, 1998.

30. This discussion relies on original court documents and memoranda from the NCAA to its membership, as well as the following articles: Jim Naughton, "Antitrust Suits Could Poke Holes in the NCAA's Rule Book, Some Predict," *Chronicle of Higher Education*, June 19, 1998; William Rhoden, "Who Collects the Eggs of the Golden Goose?" *New York Times*, May 7, 1998; Kirk Johnson, "NCAA Ordered to Pay Assistant Coaches $66 Million," *New York Times*, May 5, 1998; Jason Reynolds, "NCAA Ordered to Pay $67 Million to Assistant Coaches Who Brought Antitrust Suit," *Chronicle of Higher Education*, May 15, 1998; Marcia Chambers, "Colleges: Assistant Coaches Teach a Stubborn and Defiant NCAA a Costly Lesson," *New York Times*, July 12, 1998.

Chapter Nine

Epigraphs: Roberts is quoted in J. Carey and C. Mihoces, "NCAA: Organization in Transition," *USA Today*, June 30, 1998; Delany is quoted in *NCAA News*, June 29, 1998, as is Bowlsby; Cavanaugh is quoted in Sperber, *Onward to Victory*; McMillen and Burns are quoted in D. Lederman, "With Spate of Bills, Congress Turns Up the Heat on NCAA," *Chronicle of Higher Education*, August 7, 1991.

1. *NCAA News*, January 8, 1996, p. 10.

2. Steve Wilstein, "NCAA Faces a Risky Future, As Athletes Feel Exploited," Associated Press, December 25, 1996.

3. Douglas Lederman, "Sports Reformers Are Split over Struggles at 2 Colleges," *Chronicle of Higher Education*, February 7, 1990, p. A41.

4. McGraw et al., op. cit., p. 4.

5. These conferences are: Atlantic Coast, Big East, Big Ten, Big Twelve, Conference USA, Pacific 10, Southeaster, and Western Athletic.

6. Cited in McGraw et al., op. cit., p. 4.

7. According to *Division III News*, vol. 1, no. 2, September 1998, p. 2, the Division III allocation from the NCAA for 1998–99 increased to $8.67 million, almost all of which will be spent on Division III championships.

8. Quoted in Malcolm Moran, "Dropping Football: The Unthinkable Happens at Boston University," *New York Times*, November 2, 1997.

9. W. Byers, op. cit., p. 369.

10. One somewhat significant piece of legislation did come out of Congress in 1993. The Equity in Athletics Disclosure Act requires institutions of higher education to disclose gender participation rates and program support expenditures in college athletic programs to prospective students and, upon request, to the public. The bill was sponsored by Representative Collins from Illinois.

11. Sally Huggins, "A Capital Idea," *NCAA News*, June 6, 1996.

12. Debra Blum, "Lobbying for the NCAA," *Chronicle of Higher Education*, March 29, 1996, p. A55.

13. Of course, some constituents, the college sports fans, are delighted with the present state of affairs. Many members of Congress join them in rooting for the local college teams and are more invested in the school's athletic success than its educational mission.

14. Fax from Bill Murray, Major League Baseball, dated August 10, 1998.

15. The NBA does provide a $1.5 million-a-year subsidy to the CBA, which is often referred to as the NBA's development league. The CBA, however, has not signed players out of high school, so its players still benefit from the development provided by college basketball. Moreover, the subsidy per NBA team is a paltry $51,700.

16. Josh Gotthelf, "Agents Said to Hype Effect of NBA Lockout," *Sports Business Journal*, April 27–May 3, 1998, p. 39.

17. Under a new arrangement with the NBA, NBA scouts evaluate the top prospects and indicate what they believe their chances of success in the draft to be. This information is both indirect and quite speculative. The simpler and

more effective solution from the standpoint of the student-athletes would allow the prospects to enter the draft and then return to play in college if they are not satisfied with the outcome.

18. Some universities, like Stanford and Michigan, operate substantial industrial parks. The models here differ but a basic component is for the university to rent land out to private, profit-oriented businesses. These businesses, in turn, make ample use of professors for consulting and students for internships.

19. In the fall of 1997, CBA Commissioner Steve Patterson stated that the CBA should offer some of the top high school seniors and college players contracts of between $20,000 and $100,000 to induce them to play in the CBA. If the CBA begins such recruitment, it would constitute a fourth possible alternative for leading prospects to avoid the current, obligatory college track to the pros. See, e.g., Porto, op. cit., p. 408n.

20. Harvard was the first school to establish freshman ineligibility. Most big-time athletic schools followed suit in the years prior to World War I. Freshman ineligibility remained widespread, but was enforced on a school-by-school or conference-by-conference basis, until the 1960s.

21. Sperber, 1998, pp. 258 and 264. To be sure, there was a heated discussion between the football coach and the school administration about whether the team could take 44 players to a game in Seattle in 1949. The coach had grown fond of the two-platoon system and argued that he needed more players. The administration prevailed and Notre Dame won the game anyway.

22. NFL teams may also carry a third quarterback who can be activated only if the first two are injured in a game. Further, teams may carry a practice squad with a maximum of five players. Players from the practice squad can be activated to replace other injured players on the 45-man active roster.

23. In July 1998, the Division I Management Council rejected a recommendation to cut the number of football scholarships to 75 equivalencies, with the allowance for partial grants which would enable 95 student-athletes on full or partial scholarships.

24. Dave Caldwell, "Line of Fire," *Dallas Morning News*, August 24, 1997.

25. Sometimes schools come up with novel ways to suppress free speech. In 1998, the alumnae magazine at Rutgers University rejected an advertisement from alumni, including Nobel Prize–winner Milton Friedman, which called upon the school to stop awarding athletic scholarships, to "withdraw from professionalized athletics and resume competition at a genuinely collegiate level." *Chronicle of Higher Education*, July 7, 1998, p. A6.

26. The University of North Carolina's $7.1 million Nike contract apparently contains a clause that forbids players from concealing the Nike swoosh on their uniforms. Hal Crowther, "Games Without Shame," *The Independent*, November 12–18, 1997, p. 11.

It's been a busy eighteen months in the world of college sports since I turned in the manuscript for the first edition of *Unpaid Professionals* in December 1998. The NCAA signed a new, eleven-year, $6 billion television contract with CBS to broadcast the March Madness basketball finals. The association settled its restricted-earnings coaches' case for $54.5 million. It struggled in the courts over its standardized-test score threshold for first-year scholarships. It created a basketball reform committee and responded to its recommendations. It received and ignored a stinging critique of its 1997 restructuring from its normally placid Faculty Athletics Representatives Association. It slapped a major infraction penalty on Notre Dame for the first time, and levied the hefty punishment of reducing the school's number of football scholarships from eighty-five to eighty-four for two years. It moved its headquarters from Kansas City to Indianapolis, and sold its Learjet.

In the trenches, hypocrisy continued to flourish. Major academic fraud cases were brought to light at the universities of Minnesota and Tennessee. New corruption scandals hit the high school basketball summer leagues. Financial deficits troubled the overwhelming majority of athletic programs. Coaches' salaries skyrocketed, while coaches' behavior descended to new depths. And Nike made it clear that monitoring sweatshops was only acceptable when Phil Knight was in control.

In the end, the analysis of college sports in June 2000 is much the same as it was in December 1998. Let us take a closer look.

GRADUATION RATES

News on this front was not uplifting. While the six-year graduation rate for Division IA football players managed to improve marginally from 50 percent (for those entering college in 1991) to 51 percent (for those entering college in 1992), the rate for Division I basketball players stayed steady at 41 percent. The six-year graduation rate for black basketball players, however, fell from 37 percent to 33 percent.

More significantly, new evidence emerged to caution against using graduation rates as a meaningful guide to educational attainment. Consider first the scandal at the University of Minnesota. In March 1999, Jan Gangelhoff, a former secretary in the athletics department, revealed that she had completed more than four hundred class assignments for at least eighteen basketball players from 1993 to 1998. Following these revelations by Gangelhoff and other allegations that basketball coach Clem Haskins knew about and abetted this activity, the University of Minnesota commissioned an outside study of the basketball program. In the ensuing twenty-five-hundred-page report, the investigators concluded that there was widespread academic fraud in the program. Evidence indicated that Coach Haskins actually paid Gangelhoff handsome sums for writing papers for his players. Other administrators were also complicitous, arranging for grade changes and giving cash to players, among other things. There were also charges of sexual misconduct.[1] Haskins was fired, but only after a $1.5 million golden handshake. Together with the outside investigation, forfeited revenues, and other expenses, the scandal is estimated to have cost the university over $5 million.

While the existence of academic fraud was acknowledged and dealt with at the University of Minnesota, the University of Tennessee administration has attempted to cover up any evidence of fraud at its school. It would rather promulgate the good news: Tennessee won an award in 1999 for graduating 70 percent of its football recruits.

Yet problems have existed for many years at Tennessee. They came to the fore in 1999 with allegations made by the English Department's director of composition, Linda Bensel-Meyers, and the resignation of the longstanding director of the school's Writing Center, Robin Wright. The allegations made by Bensel-Meyers are familiar: tutors writing or typing papers for football players, physical disrespect shown for tutors by football players and athletic administrators, frequent grade changes, special courses with little academic content and lenient grading, large numbers of junior and senior football players who had no declared major (in violation of academic regulations), and so on. In fact, anonymous transcripts of thirty-seven football players released by Bensel-Meyers in April 2000 showed that academically at-risk football starters were ten times more likely to have a grade changed than nonathletes, and thirty-one times more likely to receive an incomplete and then have it changed to a passing grade than nonathletes. One not atypical member of the football team had taken credit courses in Jogging, Badminton, Basic Military Science I, Basic Officer Skills I, Weight Training, Walking, and Racquetball. Graduation rates aren't everything.[2]

ESCALATING MEDIA RIGHTS

In November 1999, CBS offered the NCAA $6 billion commencing in 2003 for eleven years of broadcast, Internet, sponsorship, and licensing rights to the annual March men's basketball tournament, plus several smaller events. The annual average revenue from this deal is $545 million, two and a half times the existing 1995–2002 contract average of $216 million.

These riches were bestowed upon the NCAA despite (a) the fact that the tournament ratings hit an all-time low in 1999 (and then fell by an additional 19 percent in March 2000), and (b) the likelihood of the emergence of a professional basketball minor league that will sap some of the talent from Division I basketball. CBS will be paying $3 million more per ratings point for its NCAA deal than it is paying for its NFL package.

But the NCAA will have money in the bank through 2013. What does this apparent bonanza mean for the troubled finances of intercollegiate athletics? Most observers have made sanguine proclamations. Some have even asserted that the financial constraints blocking the fuller implementation of Title IX will fade away in the wake of the new CBS deal. Don't count on it.

In fact, the CBS contract will have preciously little impact on the economics of college sports. Consider the following. First, the new money does not kick in until 2003, when it will be $360 million, compared to $300 million to be paid out in 2002 under the current contract (between 2003 and 2013 the annual fees then grow by around 8 percent per year). Second, the NCAA will take 6 to 10 percent off the top for administrative overhead and another 7.5 percent that will have to be shared with Divisions II and III. Third, the CBS payments include sponsorship revenues that the NCAA currently receives separately under a deal with Host Communications. Fourth, the balance will have to be divided among the 318 (or more) colleges in Division I, meaning the net increment per school in 2003 will average under $200,000. Rising coaches' salaries alone, between now and 2003, will more than eat up this gain, not to mention the ever-increasing costs for facilities, transportation, and medical insurance, among others.

ONGOING FINANCIAL DIFFICULTIES

Exploding media revenues notwithstanding, the vast majority of Division IA schools continue to run in deficit. Because no stockholders exist to demand financial discipline, new revenues are expended on higher salaries and perquisites for coaches and administrators, new facilities, additional secretaries and assistants, and the demands of gender equity.

Even the mighty University of Michigan, perennially in the top-ranked football and basketball programs, averaging over 111,000 in attendance at home football contests, and earning more than $5 million annually in licensing fees and another $5 million in corporate sponsorships,[3] has been losing money on its athletics program. Reportedly, Michigan athletics lost $3.9 million in 1998–1999, and another $3 million in 1999–2000.[4] And this was before it was jilted by Nike.

Ohio State, with its new Schottenstein Center arena and refurbished stadium, saw its athletics revenues reach an NCAA record of over $73 million during 1999–2000. Yet its athletic program has barely managed to break even the last several years and, with its large capital costs, the program is projecting deficits in the near future.

Out of 973 schools in the NCAA, in any given year there are likely to be no more than one or two dozen whose athletic programs do not run in deficit when properly accounted. There is little evidence that the situation is improving.

COACHES' SALARIES

The ineluctable upward march of head coaches' compensation packages contributes to the programs' financial woes. The norm for the top two or three dozen football and men's basketball teams now hovers around a $1 million package. Sometimes programs that would like to be considered among the top thirty also splurge. LSU, for instance, opened a few eyes when it hired Nick Saban as its head football coach in November 1999 for $1.2 million a year over five years, including $550,000 for radio, television, and Internet appearances.

There was no public report on the buyout clause in Saban's contract, but this is never a matter to be overlooked. Consider the case of Terry Bowden, the former football coach at Auburn. When Bowden was induced to resign during the 1998 season, the school paid dearly: $620,000 to buy out Bowden's contract; $210,000 to settle a lawsuit with the interim coach; $4.5 million over five years to hire Tommy Tuberville, Bowden's replacement; $1 million to buy out of a scheduled game against Florida State at Tuberville's request; and Bowden got to stay in the house that Auburn bought for him for up to five years.[5]

COACHES' BEHAVIOR

It is not unusual for a college coach to be the most important adult in an athlete's life during his or her college years. The athlete certainly spends much more time with the coach than any other adult. It is reasonable to expect the stratospherically paid Division IA coaches to model good behavior and to encourage the student to take his or her studies seriously. Many coaches do.[6]

Unfortunately, many don't. There are the Clem Haskinses and Phil Fulmers, who send their students to vacuous, gut courses and/or induce tutors to write papers for their players. And then there are the more extravagant behavioral patterns. Bobby Knight, Indiana's notorious basketball coach, chokes one player and punches another.[7] Tic Price, former basketball coach at Memphis, commits adultery with a twenty-three-year-old co-ed and physically abuses her. Kevin Bannon, basketball coach at Rutgers, has his team play strip-foul-shot, and three of his players go through practice buck naked. Mike Jarvis, basketball coach at St. John's, reacting to the NCAA's temporary suspension of one of his players, explains to the press: "I hope that none of you feel the way I have the last two days, as if someone had come into my house and raped me."[8] Mike DuBose, Alabama football coach, is accused of sexual harassment and as part of his settlement agrees to forego the last two years on his contract. After his team wins the 1999–2000 SEC championship, however, the University of Alabama modifies the settlement and adds the two years back on to his contract.[9] Apparently, winning trumps sexual harassment.

GRADUAL PROGRESS ON TITLE IX

The 1998–1999 data from the Equity in Athletics Disclosure Act revealed that women now make up 42 percent of all athletes in Division I. Further, women received 42 percent of athletic scholarship funds, 31 percent of recruiting budgets, 34 percent of coaching salary budgets, and 33 percent of total operating budgets.[10] All of these shares are up slightly from 1997–1998 and prior years.[11]

Cedric Dempsey, the NCAA's executive director, appraised the status of gender equity in college sports in October 1999 as follows: "Improvements are being made, but being made much too slowly . . . we must continue to add programs for women and dedicate more resources to women's programs on our campuses at a faster rate."[12] Dempsey's sober assessment notwithstanding, progress has been too rapid for some.

Title IX has unleashed a backlash, with detractors objecting that women's gains have meant men's losses. The actual record is considerably more ambiguous than this claim allows. For instance, between 1978 and 1996 the total number of men's sports teams in all three NCAA divisions increased by seventy-four. After falling 12 percent between 1985 and 1996, the number of male athletes grew 6 percent during the last three years.

One of the more outspoken critics of Title IX has been Kimberly Schuld, manager for special projects at the Independent Women's Forum. She asserts that Title IX implementation has created a quota system and that colleges are starting "women's programs like bowling, squash and tiddlywinks to say they have more women's programs and are in compliance."

Ms. Schuld's sarcasm aside, women have shown that they are interested in participating in intercollegiate sports when the opportunities are there. Presently, there are over 2.25 million girls playing interscholastic sports in high school—more than enough to supply enthusiastic players for larger numbers of women's college teams. (In 1997–1998 there were 203,686 male and 135,110 female athletes playing college sports.) Attendance at women's sporting contests is growing every year, as are television ratings. Until women's college sports are supported at similar levels to those of the men for close to a generation in time, it will be impossible to assess their long-run potential.

NIKE ET AL. AND THE SWEATSHOPS

Things were going along okay for Nike with the two-year-old Fair Labor Association (FLA). Nike and its industrial partners had a controlling influence on the FLA board. The FLA did not require disclosure of the location of all apparel and footwear contractors and subcontractors, did not mandate adequate minimum wage standards, and did not propose to monitor factories without advanced notification. Under the FLA's auspices there was a gradual improvement in sweatshop conditions, and Nike and its industrial partners gained the apparent legitimacy of standing for human rights and decent working conditions.

Then along came the Workers' Rights Consortium (WRC) in 1999. The WRC, the result of a grassroots student movement with ties to organized labor, wanted no corporate influence on its board, unannounced factory visits by independent monitors, and a living wage for workers. By April 2000, the WRC boasted almost 50 university members (versus around 125 university members in the FLA), and Nike had had enough.

In April, Nike began to throw its weight around. First, it canceled its sponsorship contract with Brown University athletics. Brown was one of the founding university members of the WRC. Second, Phil Knight announced that he would not make his promised $30 million donation to the University of Oregon for the renovation of its football stadium because the school had joined the WRC. Third, Nike suddenly withdrew from negotiations to extend its sponsorship contract with the University of Michigan. Nike had proposed a six-year deal worth around $4 million annually. Michigan, alas, had signed up as a provisional member of the WRC.

Adidas still requires a nondisparagement clause in its university sponsorship contracts. Colleges with Adidas money must deter their employees and students from criticizing the company. Nike has a few such clauses in its contracts as well.[13]

Jim Keady is a former assistant soccer coach from St. John's University. While coaching, Jim was also doing a research paper on Nike's labor practices for his master's degree in theology. Citing their use of sweatshop labor, Jim began to publicly protest the university's relationship with Nike. He also refused to wear the equipment that Nike provided the University. On May 12, 1998, Jim was given an ultimatum by university officials, "Wear Nike and drop this issue publicly or resign." Jim was forced to resign. It's a good thing that free trade promotes free speech and democracy.

THE PRINCIPLES OF AMATEURISM AND REFORM

When the NCAA wrote its first constitution in 1906, amateurism was identified with activities engaged in strictly for pleasure. Thus, any form of compensation (even a tuition benefit) was considered to contravene the precepts of amateurism. This concept of amateurism persisted until 1948, when the NCAA allowed that an athlete might receive a tuition benefit (but not room and board) if he was fully qualified academically and in need financially. Then the definition morphed again in 1956, this time permitting scholarships (including room and board) for athletic skills alone and with no financial need criterion.

In 1973, automatic four-year athletic scholarships were abolished. Thenceforth, all athletic scholarships would be one year at a time. Hence, if a player was not performing up to a coach's standards, he could be cut off from his scholarship no matter how well he was performing academically. The 1973 twist made it clear that athletic performance was a quid pro quo for the scholarship, lending greater credence to those who argue that college athletes are in an employment relationship with their schools.[14]

During the 1999–2000 academic year the notion of amateurism was tweaked twice more. First, at the University of Connecticut, the school decided to order championship rings in honor of the men's basketball team's first-place finish in the March 1999 NCAA tournament. The university ordered 298 rings—only 13 of which would go on the fingers of the team's players. The other recipients included: President Clinton, Governor John Rowland, former Speaker of the State House of Representatives, various corporate executives, athletics staff members, boosters, and so on. It turns out that two classes of rings were ordered: the $495.50 variety, which were made of 10-karat gold with diamond insets, and the $199 variety, which were gold-plated with zirconium stones. Members of the team received the latter. The coaching staff, athletic director, school president, and other luminaries received the former. Thus, a new stricture of amateurism was enshrined—gifts are allowed, but only up to $200 in value.

Second, several basketball players were suspended from their teams by the NCAA when it was discovered that individuals connected to AAU summer basketball teams paid part of the players' tuition at private high schools.[15] Somehow it does not violate the principles of amateurism for athletes to receive a full scholarship to attend college, but it does violate these principles for athletes to receive even a partial scholarship to high school. Equally curious, the NCAA, an association of colleges, does not hesitate to enforce rules about what students can do before they enter college.

The NCAA's evolving notion of amateurism bears little resemblance to classical ideals. Rather, it has been opportunistically shaped to respond to the economic realities and political pressures faced by college athletic departments. If there is a consistent theme, it is that amateurs cannot be directly paid for what they do, implying that there should be no direct monetary remuneration for playing a sport in school.[16]

If the NCAA adhered consistently to this view, it would, among other things: 1) allow students to be employed in jobs calling upon their athletic skills in the summertime;[17] 2) allow students to enter professional drafts and retain their collegiate eligibility if they chose not to sign with a pro team; 3) allow students to take out loans based on their future earnings power and buy career-ending injury insurance.

Not surprisingly, the NCAA's new $6 billion television contract catalyzed renewed interest among student-athletes to reform the system. A group of student-athletes at UCLA, for example, formed CASU (College Athletes' Student Union) in early 2000. CASU denounces the NCAA's Student-Athlete Advisory Committees as ineffectual and calls for substantial reform in the association's governing structure, as well as more meaningful student stipends. Hoping to head off a new movement to pay student-athletes, the NCAA has begun to entertain some of these reforms.

At its November 1999 annual meeting in New Orleans, the Faculty Athletics Representatives Association (FARA) of the NCAA passed a resolution criticizing the centralization of decision making that has taken place within the NCAA since the restructuring reform of 1997. The FARA president, Larry Gerlach, sent the NCAA Board of Directors a letter stating that the restructuring greatly diminished the voice of the faculty representatives and university presidents in the NCAA, while enhancing the power of conference commissioners. Gerlach also criticized the proposals of the NCAA's basketball reform committee as inadequate.

Among other measures in its summer 1999 report, the twenty-seven-member basketball reform committee recommended that if a basketball program graduated more than 75 percent of its players, then the team would be allowed to add one scholarship. But if it graduated less than 34 percent, the team would lose one scholarship. Gerlach questioned whether it was proper to send out the message that it was acceptable to graduate only 34 percent of the students on a basketball team.

The basketball reform committee's proposals were vetted and modified first by the NCAA Division I Management Council and then by the Division I Board of Directors in late April 2000. The Board endorsed the following reforms: a team would lose a scholarship if its graduation rate slipped below 50 percent; the recruitment period at AAU summer camps would be reduced to two weeks in 2001 and eliminated in subsequent summers;[18] a limitation of five new recruits per school year would be placed on teams; and athletes would be required to pass at least twelve hours of coursework with at least a 2.0 average by the end of their first term to retain eligibility.[19]

While clearly insufficient by themselves to curb academic fraud and exploitation of basketball players, these measures are substantive steps in the right direction. True to form, when pressure for reform reaches a certain threshold, the NCAA responds. Unfortunately, the NCAA response is usually only significant enough to dissipate the pressure, not to solve the problem. As the payoff to winning continues to grow for coaches and administrators, there is the danger that any piecemeal reform will likely be absorbed and subverted by the commercialization juggernaut.

The path to meaningful reform must begin with one simple question: what kind of system do we want to see? One possibility is to give in to commercialization, pay the star athletes, do away with athletic scholarships, and professionalize the system. If the system is professionalized but remains within the university, then three questions emerge. First, how much will it cost the colleges to pay the athletes? Second, what will happen to team morale and school spirit as a labor market for players develops? Third, do we also pay the first violinist in the college orchestra or the lead actor in the school play, and do we apply the law of supply and demand more broadly within the university? Does a professor, for instance, get paid according to enrollment in his or her classes? Beware grade inflation.

In contrast, if the system is professionalized but detached from the university, then have we done a disservice to the college sports consumer? After all, more people attend college basketball and football games than NBA and NFL games. A more apt comparison might be the first incarnation of the World League of American Football (WLAF). When it still had some teams in the United States, these teams were populated by the best college players who did not quite make the NFL. Each team was clearly better than any college team. Yet attendance was dismal compared to the nearby Division IA college teams.[20] If college football loses its branding, then will its popularity follow the sad experience of the U.S. WLAF teams? Will the new product experience the same demand and will the quantity of output be maintained?

The answers to these questions are sufficiently in doubt as to commend a more thoroughgoing effort at preserving intercollegiate sports as amateur before a professional model is adopted.[21] One serious attempt to initiate such a reform process occurred at a Drake University conference in October 1999.[22] The outgrowth of this conference was a faculty-based organization for athletic reform, dubbed the "Drake Group." At its April 2000 meeting, the group issued a five-point platform for reform:

> **1.** Remove academic counseling for athletes from the control of athletics departments and abandon the practice of providing special academic support to athletes;
>
> **2.** Eliminate athletics scholarships and expand the availability of need-based aid for all students;
>
> **3.** Publicly disclose information about the majors, advisers, and courses taken by all athletes, without revealing individual names and grades;
>
> **4.** Reduce the number of intercollegiate athletics contests; and,
>
> **5.** Stop using the term "student-athlete," and instead refer to those who participate in athletics as either students or athletes.

The implementation of point one will help to curtail the special and often fraudulent treatment given to athletes in support of their coursework. Point three will make it more difficult to channel athletes into easy classes with little or no intellectual content. Point four will make the demands of a team's schedule less incompatible with being a student.

Point two is more problematic. As long as star athletes in basketball and football generate hundreds of thousands of dollars in revenue for a school team, it seems unfair to reduce the already meager, indirect compensation they receive. For the three hundred to five hundred other student-athletes at each Division I school, it would make sense to gradually convert their athletic grants into scholarships based on academic merit and need.

Of course, if true amateur reforms are implemented, it may lead to centrifugal pressures among certain schools and the eventual emergence of a quasi-professional league. Separately, the NBA has stated its intention to begin a new developmental league in 2001. If successful, this too may help to resolve the existing tensions between amateurism and professionalism within Division I.

In the meantime, stay tuned for more litigation, more academic fraud, more bizarre behavior, more political struggle, and some good old-fashioned, competitive fun.

NOTES

1. See, for one, Welch Suggs, "U. of Minnesota Ousts 4 Top Athletics Officials in Academic-Fraud Scandal," *Chronicle of Higher Education*, December 3, 1999.

2. Another piece of disturbing academic news came out of the college football world in December 1999. James Brooks, the career-rushing leader for the Cincinnati Bengals, announced publicly that he could not get a job because he was illiterate despite having attended Auburn University for six years. Although Brooks made over a million dollars in some years while with the Bengals, he owed more than $110,000 in child support payments. *Sports Business News*, December 22, 1999.

3. For an up-to-date report on the growth of corporate sponsorships in college sports, see the "Special Report on College Sponsorships" in the *Sports Business Journal*, June 5–11, 2000, pp. 29–39. Among other things, this report chronicles the emergence of naming-rights dealing for university sports facilities. The richest deal, as of June 2000, was signed for the basketball arena at Fresno State (SaveMart Center) for $40 million over twenty-three years.

4. See, Bill King, "Unearthing the AD of the Future," *Sports Business Journal*, June 12–18, 2000, pp. 25, 32, and 35, and John Bacon, "For Athletics at Michigan, Stability No Longer Rules," *New York Times*, February 14, 2000.

5. Erik Spanberg, "Cost of Firing a Coach Can't Be Dismissed," *Sports Business Journal*, November 22–28, 1999, p. 11.

6. Dean Smith, the recently retired basketball coach at the University of North Carolina, is one such individual. See, for instance, his autobiography, *A Coach's Life: My Forty Years in College Basketball* (New York: Random House, 1999).

7. For a thoughtful treatment of the most recent Bobby Knight affair, see Alex Wolff, "Whitewash: Indiana Caves, Bobby Knight Stays," *Sports Illustrated*, May 22, 2000.

8. Quoted in William Rhoden, "In an Era of Hyperbole, People Can Go Adrift," *New York Times*, February 7, 2000.

9. Doug Segrest, "DuBose to Get Two Years Back," *The Birmingham Post*, December 6, 1999.

10. Women do relatively better regarding scholarship aid than other categories because of the large number of walk-ons in certain men's sports. According to a May 2000 study by the NCAA, women have continued to lag significantly behind men in obtaining coaching and athletic director jobs. In 1999, only 17 percent of the 995 ADs in NCAA schools were women and only 42 percent of the 7,918 head-coaching jobs for women's teams went to women, down slightly from 1995; and, minority women do worse than minority men in coaching positions. See Welch Suggs, "Top Posts in Sports Programs Still Tend to go to White Men," *Chronicle of Higher Education*, June 2, 2000.

11. Welch Suggs, "Uneven Progress for Women's Sports," *Chronicle of Higher Education*, April 7, 2000. The data is compiled by the *Chronicle of Higher Education* and is based on responses from 311 Division I schools.

12. Cited in Andrew Zimbalist, "Backlash Against Title IX: An End Run Around Female Athletes," *Chronicle of Higher Education*, March 3, 2000.

13. See, for instance, Dan Wetzel and Don Yaeger, *Sole Influence: Basketball, Corporate Greed, and the Corruption of America's Youth* (New York: Warner Books, 2000).

14. On this point and the evolution of the NCAA notion of amateurism, there is no better source than Alan Sack and Ellen Staurowsky, *College Athletes for Hire* (Westport, Conn.: Praeger, 1998).

15. These players were: Erick Barkley at St. John's, Andre Williams at Oklahoma State, DerMarr Johnson at Cincinnati, and Kevin Lyde at Temple.

16. Logically, it could be extended also to denote no athletic scholarships.

17. No other merit award winner on campus is expected to adhere to the NCAA strictures on amateurism. For instance, those who accept music scholarships can play in jazz clubs on weekends for pay without fear of losing their scholarships. They can also teach music at summer camps.

18. An alternative to the existing summer camp recruiting is to be studied by a new basketball committee established by the Board of Directors.

19. The Board sent these proposals back to either the new Basketball Issues Committee or the Management Council to further define standards and implementation details. See *NCAA News*, May 22, 2000, p. 14.

20. I thank John Siegfried for suggesting this analogy to me.

21. For an elaboration of this point, see Andrew Zimbalist, "Reforms Offer Bigger Payoffs Than Salaries," *Sports Business Journal*, May 15–21, 2000.

22. In June 2000, the Knight Commission on College Athletic Reform, discussed elsewhere in this book, was reconstituted. The Knight Commission played a significant role in generating reform pressure and specific proposals in the 1980s and early 1990s. Its reemergence is likely to contribute to the building momentum for reform in the coming years.

Index